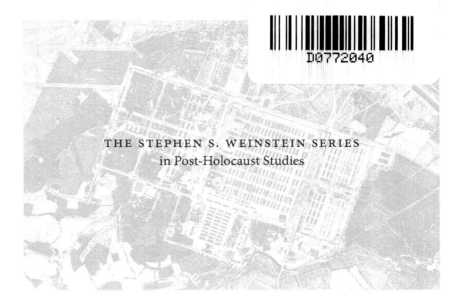

THE STEPHEN S. WEINSTEIN SERIES
in Post-Holocaust Studies

The Stephen S. Weinstein Series in Post-Holocaust Studies carries on the work and publications of the Pastora Goldner Series (2004–2007), exploring questions that continue to haunt humanity in the aftermath of Nazi Germany's attempt to destroy Jewish life and culture. Books in this series address the most current and pressing issues of our post-Holocaust world. They are grounded in scholarship undertaken by the Stephen S. Weinstein Holocaust Symposium, whose membership—international, interdisciplinary, interfaith, and intergenerational—is committed to dialogue as a fundamental form of inquiry and understanding. The symposium and the series are generously supported by Stephen S. Weinstein, who, with his wife, Nancy, is dedicated to the work of *tikkun olam,* the healing of the world, and whose commitment to combating present-day evils in our world has inspired the participants in the symposium who contribute to this series.

THE STEPHEN S. WEINSTEIN SERIES
in Post-Holocaust Studies

Encountering the Stranger

A Jewish-Christian-Muslim Trialogue

Edited and Introduced by

LEONARD GROB and JOHN K. ROTH

A Samuel and Althea Stroum Book

UNIVERSITY OF WASHINGTON PRESS
Seattle and London

For my friend
Father rick.
may we continue
on the path for
tikkun olam:
mending the
world
together.

carop

This book is published with the assistance of a grant from
the Samuel and Althea Stroum Endowed Book Fund.

UNIVERSITY OF WASHINGTON PRESS
PO Box 50096, Seattle, WA 98145, USA
www.washington.edu/uwpress

LIBRARY OF CONGRESS CATALOGING-IN-PUBLICATION DATA
Encountering the stranger : a Jewish-Christian-Muslim trialogue /
edited and introduced by Leonard Grob and John K. Roth.
p. cm. — (The Stephen S. Weinstein series in post-Holocaust studies)
Includes bibliographical references and index.
ISBN 978-0-295-99201-3 (hardcover : alk. paper) —
ISBN 978-0-295-99202-0 (pbk. : alk. paper)
1. Interpersonal relations—Religious aspects. 2. Strangers—Religious aspects.
3. Other (Philosophy)—Religious aspects. 4. Religions—Relations. 5. Christianity.
6. Judaism. 7. Islam. I. Grob, Leonard. II. Roth, John K.
BL626.33.E53 2012   201'.5—dc23   2012018866

The paper used in this publication is acid-free and meets the minimum requirements of American National Standard for Information Sciences—Permanence of Paper for Printed Library Materials, ANSI Z39.48–1984.∞

Jacket and part illustrations: *First Station: Auschwitz-Birkenau*, by Arie Galles (1998, 47 1/2 × 75 in., charcoal and white Conté on Arches with barbed wire–impressed wrought-iron frame), from the suite of fifteen drawings *Fourteen Stations/Hey Yud Dalet (Hashem Yinkom Daman)*, the latter phrase meaning, "May God avenge their blood." The title of the suite refers both to the Stations of the Cross and to the fact that the Nazi concentration camps and killing centers were near railroad stations. Galles's drawings are based on Luftwaffe and Allied aerial photographs of those sites. Within this drawing and all the others are invisibly embedded, hand-lettered phrases from the Kaddish, the ancient Jewish prayer for the dead.

To Victoria J. Barnett

Only in relationship with the other am I free.
—Dietrich Bonhoeffer, *Creation and Fall*

. . . the Stranger is one towards whom one is obligated.
　　　　　—Emmanuel Levinas, *Difficult Freedom*

CONTENTS

Prologue

Trialogue Is the Way

> There can be no peace among the nations without peace among the religions.
>
> There can be no peace among the religions without dialogue between the religions.
>
> —Hans Küng, *Global Responsibility*

Twenty-first-century strife—including but not limited to the terrorist attacks of September 11, 2001, and controversy a decade later about an Islamic community center near Ground Zero in New York, war in Iraq and Afghanistan, Iranian threats against Israel, and the Palestinian-Israeli conflict—frequently strains relationships between Judaism, Christianity, and Islam. Unavoidably, all three of these Abrahamic religions are involved and even implicated in such struggles, which endanger not only the *welfare* but also the very *survival* of individuals, ethnic groups, and nation-states. Indeed, the continued existence of our common home, the earth, is itself imperiled by violence so often spurred or, at a minimum, exacerbated by interreligious conflict.

The eighteen contributors to *Encountering the Stranger*—six Jewish, six Christian, and six Muslim scholars—are at one in the endeavor to hear and respond to the words of the Swiss theologian Hans Küng quoted above. In an age when "collisions of faith" among the Abrahamic traditions have given rise to religious violence that threatens the well-being of individuals and communities worldwide, each essayist takes responsibility to examine his or her tradition's understandings of the stranger and the "other" and to identify ways that could bridge divisions and create greater harmony among Jews, Christians, and Muslims.[1]

The contributors to this trialogue agree that tolerance and even respect, in their conventional senses, are less than adequate responses to the challenges posed by current interreligious conflict. As Mohandas Gandhi wisely proclaimed, "Tolerance may imply a gratuitous assumption of the inferiority of other faiths to one's own, and *respect* suggests a sense of patronizing."[2] Conceived throughout the centuries as *the* key to peaceful relations among traditions, tolerance has proved itself unable to tame the passions aroused in the demonization of the "other" that so frequently attends Abrahamic religious ideologies. Respect for traditions different from one's own is a far better response than tolerance. But respect does not necessarily dislodge bias that presumes the superiority of the tradition that "respects" others. The contributors to *Encountering the Stranger* agree that tolerance and respect must be surpassed by something far more radical: a welcoming of the other, an extension of hospitality enacted in genuine dialogue/trialogue.

What characterizes the *authentic* dialogue/trialogue to which the essayists in this volume aspire? We do not speak here of mere shifts in the cognitive or affective capabilities of parties to religious conflict. We aspire to a level of relationship that extends beyond both the exchange of good feeling and the sharing of ideas. Cognitive and affective growth is necessary but hardly sufficient for such dialogue. Authentic dialogue must aim to overcome *existential* mistrust of the stranger, which can still be in play even when cordial feeling and religious sharing are found. The communication we seek aims at fundamental or ontological change in the conflicting parties—a tall order—so that they become self-critical and accountable for identifying, assessing, and, where appropriate, revising their own tradition's assumptions and teachings regarding the other. Through their self-critical awareness, such dialogue/trialogue partners can open the space needed for mutual learning—individual and communal—to take place at the deepest levels. In the words of the German Jewish philosopher Martin Buber, each partner "must expose himself wholly, in a real way, in his humanly unavoidable partiality, and thereby experience himself in a real way as limited by the other, so that the two suffer together the destiny of our conditioned nature and meet one another in it."[3]

If, in the name of an uncritical embrace of my-faith-as-*the*-true-faith, I am closed off at the core of my being to possible truths to be found in the belief system of the other, that religious other will remain for me the perpetual outsider, a situation made all the more problematic by the fact that "my faith" typically links me to a community, to institutions, and involves the power and prerogatives they claim for themselves. Those who are taken to be outside "my faith"—in both the individual and communal senses of that concept—are likely to be seen, at best, as persons who are so different that I am advised to be cautious, to keep my distance, and to be on guard. At worst, such strangers are interpreted as posing a direct threat to my absolutist claims of the superiority of my religion to theirs. Such exclusivist claims can easily lead to an alleged divine sanction for violence in the name of the religion that is my own. In defense of my religion's core-ideas-become-ideology, I and my community run the risk of moving from mere verbal exhortation to acts of physical violence against those who would refuse the truths to which I and my community, alone, claim privileged access. The philosopher of religion John Hick puts the matter succinctly: "Throughout history almost all human conflicts have been validated and intensified by a religious sanction. God has been claimed to be on both sides of every war . . . exclusive claims to absolute truth have exacerbated the division of the human community into rival groups."[4]

The contributors to *Encountering the Stranger* have committed themselves to addressing the scourge of exclusivism that intensifies such rivalries. We take seriously the counsel of British rabbi Jonathan Sacks, who argues that "when religion is invoked as a justification for conflict, religious voices must be raised in protest. . . . If faith is enlisted in the cause of war, there must be an equal and opposite counter-voice in the name of peace. If religion is not part of a solution, it will certainly be part of the problem."[5] We essayists agree that insights garnered from all the Abrahamic traditions can indeed heal wounds opened, in many instances, by inauthentic renderings of these very traditions. We refuse the temptation to embrace any simplistic renunciation of religion as a source of peacemaking: In an age beset with religiously inspired conflict threatening the lives of millions, faith traditions themselves must act to heal the wounds so often incurred by bogus forms of religion posing as authentic spiritual traditions.

Given the dangers spurred by interreligious conflict, the temptation exists to search for solutions to such conflict by espousing either a facile relativism-posing-as-pluralism or a homogenizing process, which would lead to some standardized or "world religion" rooted in the lowest denominator common to all Abrahamic traditions. The discussions in this volume refuse these temptations. Our point of departure is our very embeddedness in our traditions. We endeavor to garner from each of our traditions those unique perspectives that shed light on the prospects for interreligious dialogue that goes deep down. Without claiming to represent the whole of their traditions, the eighteen essayists mine their religious heritage for those sacred resources and particularities that provide an opening to the possible truth of the religious claims of the other. In the words of theologian Paul F. Knitter, "While the renunciation of claims to be the 'only' or the 'definitive' religion may clash with past formulations of belief, there are resources within the religions themselves to justify and even require this move and to reformulate past claims of superiority."[6] Given the likely alternative to such reformulations—ongoing violence spurred by absolutist and thus conflicting religious claims—the contributors to *Encountering the Stranger* embrace trialogue as a welcoming of the stranger. Embracing this paradox—that common ground may be found and valued through mutual engagement with the distinctive particularity of diverse religious traditions—we locate reasons to hope for interreligious-trialogue-as-peacemaking in our troubled world.

The need to offer hospitality to the religious other is intensified in light of the fact that we live in a post-Holocaust world. Living in the shadow of Auschwitz disabuses us of any facile notion that long-established ethico-religious norms and rivalries can shield us from the evil that humans are capable of inflicting on one another. The contributors to *Encountering the Stranger* maintain that refuge can no longer be sought in systems of religious thought and practice that, at best, failed to prevent the Holocaust and, at worst, may themselves have been implicated in the perpetration of genocidal violence. Traditional paradigms of moral conduct or of theological understanding proved helpless to prevent the genocide perpetrated by Nazi Germany and its collaborators against the Jewish people. Other genocides and crimes against humanity have followed in the post-1945 period, giving the lie to any pretense that we humans have thus far heeded the injunction "Never Again."

Convinced that the Holocaust profoundly shows what can happen when individuals and religious traditions fail to regard the other as inviolable, the editors of this volume believed that exploration of the Holocaust's implications for interreligious engagement could shed light on and advance this book's endeavor to examine how the religious stranger might be encountered dialogically. Fortunately, Victoria J. Barnett, staff director of the Committee on Church Relations and the Holocaust at the United States Holocaust Memorial Museum (USHMM) in Washington, D.C., became aware of our project, concurred with our conviction that the Holocaust could orient and ground it, and invited all eighteen contributors to the museum for a three-day workshop. In October 2007, sixteen of the eighteen international contributors met—some for the first time—at USHMM. We were gifted with the opportunity to meet one another face-to-face as we explored ways in which engagement with the Holocaust might help inform creative approaches to Jewish-Christian-Muslim trialogue. We extend our heartfelt gratitude to USHMM, to its Committee on Church Relations and the Holocaust, and, in particular, to Victoria Barnett, an eminent scholar of the Holocaust, Jewish-Christian relations, and the work of Dietrich Bonhoeffer. Appropriately, this book is dedicated to her. We are also deeply indebted to our editors at the University of Washington Press: Jacqueline Ettinger, Beth Fuget, Mary Ribesky, and Jane Lichty. Without their capable and steadfast help, the project sparked by Victoria Barnett would not have reached completion.

In the course of visiting the museum's permanent exhibit in groups of two or three, and throughout a series of gatherings with Barnett and other members of the museum's staff, the contributors addressed concerns that moved us toward the final version of the chapters found here: What might engagement with the Holocaust teach us about key dangers of religious exclusivism? Would such engagement help us learn what inclusiveness might mean? At a time when many Jews and Christians mistrust "the Muslim other"—and at a time when many Muslims mistrust both "the Jewish other" and the "Christian" West—could our time together at the Holocaust Museum shed light on how the three traditions could work dialogically to dispel such mistrust? Our encounter—amid graphic evidence of the failure of humans to heed the command "Thou shall not murder"—not only constituted an important step in our dialogical process but also added to the distinctiveness of this book by affecting the writing it contains.

The fact that sixteen of us were able to meet in person, and in such a sobering setting, before finalizing our written contributions afforded us an unusual opportunity for collaboration as we faced the daunting challenges inherent in the nature of our project. Indeed, few minefields that threaten to explode in the face of partners-to-dialogue are more volatile than the issues raised in this volume. Addressing these issues tested even the mettle of a group committed to trialogue. Primarily provoked by interfaith disagreements about the Palestinian-Israeli conflict and by intrafaith controversies concerning how a tradition's scripture and teachings should be interpreted, unruly passions arose from time to time in our deliberations. But we were able to tame them, and our engagement encouraged friendship that will last well beyond our joint effort in producing this volume. The experience of meeting one another in person enabled us to complete our work in the spirit of that true hospitality to which we aspired. Indeed, we helped one another shape our respective contributions; we came to one another's assistance as we bore witness to the enormity of human beings' inhumanity to their fellow human beings. The reader will be the judge, but we hope that our reflections embody the message conveyed in the words of Martin Buber: "When a man is singing and cannot lift his voice, and another comes and sings with him, another who can lift his voice, the first will be able to lift his voice too."[7]

This is not to say that uniformity of message or style characterizes our collective work. Essays run the gamut from a historical account of aspects of medieval Christianity to a reflection on Jewish-gentile intermarriage, from theological discourse on Islamic scripture to personal memoir. No priority was given to consensus with regard to the content of what it might mean to "encounter the stranger." We uncovered disagreement not only among essayists representing different traditions but also among those belonging to the same tradition. Our desire was to listen well to one another. Both intra- and interreligious differences became part and parcel of creative trialogue. In such trialogue, as Buber suggests, "each of the partners, even when he stands in opposition to the other, heeds, affirms, and confirms his opponent."[8] The contributors to this volume attempted to honor the essence of Buber's declaration as they proceeded to confirm the personhood of the other.

Since this collection of essays is first and foremost a conversation among concerned colleagues who share a focus on the need for fruitful interreligious dialogue, we sought to find a format for our work that would mirror the essence of its subject matter. Each essay in this volume is followed by a series of questions distilled from queries raised by three other essayists, one from each of the three Abrahamic traditions. These constellations of questions are then addressed by the original contributor in a second essay, titled simply "Response." The volume's format is thus a concrete manifestation of its theme: there is no single way to dialogue; dialogue is the way. We thus agreed to "put our money where our mouths are": our process, hopefully, is illustrative of our product. Not only did we talk about dialogue; in our writing as well as in our face-to-face speaking, we tried to live it. Although our work as contributors to an edited volume is at an end, the larger project to which we have committed ourselves is ongoing because the task of reflecting on our traditions' understandings of the "other" is unending. We hope that our readers will join us in continuing dialogue/ trialogue that emphasizes understanding the "other" and welcoming the stranger.

Leonard Grob and John K. Roth

NOTES

Epigraph: Hans Küng, *Global Responsibility: In Search of a New World Ethic* (New York: Crossroad, 1991), xv.

1   Martin E. Marty, *When Faiths Collide* (Malden, Mass.: Blackwell, 2005), 1–4. In *Encountering the Stranger*, some but not all of the book's contributors may sometimes enclose the term *other* in quotation marks and/or capitalize it. When the term is enclosed in quotation marks and/or capitalized, it typically refers to persons insofar as they are understood, in *the essence of their being*, as other. That is, when the term is written in these ways, the intention is to underscore that human personhood, at its core, entails separation from one another but a separation that is also a relationship and, indeed, a relationship that confers obligations to one another. When the term *other* is not capitalized or enclosed in quotation marks, it also typically refers to other individuals and, in particular, to individuals whose difference and distance are likely to make us regard those individuals as strangers. The contexts in which *Other*, "*other*," and *other* are used by the book's contributors should be sufficient to make the meanings and distinctions clear, including occasional allusions to God and transcendence.

2   Quoted in Harold G. Coward, ed., *Modern Indian Responses to Religious Pluralism* (Albany: State University of New York Press, 1988), 11.

3   Martin Buber, "Dialogue," in *Between Man and Man*, trans. Ronald Gregor Smith (New York: Macmillan, 1965), 6.

4   John Hick, "Pluralism Conference," *Buddhist-Christian Studies* 24, no. 1 (2004): 253.

5   Jonathan Sacks, *The Dignity of Difference: How to Avoid the Clash of Civilizations* (New York: Continuum, 2002), 9.

6   Paul F. Knitter, ed., *The Myth of Religious Superiority: Multifaith Explorations of Religious Pluralism* (Maryknoll, N.Y.: Orbis Books, 2005), x.

7   Martin Buber, *Ten Rungs: Hasidic Sayings* (New York: Schocken Books, 1947), 84.

8   Martin Buber, *Pointing the Way* (New York: Harper & Row, 1958), 238.

ENCOUNTERING THE STRANGER

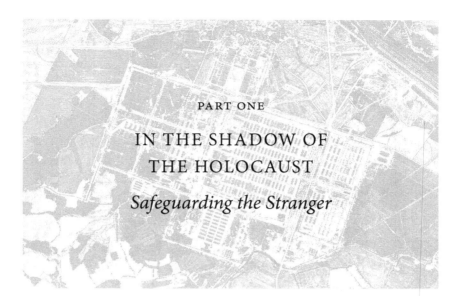

IN THE SHADOW OF
THE HOLOCAUST

Safeguarding the Stranger

The title of this book uses a term—*encountering*—whose meanings can include volatility and even violence. *Encountering* may involve meeting an enemy or an adversary, perhaps suddenly and unexpectedly, with clash and conflict ensuing. Encounters with strangers can be like that, but those possibilities do not exhaust the meanings of *encounter*, which can also entail meeting persons face-to-face and building on that experience in ways that go beyond chance, suspicion, and remaining strange, if not hostile, to one another.

In focusing on how individuals and institutions within the Abrahamic religious traditions (Jewish, Christian, and Muslim) have often encountered one another as strangers, hostile ones at that, the reflections in this book seek to show how *encounters* can be transformed—indeed become transformative—in constructive ways that are much needed in the twenty-first century, which is rife with conflict implicating those traditions. In this book, that quest begins with a claim that is as bold as it may be unexpected: to encounter the stranger face-to-face, to build on that experience in ways that go beyond remaining strange, if not hostile, to each other requires—first and foremost—safeguarding his or her life. That theme is explicitly identified in the title of Part One, whose six chapters emphasize protection for the Other and, in particular, for the stranger who stands outside "my religious tradition." True to the words of the French philosopher Emmanuel Levinas—one source of inspiration for this volume—the essayists in Part One agree that truly to encounter the Other is to hear the command "You shall not commit murder."[1] As coeditor John K. Roth notes in his chapter, Levinas does not regard this command as only a negative directive: we are enjoined to take active steps to defend the life of the Other. Prior to any act of "valuing the stranger" (Part Two of this book) or "welcoming the stranger" (Part Three), the contributors to Part One agree that we must exercise our fundamental responsibility to safeguard the stranger from harm.

As noted in the Prologue, the Holocaust presents itself as a case study of refusal on a mass scale to defend the life of the Other. Living in a post-Holocaust world, we can do no better than to turn to the Holocaust as a watershed event in human history that alerts us to the need to protect the outsider in our midst. The six essayists who have contributed to Part One address the Holocaust pointedly in their endeavor to offer a crucial instance of what may occur should we fail to heed the ethical imperative to safeguard the stranger. That the stranger must be regarded as inviolable is the point of departure for this and any study or practice of interreligious dialogue/trialogue.

Thus the title of the opening essay in this volume, Roth's "'You Shall Not Murder': A Foundation for Trialogue?" answers its own question in the affirmative. Roth goes so far as to say, "No ethical injunction is more important than 'You shall not murder.' Human civilization depends on it." Roth maintains, further, that "if that injunction is not at the heart of ethics in all three of the Abrahamic traditions, their moral stature is bereft and suspect." Writing as a Christian philosopher/theologian who is also a scholar of the Holocaust, Roth notes the extent to which the Sixth Commandment has been violated in the course of human history, a violation writ large in the genocide of the Jews at the hands of Nazi perpetrators of murder. Unless Jews, Christians, and Muslims find ways to engage in genuine trialogue, Roth argues, violations of the Sixth Commandment will continue to endanger civilization. Post-Holocaust civilization cries out for ways to ensure that "Never Again" will be realized.

Such cries may not be heeded by the God worshipped by adherents of all three Abrahamic traditions. Indeed, Roth asks if God might be considered a bystander to murder insofar as no Divine intervention has prevented genocide. Roth's conclusion: "God's refusal or inability to prevent human beings from murdering one another ramps up humankind's responsibility for itself." This call to responsibility, Roth argues, is amplified to the degree that we genuinely attend to those who have been murdered: "If we listen—carefully, thoughtfully—for what they 'say,' the humanity of their mutilated bodies, the screams that cry out in silence, demand 'You shall not murder.' . . . If we cannot heed what the murdered ones say, . . . trialogue will fall short of its potential for good." Listening to the dead in the shadow of the Holocaust and other atrocities moves us to safeguard the stranger.

Zayn Kassam opens her chapter with a reflection on the time shared by contributors to this volume at the United States Holocaust Memorial Museum (USHMM). She recalls that we witnessed "horrific reminders of the human capacity for violence against the other." Kassam notes that "unless humanity learns to appreciate and value difference, we will continue to justify violence." She adds that "in particular, religious traditions need to probe how sacred texts contribute to this problem and how they might also help correct it." Islam needs to renew the kinds of excellent relationships that existed between Jews and Muslims through the ages, for "to do otherwise would undermine a key lesson taught by the Holocaust: that the systematic 'othering' of any group is a harbinger of violence." In the endeavor to examine a possible "othering" within her own tradition, Kassam examines the Qur'an's understanding of the Other. She urges her Muslim coreligionists to rethink traditional responses to religious pluralism. Any call for constructive pluralism, she argues, will honor the teachings of the Other while allowing Muslims to retain their identity. In the course of her analyses, Kassam identifies conflicting verses in the Qur'an regarding the religious stranger and concludes that the Qur'an leaves any final judgment of the worth of the stranger to God alone. Diversity is deemed a divine creation whose purpose is to help bring communities into engagement with regard to the doing of good works. Further, any justification for violence in the Qur'an must be understood "within a particular historical and social context." Such violence, Kassam argues, represented not *calls* to aggression but rather *responses* to particular acts of enmity endangering the Muslim community.

A *novum* within human history, the Holocaust is central to David Patterson's essay on Jewish understandings of the stranger. In the process of exterminating Jews, Patterson contends, the Nazis attempted to blot out the central Jewish teaching that each human is created in the image of an infinite God and thus possesses infinite worth. The Nazis replaced this teaching with the claim that the mere accident of being born "Aryan" determines one's worth. The implications of the Jewish conception of human worth for an understanding of the Other are profound: if each soul is connected, through "the Infinite One" to every other soul, "our responsibility to and for one another is infinite." Any embrace of "*my* truth" as "*the* truth" is forbidden. Judaism accepts a pluralism of religions in its desire to realize genuine interreligious dialogue.

Patterson's defense of the morality of numerous Israeli Jewish actions in the course of the ongoing Palestinian-Israeli conflict calls attention to a fundamental ambiguity inherent in the meaning of "the stranger." In periods of conflict, the moral imperative to defend the stranger leads us to ask, "Who is a stranger to whom?" Clearly, there are multiple meanings of "the stranger"; indeed, it can be argued that we are all strangers to one another! Patterson asserts that with regard to at least some Palestinians, the Jewish stranger most often stands in need of protection from the Palestinian outsider. While asserting the need to protect the non-Muslim stranger, several Muslim contributors also write of the need to defend the lives and well-being of Muslims deemed hostile strangers themselves. Contributors to Part One of this volume—indeed, all contributors to *Encountering the Stranger*—are committed to a *reciprocal* heeding of the imperative to safeguard the stranger.

For Henry F. Knight, the Holocaust poses a serious challenge to Christianity: "Christianity faces the complicity of its own family in a crisis of moral integrity regarding Christian attitudes and behavior toward Jews before and during the Holocaust." And the problem lingers in the form of an ongoing embrace of supersessionism by many Christians—a disposition to privilege "Christian truth" in ways that give it dominance over every other religious stance. Supersessionism fails to make room for the Jewish other, thus ending any possibility of authentic interreligious dialogue. Contrasting what scholar Regina M. Schwartz has called an exclusivist "logic of scarcity" with an inclusive "logic of plenitude" resting on the notion that truth can be expressed in diverse ways, Knight holds out the hope that Christians may yet come to honor the Jewish other. If, on the one hand, we follow the logic of scarcity to its endpoint, claims Knight, we come to the Nazi selection process at Auschwitz: the absolute negation of any attempt to safeguard the Other. If, on the other hand, we follow the logic of plenitude, Christians will confront a "wounded" post-Holocaust world together with Jews, doing so in genuine dialogue. And just as the logic of plenitude negates a supersessionism that endangers the integrity—and perhaps the very existence—of the Jewish other, so does it extend a protective shield around the third party in the Abrahamic tradition, the Muslim other.

How does Knight propose, concretely, to begin the healing process in a post-Holocaust world? "Minimally," he argues, "Christians need to read the works of post-Shoah Jewish thinkers and hear the testimonies of Jewish survivors" because, together, Jews and Christians face a damaged world in a spirit characterized by Knight as "a wager for life." Christians need to sit shivah (days of mourning in the Jewish tradition) along with their Jewish brothers and sisters. The Holocaust, according to Knight, "does fundamental violence to God's gift of life in creation." The inhabitants of a post-Holocaust wounded world are thus alerted to the need to safeguard one another's existence.

Bassam Tibi, having spent a research term at the USHMM Center for Advanced Holocaust Studies, where he studied antisemitism in his own Islamic tradition, feels renewed confidence in addressing questions concerning the need to safeguard the religious other. Tibi notes that his findings regarding contemporary Islam evoke "memory of a time preceding the Holocaust." "As a liberal Muslim," he continues, "I am shocked to the bone by what is said about Jews in the writings of Islamists. There is a conflict within Islam . . . between a humanist Islam and a jihadist-xenophobic Islam." The latter, Tibi contends—"lacking authentic roots in Islam"—constitutes a major obstacle to an acknowledgment of religious pluralism. "There is need," he argues, "for a pluralism that promotes peace not only between Muslims and others . . . but also among Muslims, who are themselves a diverse people."

Tibi's essay is devoted to a defense of an Islam open to the possibility of pluralism in the face of what Tibi calls *Islamism*, a political, militant, and, in his view, misguided version of Islam. Islamism, Tibi argues, is not supported by a careful reading of the Qur'an. He advocates a rethinking of key Islamic concepts derived from both the Qur'an and later exegetical writings. Such a rethinking allows for the promotion of what Tibi calls a "civil Islam." Support for such a concept is to be found in the legacy bequeathed to Islam by a Hellenistic rationalism. Such a tradition provides a model for the establishment of cross-cultural dialogue. A revival of this rationalist legacy, he claims, "would help reverse recent developments and could promote the Islamic adoption of pluralism and democracy." Tibi is outspoken in his assertion that the hope for world peace lies in the balance.

Leonard Grob argues that not only the moral fiber of interreligious dialogue but the tradition of ethics as a whole must be called into question in a post-Holocaust world. Citing the work of Emmanuel Levinas and the prophetic tradition to which Levinas is heir, Grob contends that "Judaism's core teachings concerning the stranger can help heal our wounded world." Approvingly, Grob quotes Levinas: "[This is a world] of which Judaism is not only the conscience, but also the testimony . . . ; the cruelty where the burning of *my* suffering and the anguish of *my* death were able to be transfigured into . . . concern for the *other*." In other words, the Holocaust has given renewed emphasis to the absolute imperative to protect the stranger at all costs: we must invert a fear of our own death into a primordial fear of committing murder.

As an appropriate closing both to his essay and to Part One of this volume, Grob, again following Levinas, argues that safeguarding the Other is the foundation upon which all post-Holocaust ethics must be built. Such safeguarding thus provides the framework within which authentic trialogue among the Abrahamic traditions can emerge. "Being taught responsibility for the Other," Grob contends, "is a precondition for all meaningful trialogue." Such trialogue occurs when all parties recognize that although they come upon "insoluble problems" in interreligious dialogue, they must work vigilantly to ensure that such problems do not result in violence. In a post-Holocaust world, "where hatred of the religious other . . . continues to contribute to ongoing violence, including genocide," Grob emphasizes that we must "honor the sacredness of each individual of each faith tradition in the endeavor to overcome the urge toward domination." Encountering the stranger must mean safeguarding the stranger.

NOTE

1   Emmanuel Levinas, *Totality and Infinity: An Essay on Exteriority*, trans. Alphonso Lingis (Pittsburgh: Duquesne University Press, 1969), 199.

1

"You Shall Not Murder"

A Foundation for Trialogue?

JOHN K. ROTH

You shall not murder.
—Exodus 20:13

No ethical injunction is more important than "You shall not murder." Human civilization depends on it. So does the value of religion, including Judaism, Christianity, and Islam. In one way or another, all three of those traditions affirm that murder is wrong. It violates God's commandment.

Christianity, my religious tradition, emphasizes the Ten Commandments, especially as they are stated in Exodus 20 within the Hebrew Bible. Yet Christians—individually and collectively—have often disobeyed the Sixth Commandment, which says "You shall not murder." Indeed, Christians have even incited and committed murder in God's name. Jews and Muslims have been victims of that crime. When it comes to murder, there is much need for Christian repentance and atonement.

Questions

The facts stated above have many implications for me. How, for example, should I respond to Christianity's violations of the commandment against murder? Where does Christianity's sometimes murderous history allow me—require me—to stand when it comes to dialogue with Jews and Muslims? Are those traditions innocent when judged by the Sixth Commandment? What if all three, in their own particular and distinctive ways, are guilty of violating the Sixth Commandment? How can and should "trialogue" go forward in response to the possibility that murder must be faced by all three of these traditions? Is it possible, crucial even, for Jews, Christians, and Muslims to explore whether God's injunction against murder might provide a foundation for trialogue that could benefit these traditions individually and in relation to one another?

Definitions

This essay explores background that is important for sound responses to such questions. One starting point is to note that some versions of the Decalogue's sixth commandment substitute *kill* for *murder*. In either case, those key words require definition if the commandment is to make sense, but how much difference does it make if the Sixth Commandment contains one word rather than the other? The answer is *a great deal*.

According to the most reliable biblical scholarship, *murder*, not *kill*, is the best English term to use in translating the Hebrew text. That decision is significant, for the meanings of *murder* and *kill*, although closely related, are not identical. All murder is killing, but not all killing is murder. To kill means to inflict or cause death, which also happens in murder, but distinctions exist because killing acts can be accidental and unintentional. Killing acts of that kind are not murder, which typically requires an intention, often including premeditation and careful planning, to inflict or cause death. In addition, murderous intentions are usually inflamed by anger, malice, envy, greed, fear, hate, revenge, or some other violence-inciting emotion. Not all killing actions fit that description, but murderous ones typically do.

Historically, the Sixth Commandment, along with others in the Decalogue, has been understood to be addressed to human beings—to Jews, Christians, Muslims, and, indeed, to all persons and communities—whose distinctiveness includes a capacity for murder that is not found in any other part of the natural world. Various interpretations of its meaning can be found, but they all share and depend upon the understanding that the imperative applies to human beings who are commanded not to do certain things that are within their power. Obvious though this point may be, awareness of it helps underscore other crucial differences between *kill* and *murder*.

The Sixth Commandment is unequivocal and absolute. Allowing no exceptions, it does not say that "murder is wrong in situation X, but it may be permissible in situation Y." Murder, the commandment entails, is wrong—period. Killing, however, is not so easily interpreted that way, unless one stipulates that *killing* means *murder*. In fact, unless *killing* is qualified in that way, or in some other way that restricts the meaning of that term to forms of killing that are intentional but wrongful, unjustifiable, or inexcusable, a commandment that says "You shall not kill" would be so ambiguous, even nonsensical, that it would be impossible for human beings to obey it no matter how good they might be or how hard they might try.

To see why that situation holds, notice that human life depends on killing. That statement, of course, is as problematic as it is evident, as much in need of qualification as it is bold. Therefore, to avoid misunderstanding, I need to clarify what I do and do not mean by it. I do not mean, for example, that human life depends on war; it does not, although sometimes war is unavoidable and even necessary to defend human life. Nor do I mean that human civilization depends on capital punishment; it does not, although there may be times and places where justifiable reasons for executions can be found. What I do mean is that human life and civilization cannot exist, let alone thrive, unless people eat, quench their thirst, obtain shelter, raise and educate their young, and, in short, take the actions that are necessary to sustain human life. Unfortunately, those actions cannot be taken without killing. As the philosopher Philip Hallie cogently put the point, "We are in the food web. We are killers, if only of plants."[1]

An absolute and unequivocal prohibition against killing is not what the Sixth Commandment can mean if it is coherent. With due qualification, human life depends on killing, but a corollary of that truth is that human existence and especially its *quality* also depend on careful discrimination between killing that is justifiable or excusable and killing that is not. Absent such discrimination, including laws and sanctions to implement the difference socially and politically, it is hard to imagine that human civilization could long endure.

Perspectives

Much but not all killing is murder, but now two more questions must be addressed for the Sixth Commandment to make sense: When is killing murder? What constitutes murder? My response to those questions emerges from the perspectives that inform my thinking about the Sixth Commandment. My perspectives are those of a Protestant Christian philosopher/theologian whose work has concentrated for more than forty years on the Holocaust, Nazi Germany's attempt to destroy the Jewish people, and on other genocides as well. This outlook reminds me, again and again, of an unmistakable instance of murder, namely, the murder that the Hebrew Bible identifies as the first one. Genesis 4:1–16 tells that story, which depicts Cain's slaying of his brother Abel.[2]

When God favored an offering by Abel but "had no regard" for one by Cain, the latter's anger got the best of him. "Let us go out to the field," said Cain to the apparently unsuspecting Abel. "And when they were in the field," the biblical text continues, "Cain rose up against his brother Abel, and killed him." The story reports that God responded: "What have you done? Listen; your brother's blood is crying out to me from the ground!" Cain's killing act made him "a fugitive and a wanderer on the earth," one who "went away from the presence of the Lord," but God spared Cain's life, marking him "so that no one who came upon him would kill him."

At rock bottom, murder takes place when one person kills another intentionally, deliberately, and unjustifiably. (Much hinges on the last term in particular, a point to which I return in due course.) Cain's killing of Abel was murder—*homicide*—or no act could be. Moreover, like the Sixth Commandment itself, the Genesis narrative leaves no doubt that murder is wrong. That same account, however, raises as many questions as it answers. For instance, was Cain's killing of Abel clearly premeditated? Genesis does not say so explicitly, although far from being excluded, the text definitely invites such an inference. Furthermore, when Cain "rose up against his brother," was that action murderous from the outset? Again, the text allows for the possibility that it might not have been that way, although Cain's "rising up" resulted in killing that was unlikely to have been accidental. Otherwise, Cain probably would not have tried to fend off God's question—"Where is your brother Abel?"—by denial and evasion: "I do not know; am I my brother's keeper?" (Genesis 4:9).

The ambiguities do not end there. When Cain questioned whether he should be held accountable as his brother's keeper, was he implying that creation did not yet have a moral structure that condemned murder, as the

Sixth Commandment would do explicitly later on? Cain's defense might have been that he unfairly received an ex post facto judgment from God. Who says, and where and when was it said, Cain might have protested, that I am to be Abel's keeper? However, if Cain made a legalistic move of this kind, Genesis shows that God had none of it. Prior to its story about Cain's murder of Abel, the biblical account in Genesis brims with language about what is good, about the knowledge of good and evil, about obedience and disobedience. The Genesis tradition, moreover, makes clear not only that God "created humankind in his image, in the image of God he created them; male and female he created them," but also that "God blessed them" (Genesis 1:27–28). Could it make any good sense for God to create human beings in God's image, bless them, and then permit them with impunity to slaughter one another intentionally? At the end of the day, ambiguity notwithstanding, no credible reading could interpret Genesis as doing less than defining murder quintessentially or as doing anything other than finding murder wrong—period.

The clarity notwithstanding, a troubling shadow still lurks in the questions and responses above. It will need revisiting. Meanwhile, a basic point is maintained within Jewish tradition, which, among other things, holds that when God gave Moses the Ten Commandments at Sinai, those imperatives were etched on two stone tablets, five commandments on each. The first five identified human duties to God; the second five underscored obligations that persons have to one another. Tradition holds further that there are parallels between the two sets of five commandments. Thus the Sixth Commandment, "You shall not murder," is especially linked to the First Commandment, "I am the Lord your God, who brought you out of the land of Egypt, out of the house of slavery; you shall have no other gods before me." Murder—the intentional, deliberate, and unjustifiable killing of one human being by another—is wrong for reasons that go deep down because they violate the First Commandment.

God created human life in God's image. In God's sight, and surely in ours, that act was good. It was also awesome, even sacred, for in the ultimate sense, no human being has the power to create human life—not even the wonders of twenty-first-century science contradict that fact—and murder destroys human life in ways that are beyond our repair and recovery. God may or may not resurrect the dead, but human beings utterly lack the power to do so. The result is that no human act rivals murder in defying, disrespecting, and denying God.

Here it is worth noting that, according to the biblical scholar David Flusser, the Christian New Testament "does not use the term 'Ten Commandments' even once," but the injunction against murder is emphasized in multiple instances, and especially by Jesus in ways that are thoroughly consistent with the Jewish tradition that he observed.[3] In Matthew 19:16–22, Mark 10:17–22, and Luke 18:18–23, for example, Jesus stresses the importance of obeying God's commandments and explicitly condemns murder. Paul does the same in Romans 13:9, adding that the Sixth Commandment, along with those prohibiting adultery and theft, "are summed up in this word, 'Love your neighbor as yourself.'"

Flusser's observation about the Christian New Testament may be appropriate for the Qur'an as well. If the latter does not use the term *Ten Commandments*, it prohibits murder both explicitly and implicitly. Representative passages such as the following bear witness to that claim: (1) ". . . Whoever kill[s] a human being, except as a punishment for murder or other villainy in the land, shall be looked upon as though he had killed all mankind . . ." (Qur'an 5:32); (2) ". . . You shall not kill—for that is forbidden by God—except for a just cause" (6:151); (3) "Do not kill except for a just cause (manslaughter is forbidden by Him)" (25:68).[4] These texts use *kill* more than *murder*. If qualifications such as "except for a just cause" surround the former, as they often do in Jewish and Christian interpretations as well, at least an implied imperative against murder exists in these texts. That imperative is without qualification—unless, of course, one argues that an instance of murder is really an instance of justifiable killing and thus not murder at all. All three traditions have employed such dubious reasoning when it suited them, a fact that complicates but by no means invalidates the injunction against murder. It is in this fraught area that some of the most crucial aspects of contemporary Jewish-Christian-Muslim trialogue are to be found, particularly as violence rages in the Middle East, suicide bombers deal death, and problematic claims about the "justice" of what are murderous actions are sounded on all sides of conflicts in which Jews, Christians, and Muslims are deeply embroiled and implicated.

What Have We Done?

To some extent the Sixth Commandment has had a braking effect on humankind's propensity for violence. Arguably, however, an honest historical appraisal leads to the conclusion that the most distinctive quality about the Sixth Commandment is the extent to which it has been violated—disregarded, dismissed, and disrespected. Coupled with those characteristics, one must add that the Sixth Commandment has never been backed sufficiently by credible sanctions, divine or human, that would ensure full respect for and obedience to it.[5]

"What have you done?" God asked Cain after he murdered Abel. In the early twenty-first century, Jews, Christians, and Muslims alike need to hear God putting that question to them with particular reference to murder and other forms of killing as well. In more ways than one, such hearing is not easy. The slaughter-bench of history, to use G. W. F. Hegel's phrase, calls into question the functional status of the Sixth Commandment. A commandment that is not obeyed may still be a commandment, but its functional status depends on obedience and credible sanctions against disobedience.

An injunction that is not heeded lacks credibility. When Nazi Germany, supported by many German Christians, unleashed the Holocaust, the force of the imperative "You shall not murder" was impugned to the degree that millions of Jews were slaughtered. It took the violence of a massive world war, which left tens of millions more corpses in its wake, before the Third Reich was crushed and the Holocaust's genocidal killing centers were shut down. At least in the three major monotheistic traditions, God is the source and the ultimate vindicator of the Sixth Commandment. If God is not acknowledged and obeyed, God's existence is not necessarily eliminated, but God's authority is curtailed. And if God's authority lacks credibility, then the nature of God's existence is affected too. How has the Sixth Commandment functioned and fared in history? Two of the words that must be used in response to that question are *poorly* and *badly*. Unless Jews, Christians, and Muslims find ways to work together to reverse that situation, human civilization itself is imperiled more than ever.

What Has God Done?

When one wrestles with the Sixth Commandment, God's question to Cain—"What have you done?"—can be put to God as well. God's prohibition of murder is clear, but arguably not clear enough because the commandment's meaning is neither completely self-evident nor as thoroughly detailed and forceful as it might be. Even if the taking of any life is in some sense wrong, and such a case can be made, God's specific positions—

to the extent that they exist—on war, capital punishment, abortion, and euthanasia appear not to be entirely free of ambiguity, leaving men and women to contend for and about the interpretations that make the best sense. The complications, however, are not restricted to matters of interpretation. They also involve God's relation to murder, which is made the more troublesome because of the Sixth Commandment.

Could it be that the Sixth Commandment is violated by God, the very One who established it? That question does not imply, God forbid, that God is a murderer, but it does raise the possibility that God can be found wanting for failing to intervene against murderers and, to that extent, for being a bystander if not an accomplice when murder takes place.

When that possibility is raised, theology usually offers justifications or excuses for God in an exercise called *theodicy*. Such thinking usually maintains that, no matter what happens, God is just and good. Where murder is concerned, theodicy typically gives God a pass by arguing that human beings and they alone are responsible for their actions because God gave them freedom to choose and act. Freedom's defense for God, however, is more problematic than it seems.[6] As homicide and genocide make clear, God's gift of freedom has taken an immensely murderous toll. History shows that human beings can and will use their freedom to murder wantonly, and to a large extent with impunity, because the murdering is never stopped soon enough. Auschwitz makes us ask, "Where was humanity?" Auschwitz can also make us ask, "Where is God?" and it does so because of the Sixth Commandment.

"You shall not murder"—this commandment reveals much about God. The revelation is awesome but not only because God's commanding moral voice resounds within it. The revelation is also awesome because God's refusal or inability to prevent human beings from murdering one another ramps up humankind's responsibility for itself. The Sixth Commandment reveals God to be One who takes human accountability far more seriously than men and women—Jews, Christians, and Muslims included—are likely to do.

The Sixth Commandment and the Future

The Sixth Commandment will continue to be what I called it at the outset: the imperative that is the most necessary, although not sufficient, condition for human civilization. No less clear is the fact that this commandment will continue to be violated, often immensely and with a large measure of impunity. Furthermore, the God who prohibits murder is also the One who will do relatively little, if anything, to stop human beings from committing homicide or genocide.

The Jewish philosopher Emmanuel Levinas, who lost much of his family in the Holocaust, insisted that "You shall not murder" means nothing less than "you shall defend the life of the other."[7] The Sixth Commandment and the task that Levinas rightly identifies as following from it show that nothing human, natural, or divine guarantees respect for either imperative, but nothing is more important than making them a key responsibility in Jewish-Christian-Muslim understanding, for they remain as fundamental as they are in jeopardy, as vitally important as they are threatened by humankind's murderous destructiveness and indifference.

CONTRIBUTORS' QUESTIONS FOR JOHN K. ROTH

1. Does your conclusion that "the God who prohibits murder is also the One who will do relatively little, if anything, to stop human beings from committing homicide or genocide" imply that we must somehow transcend our theological representations of God? We know that God is capable of adhering to His own Sixth Commandment; for example, God rescues Isaac from Abraham's knife. If God does not act "otherwise," is it not the case that our failure to transcend the murderous in the three Abrahamic traditions reflects at least partly the fact that we have been unwilling, if not unable, to imagine or transformatively experience divinity that is not also, at times, murderous? Is a non-murderous God even conceivable within the constructs of our three faiths?

2. You write: "Auschwitz can . . . make us ask, 'Where is God?'" What do you make of the views of Auschwitz survivors Hugo Gryn and Elie Wiesel that God was, in some sense, *within* Auschwitz among those suffering and dying? Does this argument in any way temper the judgment regarding "God's refusal or inability to prevent human beings from murdering one another"? Might this kind of thinking take God "off the hook" for the murders at Auschwitz? Might even hints of "theodicy" blunt the force of your observation that "God's refusal or inability to prevent human beings from murdering one another ramps up humankind's responsibility for itself," which returns to the Sixth Com-

mandment a sense of sacred obligation that might help foster trialogue among the Abrahamic traditions?

RESPONSE BY JOHN K. ROTH

The questions that my colleagues pose are mostly about God, an understandable result because my discussion of the Sixth Commandment—"You shall not murder"—reflects on God's relationship to that divine injunction, arguing that both humankind and God fail to honor sufficiently the imperative that is the most necessary, though insufficient alone, for human flourishing. One line of questioning asks whether trialogue would be facilitated if Jews, Christians, and Muslims went beyond their typical theological representations of God or at least tried to conceive of a non-murderous God. A second and related line of questioning asks whether trialogue among Jews, Christians, and Muslims could be advanced if it emphasized God's presence and solidarity with those who suffer and die by violent means. By concentrating on God as the One who is ultimately merciful, loving, and compassionate, might the divine injunction against murder achieve a degree of persuasiveness that otherwise would be unachievable?

These suggestions have merit. If the identities of Jews, Christians, and Muslims and trialogue among these traditions are to be deeply ethical, as they surely ought to be, then ideally every Jew, Christian, and Muslim must take a stand against murder, including a commitment not to take murderous revenge when killing takes place. How Jews, Christians, and Muslims think about God has crucial parts to play in encouraging such stands and commitments. I do not believe, however, that a one-size-fits-all theology for the three traditions should be sought, even if it could be found.

If credible theologies can be found that in no way leave God implicated in violence or even murder, more power to them. Finding such a God within the three Abrahamic traditions, however, is easier said than done. Nevertheless, the commandment against murder remains, disrespected and impotent though it often is. If that injunction is not at the heart of ethics in all three of the Abrahamic traditions, their moral stature is bereft and suspect.

To my mind, the point of Jewish-Christian-Muslim trialogue is much more ethical than theological. Granted, ethical and theological perspectives are often related and even inseparable, but they are not identical. Ethical relationships, characterized by caring for one another, are what trialogue most needs to achieve. At the core of those relationships stands the commandment and commitment not to murder one another. I doubt that trialogical discussion about God, important though it can be, is likely to advance this cause much beyond a basic agreement that murder is wrong. What may be more helpful, but only by a little, I expect, is discussion that clarifies what is included or excluded in the concept of murder. The problem here is that the human propensity for rationalization and self-righteousness will try to justify killing as non-murder, thus explaining murder away, while at the same time indicting opponents as murderers when their actions attack one's own people. If agreement that murder is wrong can serve as a basis for Jewish-Christian-Muslim trialogue, it will need to get beyond rationalization, self-righteousness, and every other impulse that finds "them" murderous but never "us."

My essay maintains that killing acts can be accidental and unintentional. Killing acts of that kind are not murder, nor are those carried out in self-defense or to protect others from life-threatening violence. But those qualifications still leave murder taking an immense toll, not only in individual homicidal acts but also in war crimes, crimes against humanity, and genocide. Typically, as my essay notes, murderous actions require an intention, often including premeditation and careful planning, to inflict or cause death. Importantly, intent ought not to be construed too narrowly lest murderous acts are falsely denied and swept away by the defining strokes of self-serving pens. Where murder is concerned, particularly the mass murder associated with war crimes and crimes against humanity, intent should not be restricted to premeditation and careful planning but should also leave room for indictments based on considered judgments that there are good reasons to think that the actions a person or group has carried out or is undertaking were/are likely to inflict death in ways that exceed reasonable understandings of self-defense or the protection of others against life-threatening violence. Again, there is no one-size-fits-all rationale for deciding these cases, or even for defining the terms that are unavoidably in play within such judgments. For that reason, I suggest a different approach that might make the injunction against murder a more credible and fruitful basis for Jewish-Christian-Muslim trialogue. This approach concentrates neither on God nor on concepts but on the dead.

So many of the dead are dead not because they lived to a ripe old age or even because disease, untimely though it may have been, ended their lives. So many of the dead are dead—children and women as well as men, the young and the old—because they were murdered. If most of the murdered do not have their lives stolen by what we typically mean by homicide, neither are the murdered killed as enemy combatants in warfare, nor are they the unfortunate civilian casualties of euphemistic "collateral damage" during military operations, a category that unethically washes murder away. The murdered ones include the innocent—a real and valid category, notwithstanding ideologies that make all victims "guilty"—especially those slaughtered in rocket attacks and air strikes, wiped out in suicide bombings, annihilated in mass shootings, starved to death, butchered in hundreds of lethal ways. In various ways, places, and times—past, present, and probably yet to come—Jews, Christians, and Muslims have done these things to others, to one another, and to their own, not in the same measure or in equivalent ways but with enough bloodshed to say that all three traditions harbor murder(ers) within them.

Those unjustly robbed of life by human decisions and human actions are the ones we need especially to see and to heed. But if we settle for calling these dead *victims*, we misplace where key aspects of the emphasis need to be placed. By speaking of victims, we rightly call attention to the victimizers, to the murderers. By speaking only of victims, however, we obscure the faces of the dead and the humanity of the murdered, those who, in George Steiner's words, have been "done to death."[8]

"Try to look," wrote the Auschwitz survivor Charlotte Delbo, "just try and see."[9] She wanted people to see the defaced faces of the dead (especially the murdered dead), to discern what those faces say about right and wrong, to take to heart how the humanity of the dead—even, indeed especially, in their silence—resounds the imperative against murder. Another French voice, that of the Catholic priest Patrick Desbois, echoes Delbo's. Desbois's mission has been to help us—Jews, Christians, Muslims, and more—remember the humanity of more than 1.5 million Jews who were shot to death at hundreds of extermination sites in Eastern Europe during the Holocaust. They were murdered by Germans and their collaborators—baptized Christians undoubtedly and overwhelmingly among them—and then left to rot in unmarked mass graves that scar the earth in Ukraine, Belarus, and Russia long after the Holocaust. By interviewing hundreds of witnesses who did see the dead, Desbois says that he seeks "to establish the truth and justice."[10] Surely, fidelity to the injunction against murder is inseparable from that task.

Some of the interviews conducted in 1946 by the American psychologist David P. Boder are among the earliest with persons who survived the

Holocaust. Using the wire recording technology that was state of the art at the time, Boder interviewed "about seventy people, representing nearly all creeds and nationalities in the DP [displaced persons] installations in the American Zone." He recorded 120 hours of testimony, which was translated, he said, "to keep the material as near to the text of the original narratives as the most elementary rules of grammar would permit."[11] Eight of these interviews were published by the University of Illinois Press in 1949. The last one contains the testimony given in Munich by a man named Jack Matzner on September 26, 1946.

Born in Wiesbaden, Germany, Matzner, forty-two when the interview took place, was a Jew of Polish descent. Deported from Germany to Poland in 1938, he illegally returned to Germany for a time, and then he and his family were reunited in Antwerp, Belgium. On May 14, 1940, soon after the Germans occupied Belgium, Matzner went to France. Eventually arrested, he was deported to the East. The account he gave to Boder after surviving "fifty-five months of concentration camps" included episodes that were deeply embedded in his memory (200).

On one occasion in 1945, Matzner was inside Germany as a slave laborer for Heinkel Aviation Industries. He reports that his captors beat him and then imprisoned him in a flooded cellar with "about ninety or ninety-five people," many of them in water that was already "chest high." Matzner's account to Boder continued as follows: "Those who were lying there were already dead. And those who were standing had arranged the bodies of the dead in such a manner that they could stand or sit on them. Otherwise, the ones who were still living would also have drowned. I did the same thing. I found myself a place at the wall. I dragged two bodies which were under the water and arranged them against the wall, and I sat on them. And so I remained in the water, counting from that morning, exactly two days and two nights" (217).

Boder interviewed Matzner, but perhaps with those drowned Jews from Matzner's account in mind—to say nothing of the millions who had been starved and beaten to death, shot, or gassed—he ended the introduction to his book with these words: "The verbatim records presented in this book make uneasy reading. And yet," he added, "they are not the grimmest stories that could be told—I did not interview the dead" (xix). That last thought-provoking phrase—I did not interview the dead—became his book's title.

If we see the dead, if we listen—carefully, thoughtfully—for what they "say," the humanity of their mutilated bodies, the screams that cry out in silence, demand "You shall not murder." How could they not? No voice divine or human can speak with more authority, more passion and urgency, than that. Neither the figurative face of God nor the face of the actual living other can exceed what the faces of the murdered ones tell us about the fragile preciousness of the gift of human life. If we cannot heed what the murdered ones say, Jewish-Christian-Muslim trialogue will fall short of its potential for good.

During the development of this book, most of the contributors were privileged to meet for discussion at the United States Holocaust Memorial Museum in Washington, D.C. We took time to experience the museum's permanent exhibition and its presentation about *The Protocols of the Elders of Zion*, the notorious early twentieth-century forgery—still circulating to this day—that has inflamed antisemitism by falsely and perversely alleging that there is an invidious, destructive, and murderous Jewish conspiracy to dominate and control the world. During our time together, I think that we saw and heard some of the murdered ones. When we looked into one another's eyes, when we listened to one another's voices, when we considered what we ought to say, and later what we ought to write as we revised the essays that we shared at the museum and that now form the contents of this book, our encounters with the dead made a difference. The murdered ones made us see, I believe, not only how the injunction against murder can be a basis for Jewish-Christian-Muslim trialogue but also why it must be.

NOTES

1   Philip Paul Hallie, "Cruelty: The Empirical Evil," in *Facing Evil: Light at the Core of Darkness*, ed. Paul Woodruff and Harry A. Wilmer (LaSalle, Ill.: Open Court, 1988), 128.

2   The biblical quotations in this chapter come from the New Revised Standard Version.

3   David Flusser, "The Decalogue in the New Testament," in *The Ten Commandments in History and Tradition*, ed. Ben-Zion Segal and Gershon Levi (Jerusalem: Magnes Press, Hebrew University of Jerusalem, 1990), 221.

4   The quotations from the Qur'an are from N. J. Dawood's translation, *The Koran: With a Parallel Arabic Text* (New York: Penguin Books, 1990).

5   If there is life beyond death, God's judgment may provide sanctions that condemn murder beyond all doubt and without remainder. Unfortunately, that result comes

too late to be effective in history, for neither the murdered nor their murderers have returned to tell what God may have done with them. Nor has God made that situation crystal clear. Meanwhile, within history, murder is sometimes punished but not with sufficiently credible deterring impact. History's mounds of murdered dead grow larger and larger.

6   For elaborations of my views on these matters. *See,* for example, my contributions to Stephen T. Davis, ed., *Encountering Evil: Live Options in Theodicy,* rev. ed. (Louisville, Ky.: Westminster John Knox Press, 2001).

7   Emmanuel Levinas, "In the Name of the Other," trans. Maureen V. Gedney, in *Is It Righteous to Be? Interviews with Emmanuel Levinas,* ed. Jill Robbins (Stanford, Calif.: Stanford University Press, 2001), 192.

8   George Steiner, *Language and Silence: Essays on Language, Literature, and the Inhuman* (New York: Atheneum, 1967), 157. I am indebted to Paul C. Santilli for this reference. On the importance of encountering the face of the dead, especially the murdered dead, Santilli's thought influences mine. See especially Paul C. Santilli, "Philosophy's Obligation to the Human Being in the Aftermath of Genocide," in *Genocide and Human Rights: A Philosophical Guide,* ed. John K. Roth (New York: Palgrave Macmillan, 2005), 220–32.

9   Charlotte Delbo, *Auschwitz and After,* trans. Rosette C. Lamont (New Haven, Conn.: Yale University Press, 1995), 84–86.

10   See Patrick Desbois, *The Holocaust by Bullets: A Priest's Journey to Uncover the Truth behind the Murder of 1.5 Million Jews* (New York: Palgrave Macmillan, 2008). For more information about Desbois and his findings. *See* http://www.yahadinunum.org. See also Maria Danilova and Randy Herschaft, "Ukraine Slaughter Was Opening Salvo of Nazis' Final Solution," *Seattle Times,* February 1, 2009. The Desbois quotation is taken from Danilova and Herschaft's Associated Press article. Desbois heads Yahad–In Unum (Hebrew and Latin for "together"), an association of Catholics and Jews that seeks reconciliation between their traditions. Its website is noted above.

11   David P. Boder, *I Did Not Interview the Dead* (Urbana: University of Illinois Press, 1949), xiii. Further citations to this volume are indicated in parentheses.

2

Whom May I Kill?

ZAYN KASSAM

When participants in this trialogue spent time together at the United States Holocaust Memorial Museum (USHMM) in Washington, D.C., they obtained horrific reminders of the human capacity for violence against the other, whose allegedly "essential" characteristics often are depicted as negative and threatening. Even though a collective call for "Never Again" was articulated by Jews as a warning to the world after the Holocaust, violence—including genocide—continues to mar our lives.

One of the most chilling aspects of the evidence collected and displayed at USHMM is that ordinary people acted in ways large and small that resulted in extraordinary violence, justifying these actions to themselves in the process. Time spent at USHMM can daze the visitor, but one realization becomes inescapably clear: unless humanity learns to appreciate and value difference, we will continue to justify violence against one another by employing rhetoric that depicts the other as vile and menacing. In particular, religious traditions need to probe how sacred texts contribute to this problem and how they might also help correct it.

This chapter examines relevant verses in the Qur'an to discern how Islamic scripture identifies the stranger, the actions that should follow such identification, and the conditions in which those actions may include violence. Beginning with commentary on how the Qur'an views non-Muslims, the chapter specifically proceeds to consider Islamic views regarding Jews and Christians as well as those traditionally known as the hypocrites and the polytheists. Finally, the analysis points in directions that may enable Muslims to rethink religious pluralism while retaining their primary identity as Muslims.

The Stranger

Strangers are not understood monolithically in the Qur'an; generally, the Qur'an enjoins doing good to them: "Serve Allah, and join not any partners with Him; and do good—to parents, kinsfolk, orphans, those in need, neighbors who are near, neighbors who are strangers, the companion by your side, the wayfarer (ye meet), and what your right hands possess: For Allah loveth not the arrogant, the vainglorious" (4:36).[1] However, it could be argued that Muslims might consider the unbeliever as an outsider or a different kind of "stranger." The term *kāfir*, literally meaning "the ungrateful one," connotes one who is an unbeliever, who does not recognize God's bounties and hence does not accede to the lordship and creatorship of the one God. Some monotheists may fall into this category if, despite being monotheists, they are ungrateful for the bounties of creation. It may also be extrapolated that all polytheists (*mushriqūn*)—those who hold the view that different divinities are responsible for the bounties found in creation—are, therefore, unbelievers and hence outsiders. In the Qur'an's own time, such folk were clearly considered a potential physical threat to Muslims, as can be extrapolated from the Qur'an's caution to the Muslims of its time that prayer may be shortened while traveling, should there be any fear of being attacked by unbelievers (4:101).

Islam takes Abraham to be the quintessential *muslim*, anyone who has performed the act of *islām* (surrendering to divine will). While this designation applies to Muslims, it also fits those who are not Muslim by faith but are monotheistic by persuasion, before or after Islam was revealed as a historical religious tradition through the prophecy of Muhammad in the seventh century. The Qur'an relates the story of Abraham's watching the sun, moon, and stars and determining that he could not worship them because they were not constant and abiding but subject to rising and setting. For Abraham, the only being worthy of worship is not one that rises and sets but one who created those who rise and set (Qur'an 6:76–80). Thus, by implication, the ungrateful one, or *kāfir*, is identified as one who has not acknowledged the lordship and creatorship of God.

The Qur'an further specifies that God is not multiple but single. In

Qur'an 112, the chapter most often cited as revealing the oneness or unicity of God, it is said that God is One, that God did not beget, nor was God begotten. This outlook may well have been emphasized to contrast with the pre-Islamic Arab belief that Allah had three daughters who were divinities in their own right; the Christian belief that that God had a son, Jesus, who was also divine; and the common Greek notions of divinities giving birth to other divinities. Furthermore, this crucial chapter asserts that nothing in creation has the likeness of divinity: God is sui generis. Hence the Qur'an takes polytheists—all those who believe in a plurality of divinities—to be among those who refuse to acknowledge the truth about the unitary nature of divinity.

Importantly, the Qur'an also states, "Let there be no compulsion in religion" (2:256), thereby suggesting that acceptance of the Qur'an's revelations about divinity is a matter of individual choice. Another verse directs Muhammad to say to his detractors, "To you be your Way, and to me mine" (109:6), suggesting that just as others have the freedom to follow their own gods, Muhammad has the freedom to follow his. A third example indicates that it is within the purview of divine wisdom that many communities and nations exist: "We created you from a single (pair) of a male and a female, and made you into nations and tribes, that ye may know each other" (49:13), suggesting that a diversity of nations—and by implication, a diversity of belief systems—is part of the divine organization of humanity. Another verse testifies that the Qur'an was sent specifically as a scripture in the Arabic language for Arabs to understand (12:2), but the Qur'an came from the same God who created Moses and other prophets mentioned in the Bible (5:48), thereby suggesting that God has sent emissaries to other peoples and that Muslims are not alone in having received divine revelation and guidance.

Such verses complicate and problematize the identity of the outsider. If a Muslim acknowledges that God is Lord and Creator of all that exists in creation, then who can properly be called an outsider? Whether a Muslim or not, no person can properly fall outside the range of God's mercy and compassion. By the very fact of being part of creation, a non-Muslim cannot fall outside of God's grace. Similarly, if a person persists in unbelief despite having had access to revelation and despite partaking of and observing God's bounties, then the matter is left to God rather than Muslims to deal with.

Jews and Christians

Chapter 5 of the Qur'an, titled *Al-Maidah* (The Table Spread with Food), deals specifically with Jews, Christians, and Sabaeans.[2] The Qur'an clearly states that divine revelations were given to Moses and to Jesus and that Jewish and Christian communities were given guidance by God to judge between truth and falsehood. Two verses are especially relevant in this regard. After declaring that God set forth and confirmed the truth for both Jews and Christians, the first (Qur'an 5:48) exhorts Muslims not to follow those among Jews and Christians who are errant in their views: "If Allah had so willed, He would have made you a single people, but (His plan is) to test you in what He hath given you: so strive as in a race in all virtues. The goal of you all is to Allah; it is He that will show you the truth of the matters in which ye dispute." The intent of the portions of this chapter that deal with Jews and Christians is clearly that members of these traditions are recipients of divine revelation. While there are among them those who, nonetheless, choose to ignore the truth and guidance to be found therein, such folk will be dealt with by God as God wishes.

The second crucial verse (Qur'an 5:51) exhorts Muslims not to take Jews and Christians as *awlīyā'* (often translated as "friends"), for they are *awlīyā'* to one another. A Muslim who takes them as such thus becomes one among them; God will not guide these Muslims. Such a verse is no doubt quite perplexing and distressing to Jews and Christians, given that, as we have seen, God declared that Jews and Christians are recipients of divine revelation and guidance. However, the context suggests that the term *walī* (pl. *awlīyā'*), although frequently rendered as "friend," is meant here in the sense of *one who has authority*. Thus the verse asks that Muslims not cede authority to Jews and Christians with respect to the matter of God's guidance, because Muslims have been given their own revelation and guidance; Muslims accepting Jews and Christians as *awlīyā'* would mean, in essence, that "as one of them," they are to adhere to the guidance given to Jews or Christians.

The verse in question suggests that while Jews and Christians have been given divine guidance, some of them have erred. How is one to distinguish between those Jews and Christians who are righteous and those who are errant? Muslims have their own scripture to guide them. Therefore for Muslims to take as authorities in matters of morality those Jews and Christians who are errant in their understanding of their scripture is to lead these Muslims toward tyranny. At this point, they are in danger of losing God's guidance, for, as is quoted in Qur'an 6:144, "Allah guideth not people who do wrong."

Verses such as these run the danger of being misinterpreted, mistakenly bearing the burden of suggesting that the Qur'an unequivocally condemns association with Jews and Christians. A closer examination suggests that the Qur'an on the whole upholds the sanctity and veracity of divine revelation to Jews and Christians, while holding the view that some among the Jews and the Christians have erred, thus making it prudent for Muslims to follow their own divine revelation. As I have argued, Muslims should not take Jews and Christians as authorities on God's guidance lest they cede authority to errant Jews and Christians and have turned themselves, inadvertently if not intentionally, into what the Qur'an understands as "tyrants."

The Qur'an insists that God is displeased with unrighteous and tyrannical behavior regardless of the monotheism in which it is found. God is the source of guidance through revelation for the three monotheisms of Judaism, Christianity, and Islam, a point stressed in verse 5:69: "Lo! those who believe, and those who are Jews, and Sabaeans, and Christians—Whosoever believeth in Allah and the Last Day and doeth right—there shall no fear come upon them neither shall they grieve" (Pickthall translation). In numerous places, the Qur'an distinguishes between those who believe and do good works and those who do not. Thus all such Jews, Christians, and Muslims will enjoy the pleasure of their Lord (Qur'an 98:7–8). Consistently, however, the Qur'an also distinguishes between monotheists who are within the pale of accepted religiosity and those who fall outside the pale of righteousness by dint of their errant beliefs and unrighteous actions. Even though one is a monotheist acknowledging the one Creator, unrighteous conduct makes one an outsider.

The Hypocrites (Munāfiqūn)

The majority of Qur'anic verses that focus on killing aim at its prohibition. When verses give divine permission to kill, careful examination reveals that such verses are directed against specific groups and acts, all of which must be viewed within the context of seventh-century Arabia, when Muhammad was establishing his mission. For instance, Qur'an 6:151 forbids killing except for just cause: "Say: 'Come, I will rehearse what Allah hath (really) prohibited you from': Join not anything as equal with Him;

be good to your parents; kill not your children on a plea of want;—We provide sustenance for you and for them;—come not nigh to shameful deeds. Whether open or secret; take not life, which Allah hath made sacred, except by way of justice and law: thus doth He command you, that ye may learn wisdom."

Verses 4:88–92 lay out the parameters regarding who may be killed, that is, those instances in which just cause for killing may be found. These verses apply specifically to the *munāfiqūn* (hypocrites). The context of the verses indicates that the *munāfiqūn* are those polytheistic Arabs who heard the revelations but rejected them. Qur'an 4:88 declares: "Why should ye be divided into two parties about the Hypocrites? Allah hath upset them for their (evil) deeds. Would ye guide those whom Allah hath thrown out of the Way? For those whom Allah hath thrown out of the Way, never shalt thou find the Way." Verse 4:89 continues: "They but wish that ye should reject Faith, as they do, and thus be on the same footing (as they): But take not friends [*awlīyā'*] from their ranks until they flee in the way of Allah (From what is forbidden). But if they turn renegades, seize them and slay them wherever ye find them; and (in any case) take no friends or helpers from their ranks." In this verse, the command to kill applies solely to those who were considered hypocrites within the social environs of the early Muslims.

The following verse, 4:90, further restricts the license or right to kill: "Except those who join a group between whom and you there is a treaty (of peace), or those who approach you with hearts restraining them from fighting you as well as fighting their own people. If Allah had pleased, He could have given them power over you, and they would have fought you: Therefore if they withdraw from you but fight you not, and (instead) send you (Guarantees of) peace, then Allah Hath opened no way for you (to war against them)." The verse makes clear that those having joined the Muslims in the path of God and then having departed from or rejected the faith—thus being among those who may be killed (4:89)—still may not be killed if they have formed a treaty with the Muslims or are not aggressors against them (4:90). In such cases, God withdraws the right to kill *munāfiqūn*. Lest God's commandments still be considered unclear, the final verse included among the group noted here (4:91) specifies once more the circumstances in which killing is forbidden or permissible: "Others you will find that wish to gain your confidence as well as that of their people: Every time they are sent back to temptation, they succumb thereto: if they withdraw not from you nor give you (guarantees) of peace besides restraining their hands, seize them and slay them wherever ye get them: In their case We have provided you with a clear argument against them."

Qur'anic verses that legitimize killing focus on the *munāfiqūn* and do so only in relation to specific contexts defined and restricted by God's revelation. Even members of this group may not be killed if they withdraw, offer peace, or restrain their hands; killing them is justifiable only if they persist in violence against Muslims. But now a moral quandary arises for contemporary Muslims: Should these verses about killing—verses that pertained historically to a specific group known to the nascent Muslim community in its particular historical context—be interpreted in ways that also make them applicable to contemporary human beings who may be identifiable as *munāfiqūn* and, under the license given by God, as people permitted to be killed? If the answer is yes, then difficulties arise. There is the danger that such an interpretation leaves the Qur'an open to those who will (mis)use it for political expediency. No doubt those with whom the Muslims have political or sectarian conflicts sometimes have been conflated with the historic *munāfiqūn*. In my view, however, a Qur'anic verse should not be taken out of its historical context to justify killing, nor should contemporary groups be retroactively identified with the *munāfiqūn*, since such interpretations do violence to the intention of God's words in the Qur'an, which clearly hold life to be sacred and inviolable.

A similar argument could be made regarding verses 33:60–61, which state: "Truly, if the Hypocrites, and those in whose hearts is a disease, and those who stir up sedition in the City, desist not, We shall certainly stir thee up against them: Then will they not be able to stay in it as thy neighbors for any length of time: They shall have a curse on them: whenever they are found, they shall be seized and slain (without mercy)." These verses do not call for killing of all those deemed hypocrites, all those whose hearts are diseased, or all those who spread falsehoods in Medina. Rather, they are directed toward those in these groups who "desist not." The early Muslim community was under physical threat by members of such groups. These verses indicate that if members of such groups persisted in their hostilities, then God would allow the Muslims to kill the hostile group.

The Polytheists (Mushriqūn)

Verses 2:190–94 reiterate God's command to fight those who fight and banish the Muslims but to cease fighting if the opponents relent. Here the phrase "have turned them out" (2:191) refers to the polytheist Meccans displaced by the Muslims from Mecca. In addition, God commands that there be no transgression except against those who are wrongdoers and, in particular, those who are tyrannical. Tyrants are mentioned separately from the Meccan aggressors. By extrapolation, among them may be people who are not polytheists, including Muslims. Here the principle of restraint—that reprisals against tyrants, including killing, should cease when tyranny stops—remains in force.

Further, the Qur'an calls for killing those who wage war or cause corruption or mischief in the land. This call may be interpreted as referring to the killing of polytheists and criminals, as well as to those who cause *fitnah*, the act of breeding social chaos or spreading misinformation (also understood as a reference to polytheists). Verses 5:33–34 specify that the punishment for those who "wage war against Allah and His Messenger, and strive with might and main for mischief through the land is: execution, or crucifixion, or the cutting off of hands and feet from opposite sides, or exile from the land: that is their disgrace in this world, and a heavy punishment is theirs in the Hereafter; Except for those who repent before they fall into your power: in that case, know that Allah is Oft-forgiving, Most Merciful." Verse 8:39 states: "And fight them on until there is no more tumult or oppression, and there prevail justice and faith in Allah altogether and everywhere; but if they cease [their *fitnah*], verily Allah doth see all that they do."

It may be tempting (for some) to read this last verse to mean that all polytheists should be killed until Allah's religion has been universally established. However, this verse, especially with regard to the context from which it first emerged, suggests rather that aggression and killing be employed against those who cause *fitnah* until they cease doing so. Without *fitnah*, there is no cause for killing. Verse 2:217 states that *fitnah* consists in actions intended "to prevent access to the Sacred Mosque [in Mecca], and drive out its members." Further, *fitnah* is "worse than slaughter."

Chapter 9 of the Qur'an continues the discussion about how polytheists (*mushriqūn*) are to be treated. Verse 12 follows the principle that has been illustrated by the evidence cited thus far, namely, that the polytheists are to be fought only if they "violate their oaths after their covenant [with Muslims], and taunt you for your Faith." The verse that follows calls on Muslims to fight those (polytheists) who have violated their oaths and attacked first, suggesting that fighting in self-defense is permitted. In all these instances, it appears that the Qur'an justifies killing in response to hostile acts that prevent Muslims from following their faith; it does not justify killing people just because they are polytheists.

The Qur'an suggests that Muslims are not alone when it comes to killing in self-defense. Verse 5:32 states that God "ordained for the Children of Israel that if any one slew a person—unless it be for murder or for spreading mischief [*fasād*] in the land—it would be as if he slew the whole people [i.e., killed all humankind]." Verse 17:33 again affirms the principle that life is not to be treated wantonly: "And if anyone is slain wrongfully, we have given his heir authority (to demand qisas [blood money] or to forgive): but let him not exceed bounds in the matter of taking life."

Rethinking Pluralism

When the Qur'an justifies violence and killing, the verses in question are directed toward specific groups of people within a particular historical and social context. They are calls not for aggression but for responses to aggression. Violence is never justified when a threat is withdrawn. This analysis indicates that the Qur'an supports constructive forms of religious pluralism. The Qur'anic account that diversity was created among humans so that they might know one another implies that such diversity is intended to be beneficial in bringing the various communities into relation for the purpose of vying with one another in good works. Additionally, the idea that Muhammad is simply another prophet—even if, according to the Qur'an, the last—in a long line of messengers and prophets divinely chosen to reveal God's guidance to humanity suggests that certainly all biblical peoples should be considered part of the *muslim* family: those who have had access to divine revelation and who have acknowledged God as Lord and Creator. As such, these peoples cannot be considered the other, or the stranger, except in matters of righteousness as a distinguishing mark. Thus individuals of each of these faiths might err, but the faith itself is not in error. Given that the Qur'an considers God to be merciful and compassionate and the creator of all that exists, then even those who stand outside the biblical fold should not simply be written off as outside the purview of divine guidance, which may manifest itself to them in ways consistent with their own linguistic and cultural frameworks. For, it could be argued, only God knows best how divine self-revelation has been conveyed in each corner of creation.

One of the most significant barriers to facilitating pluralistic attitudes within the Abrahamic traditions lies in the self-understanding of these religions as universal. All may be led to feel that the entire world should benefit from their teachings. In particular, missionizing impulses within Christianity and Islam seemingly cannot subside until the entire world is converted either to Christianity and the saving power of Christ or to Islam and surrender to God (Allah). However, while the motivation for missionizing leading to conversion is rooted in "sharing the good news," such motivation necessarily entails thinking less of the other, "othering" the other or thinking that the other has no path to salvation unless one does them the favor of granting them the opportunity to convert. Resistance to conversion only reinforces the perceived intractability of the other. Thus, a major challenge to thinking constructively about the role of the outsider is presented in the need to balance missionary impulses with the need to live peacefully and respectfully in a world of diverse faiths, recognizing that difference holds value as an expression of the divine. Both perspectives—those of missionizing and those of pluralism—exist in a quintessentially Islamic framework that emphasizes the unicity of all reality. Together they underscore the importance of difference—or strangeness. Yet difference reveals that there is always "something more," for difference as such can neither express nor contain the full truth. As mystical traditions within Islam suggest, the ultimate goal may be to transcend the specificity of boundaries, to re-center toward the source of existence, to reorient the purpose of life toward harmony with the ground of being and the well-being of others.

CONTRIBUTORS' QUESTIONS FOR ZAYN KASSAM

1. With regard to Jews and Christians, you argue that "the Qur'an on the whole upholds the sanctity and veracity of divine revelation to Jews and Christians, while holding the view that some among the Jews and the Christians have erred." You also stress that caution dominates many Muslims' considerations of Judaism and Christianity: "How is one to distinguish between those Jews and Christians who are righteous and those who are errant?" Do the Qur'an and other Islamic teachings provide criteria for either the righteousness or the errors of Jews and Christians? Have such criteria been developed and/or served as issues for discussion among Islamic teachers? How might your responses to

these questions be affected by the fact that ours is a post-Holocaust world whose political context contains twenty-first-century violence implicating all three Abrahamic traditions?

2. In Islam, is the outsider one who does not believe in a certain creed, or is he or she one who fails to engage in a certain action? In other words, does the accent fall on belief or on action? Can a "nonbeliever" who does good works have a place in "heaven"? If not, then how is true dialogue—not merely an effort to convince the other of this or that doctrine—possible? And if the nonbeliever, on the Islamic view, does have a place in the next world, then why should Islam, as sometimes argued, become the religion of all humankind?

RESPONSE BY ZAYN KASSAM

It would be presumptuous and mistaken to distinguish between those Jews and Christians who are righteous and those who are errant, because doing so would suggest that Muslims are able to judge between righteousness and errancy. Rather, the Qur'an insists that God alone is ultimately the judge over Muslims, Jews, Sabians (Sabaeans), Christians, polytheists, and Magians (Qur'an 22:17). It is not a Muslim's place to determine whether a Jew or a Christian is righteous or errant; it is God's prerogative to do so at the final judgment. The Qur'an, moreover, makes no distinctions among Muslims, Jews, Christians, and Sabaeans in stating that those who believe in God and the Last Day (or Day of Judgment) and who do righteous deeds will receive their reward from God, that they have nothing to fear and will not come to grief (Qur'an 2:62). While the Qur'an admonishes Muslims against following Jews and Christians as religious authorities, it does not advocate against cooperating with them on causes of mutual interest.

Even though the Qur'an clarifies that God will decide on the righteousness or errancy of Jews and Christians on the Day of Resurrection, this does not mean that Muslims have withheld judgment of Jews and Christians, especially in contemporary postcolonial and post-Holocaust periods. It is one thing, however, to blame Jews and Christians for perceived and real injustices directed against Muslims, but it is quite another to assume a divine mantle in presuming that the level of righteousness of any person, regardless of faith, can be determined. The terms most often used to denote righteousness are piety (*taqwa*), meaning "God-fearing" or awareness of God as witness to all one does and to whom one is accountable, and "doing good deeds" (*amila salihan*). Another term used to denote righteousness is *al-birr*, translated both as "piety" and as "righteousness." In Qur'an 2:177, righteousness means

> to believe in Allah and the Last Day, and the Angels, and the Book, and the Messengers; to spend of your substance, out of love for Him, for your kin, for orphans, for the needy, for the wayfarer, for those who ask, and for the ransom of slaves; to be steadfast in prayer, and practice regular charity; to fulfill the contracts which ye have made; and to be firm and patient, in pain (or suffering) and adversity, and throughout all periods of panic. Such are the people of truth, the Allah-fearing.

An example of errancy can be found in Qur'an 9:30, which takes issue with Jews who claim that Ezra is the son of God and with Christians who claim that Christ is the son of God, while transgressors among the Children of Israel are said to have been rebuked by both David and Jesus (Qur'an 5:78). God finds transgression in any faith community reprehensible but not unforgivable: "If only the People of the Book had believed and been righteous, We should indeed have blotted out their iniquities and admitted them to gardens of bliss" (Qur'an 5:65). Thus if God can overlook errors, then Muslims should withhold judgment, for judgment is a divine prerogative.

The Qur'an suggests that God is concerned that Jews and Christians are faithful to their own traditions. Some Jews and Christians are evildoers; others are righteous. The difference depends on whether they adhere to divine guidance, which for Jews and Christians, respectively, depends on how well they "stand fast by the Law, the Gospel, and all the revelation that has come to [them]" (Qur'an 5:68). The latter condition suggests two points: first, that Jews and Christians have been given divine guidance in their own scriptures, and thus the Qur'an tacitly embodies what we would call a religiously pluralist position; second, that Jews and Christians are not, as a whole, to be dismissed as either righteous folk or errant in their ways. Rather, they are held accountable to the same standards as Muslims. That is, they are minimally required to believe in God and in the Day of Judgment; further, they are to do good works, as outlined in Qur'an 5:69: "Lo! those who believe, and those who are Jews, and Sabaeans, and Christians—Whosoever believeth in Allah and the Last Day and doeth right—there shall no fear come upon them neither shall they grieve" (Pickthall translation). In other words, generalizations about Jews and Christians are not valid, nor may any judgments be offered that are based on alleged degrees of righteousness or errancy.

In a post-Holocaust and postcolonial world, however, political issues that have an impact on Muslims are often cast as religious, especially when religion becomes the uniting factor in identifying a group. So, for instance, the Third Reich's genocide against the Jews and others led to the creation of the State of Israel, so that Jews would be guaranteed a homeland that would provide sanctuary against the recurrence of that horror. The creation of the State of Israel had implications and consequences for Palestinians living on the lands of the new state. Many of them feel that they were unfairly ejected from their homeland or barred from reentering once they had left as refugees. Representation of the political struggle of Palestinians for control over and/or political autonomy in what they consider to be their homeland has gradually been transformed into a religious struggle, particularly as more secular political parties fail to deliver on the promise that the struggle for political autonomy will advance through their efforts.

Palestinian Arab Jews, Christians, and Muslims all lived in territory that became the State of Israel, a reality eclipsed by the popularly held monolithic view that Palestinians are fundamentalist and militant Muslims. This view ignores other faith communities that are also Palestinian as well as the many Palestinian Muslims—religious or secular—who are neither fundamentalist nor militant. On the Israeli side, politically secular Jews increasingly contend with religious Jews whose political perspectives maintain that God gave the Promised Land—stretching from the Mediterranean to the River Jordan—to the Jews and that this fact cannot change. According to this outlook, the State of Israel should not attempt to accommodate the Palestinians.

Further complicating relationships between Israelis and Palestinians are allegations that Muslim hatred for Jews began with the founding of Islam, a misguided claim that takes Qur'anic verses out of context to "prove the point." On the other side, Muslims—but not necessarily Palestinian Muslims—criticize the State of Israel's treatment of Palestinians in rhetoric similar to that employed by many Jews with respect to Muslims. Since the founding of Islam, these Muslims claim, Jews have been treacherous infidels and no friends of Muslims.

Fortunately, these hostile perspectives are not representative of the views of a majority of Jews or Muslims. History and contemporary life provide many examples of good relations between Jews and Muslims that have benefited both communities. These relationships and benefits must be underscored and supported. To do otherwise would undermine a key lesson taught by the Holocaust: that the systematic "othering" of any group is a harbinger of violence and indifference toward the suffering of the other.

Meanwhile, the conflict in the Middle East is primarily not religious but political. Indeed, within the rich and multifaceted Jewish, Christian, and Islamic traditions significant resources exist to work toward addressing the issues that most need to be resolved to achieve a just and lasting peace in the region. All three traditions stress the value of forgiveness, kindness and hospitality to strangers, social justice, stewardship of the earth, justice and fairness, generosity, and caring for the other.

Interpretations of sacred texts are necessarily connected to the contexts in which the interpreters do the interpreting, for otherwise our sacred texts cease to be relevant. With regard to the principles of coexistence they put forward, all the major religious traditions of the world manifest a dimension of universality; aggressive proselytizing would thus bespeak a fundamental lack of respect for both religious pluralism and the truths to be found in all religious traditions. Colonialism's history shows that attempts to "save" the other in the name of religion and "civilization" often mask intentions to rob the other of their material, cultural, and religious riches. Using religious traditions to perpetuate injustice, violence, and war disrespects the best of those traditions. It behooves people of all faiths to resist such disrespect of their traditions.

NOTES

1   All of this chapter's translations from the Qur'an can be found online in the database of the Center for Muslim-Jewish Engagement, University of Southern California, http://www.cmje.org/religious-texts/quran. This online version of the Qur'an contains English translations by Abdullah Yusuf Ali, Marmaduke Pickthall, and M. H. Shakir. Except where noted parenthetically in the text, I have used the translations by Yusuf Ali.

2   A small monotheistic religious sect, also known as Mandaeans, originating in what is today southern Iraq, the Sabaeans (sometimes rendered Sabians), spelled with the Arabic consonant "sad" and mentioned in the Qur'an, are to be distinguished from the Sabaeans, spelled with the Arabic consonant "sin," who were polytheistic inhabitants of southwestern Yemen. See Şinasi Gündüz, "Problems on the Muslim Understanding of the Mandaeans," *ARAM Periodical* 11, no. 2 (1999): 269–79. Available online at http://poj.peeters-leuven.be/content.php?url=issue&journal _code=ARAM&issue=2&vol=11.

3

"Where Is Your Brother?"

Jewish Teachings on the "Stranger"

DAVID PATTERSON

> We encounter God in the face of the stranger. That, I believe,
> is the Hebrew Bible's single greatest and most counterintuitive
> contribution to ethics. . . . The human other is a trace of the
> Divine Other.
> —Rabbi Jonathan Sacks, *The Dignity of Difference*

Contemporary philosopher Emil L. Fackenheim penetrates the core of the
Holocaust when he writes that, in the aftermath of this genocide, "philosophers must face a *novum* within a question as old as Socrates: what does it
mean to be human?"[1] By exterminating the Jews, the Nazis attempted to
obliterate the millennial testimony that the Jews represent by their very
presence in the world. Central to that testimony is a teaching on what gives
meaning and value to the human being. The Nazis' determination of the
value of a human being rests upon an accident of nature: one who is born
an "Aryan" has more value than one who is not born an "Aryan." And one
who is an "Aryan" takes on even greater value according to a will to power.
Further, an "Aryan" has no essential connection to a non-"Aryan," and
certainly not to a Jew.

The Jewish teaching is that a human soul enters the world not by accident but by divine will. Created in the divine image of the Infinite One, a
human being has infinite value, a value that rests upon nothing that can

be weighed, measured, or observed. God begins His creation of humanity, moreover, from a single human being, and not from two, so that no one can say to another, "My side of the family is better than your side of the family" (see *Tosefta Sanhedrin* 8:4–5). There is only one side of the family, and each of us is both *physically* and *spiritually* tied to the other; to be sure, the Hebrew term for "human being" is *ben adam*, a child of Adam. Just as each beam of light that radiates from a star is connected, through the star, to every other beam of light, so is each soul connected, through God, to every other soul. And since God is the Infinite One, our responsibility to and for one another is infinite.

In this post-Holocaust world, the question raised by Fackenheim remains to be decided. Indeed, diarist Chaim Kaplan raised the question from along the edge of the annihilation itself: after the Holocaust, he said in his Warsaw Ghetto diary, "either humanity would be Judaic, or it would be idolatrous-German."[2] The Judaic view of the one who is not "one of us" begins with the Covenant of Abraham.

The Covenant of Abraham

In the biblical account of Abraham's entry into the Covenant with God, we have the basis for the fundamental Jewish teaching concerning the stranger, something made famous in the Holocaust: it is the concept of the *chasidei umot haolam*, or the Righteous Among the Nations. Like the fundamental view of the human being, this notion of the Righteous Among the Nations is tied to the Jewish account of creation. The Talmudic sage Rabbi Yochanan ben Zakkai, for example, teaches that when God created the heavens and the earth, His first utterance broke into seventy sparks. From those seventy sparks emerged the seventy languages of the seventy nations (*Shabbat* 88b). This means: each nation bears a trace of a revelation from God. Thus, according to Jewish teaching, a person does not have to be an adherent of Judaism to be counted among the righteous and to have a place with God.

In Abraham's story, this point is illustrated through his encounter with the king of Salem, Melchizedek, in which the king went out to offer bread and wine to Abraham on his way home from saving Lot, who had been kidnapped during a battle among the kings of the region (see Genesis 14:18). The lesson? It is this: the stranger, the non-Jew, may well be among the righteous whom God has sent into the world to elevate creation. Thus, in his first conversation with God after sealing the Covenant, Abraham argues for the sake of the righteous in Sodom and Gomorrah (Genesis 18:20–32).

According to the Torah, Abraham was chosen to enter into a covenant with the Creator not for the sake of his own household but so that through the Covenant "all the families of the earth shall be blessed" (Genesis 12:3). And the blessing lies in the testimony that the Covenant requires the children of Abraham to deliver to the world; thus, says the Lord through the prophet Isaiah, "[I] set thee for a covenant of the people, as a light unto the nations" (Isaiah 42:6). In a word, the Jews are chosen to say to the world that every human being is chosen, every human life has meaning and value, and each of us is infinitely responsible to and for the other. Indeed, this covenantal interrelation of responsibility to and for one another belongs to the fabric of creation itself: as Nachmanides has noted, *brit*, the word for "covenant," is a cognate of *bara*, which is to "create."[3] Inasmuch as creation and covenant are interwoven, creation is the creation of a relation. It is the coming into being of the You, where the You is not our fellow Jew but our fellow human being, any *ben adam*.

Thus the Kabbalist text, the *Zohar*, reads the opening line of the Torah as "bereshit bara Elokim at," or "In the beginning God created the 'you.'" That is to say, "In the beginning God created the letters from *alef* to *tav*, the stuff of the word, which is *at*: You [in its feminine form]" (*Zohar* 1:15b). In the beginning, God created the avenue through which we may enter into a relation to Him, which is precisely the other human being, including—or beginning with—the stranger. Through the word *you* that we say to the other human being with our whole being we enter into a relation with the Eternal You.

Why does God give Moses two tablets rather than one? Not because He cannot write small enough to fit it on one tablet. No, it is to articulate two realms of relation: the first tablet pertains to the relation *ben adam leMakom* and the second to the relation *ben adam lechevero*, "between human and God" and "between human and human," respectively. And yet *there is only one relation*. What, then, is the holiest space in this world? It is not the Temple Mount, or even the Holy of Holies. The holiest space in this world is the space *between* the *cheruvim* (cherub angels) facing each other atop the ark that contains the Torah. *Atop* the ark, this between-space is higher than the contents of the ark. This single space signifies the single realm of relation between God and human, between human and human. That is where the Divine Voice speaks. That is where the human voice answers. And it answers most fundamentally in its response to the commandments of Torah regarding the stranger.

The Commandments of Torah

The root of the Hebrew word for "commandment," *mitzvah*, is *tzavta*, which means "connection." A commandment is not a rule or a dictate that must be followed; rather, it is a means of connecting with God. As we have seen, the most fundamental means of connecting with God lies in our connection with the other human being. And the most fundamental of those connections can be found in the commandments concerning our relation to the "stranger," or the *ger*.

In Exodus 22:20, for example, we read, "You shall not wrong a stranger, nor shall you oppress him; for you were strangers in Egypt." In our world, having been abused has become an excuse for becoming an abuser, just as having been oppressed has become an excuse for strapping bombs to one's children to commit murder; in Judaism, the fact that you were oppressed as a stranger means precisely that you will *not* oppress non-Jews. Why? Because "you know the soul of a stranger, as you were strangers in Egypt" (Exodus 23:9). The phrase "for you know the soul of the stranger" is "yedaatem et-nefesh hager." Now the word for "know," *daat*, also means to "be joined together with." This suggests that because every soul is an emanation from the Holy One, each is bound to the other, Jewish and non-Jewish. The stranger who dwells among you shall be as one of your own, because you are *essentially* and *physically* tied to him or her as a *ben adam*, a child of Adam.

Hence "the stranger who dwells among you shall be as one of your own, and you shall love him as yourself. For you were strangers in the land of Egypt: I am the Lord" (Leviticus 19:34). That is, you shall love him *k'mokha*, "as yourself," an echo of the commandment to love your neighbor, your fellow Jew, *k'mokha* (Leviticus 19:18). What does it mean? A better rendering of *k'mokha* is "that is what you are like." In other words, "you shall love the stranger, for love for the stranger *is* your self": that loving is the *who* that you are in the depths of your being. On this basis we have the Chasidic teaching that this love for the other human being—for the stranger—is the foundation of Torah (*Toledot Yaakov Yosef, Korach* 2). Oriented toward Torah, then, Jewish teaching is oriented toward the other human being, who is the stranger, *but who is no alien other*. And the phrase "I am the Lord"? It means that we can have no connection to God without this fundamental connection with the *ger*.

Because the *ger* is not an alien other, but one to whom the Jew is connected in the depths of his soul, we have this commandment: "You shall not pervert the justice due to a stranger or to the fatherless, nor take a widow's clothing as a pledge. But you shall remember that you were a slave in Egypt, and the Lord your God redeemed you" (Deuteronomy 24:17–18). Here we have a revelation of the *absolute* responsibility each of us has for those who have nowhere to turn, as exemplified by the widow, the orphan, and the stranger. These commandments, moreover, are revealed both in the singular and in the plural: they apply both to you as a community and to you as an individual.

What must be kept in mind, of course, is that in these commandments of Torah the word for "stranger" is *ger*: a *ger* is a non-Jew who dwells among the Jews. Seeking only peace, only to be a good neighbor, only the human-to-human relation that makes dwelling possible. Two other words for "stranger" are *zar* and *nakhar*. *Nakhar* simply refers to someone who is foreign and unfamiliar, but with whom one might become familiar. The *nakhar* is one who might become a *ger*. *Zar*, however, refers to one who is utterly alien, who is beyond anything that can become familiar, as in *avodah zarah*, the alien worship that is "idolatry." And the height of idolatry is to be found among those who make their children "pass through the fire" (Deuteronomy 18:10), whether through child sacrifice or by strapping bombs to their children, tragically making them into murderers who would pass as "martyrs." According to Jewish teaching, there is no obligation to the "stranger" as *zar*, that is, as one who is bent upon your extermination.

These are the basic Jewish teachings with regard to the stranger in the Written Torah. Let us consider how the Oral Torah—the Talmud and the midrash—elaborate on these teachings.

Teachings from the Oral Tradition

Here it must be acknowledged that the Talmud contains teachings on the stranger such as the following: "A Jew must not associate with the Gentiles because they are shedders of blood" (*Avodah Zarah* 22a). The context of such teachings, however, must be kept in mind. At various times in Jewish history, non-Jews have been at best informers, at worst murderers, against Jews. Wherever the stranger has not posed such a threat, Jewish teachings from the oral tradition have treated him or her as a child of God; generally speaking, this is where the term *ger* applies.

While Judaism understands the Jews to be a "people apart" (see Leviticus 20:24), their distinction among the nations lies in their singled-out mission to transmit certain teachings concerning, among other things, the treatment of the stranger. If a human being is distinguished as a "speaking being," for example, his or her basic connection with other human beings lies in the word: for a Jew, the urgency of saying the word *you* to another Jew is equal to the urgency of saying the word *you* to a non-Jew. Thus the Mishnah teaches that the prohibition against wronging someone in buying and selling also applies to wronging someone, including the stranger, *with words* (*Bava Metzia* 4:4). And chief among the words that a Jew must utter to another human being, so as not to wrong him or her with words, is the word *you*.

Similarly, with respect to the *ger* the Talmud teaches, "Do not taunt your neighbor with the same blemish you have" (*Bava Metzia* 59b). What applies to the Jew applies to the non-Jew: do not judge. Let God be the judge of who is righteous and who is not, of who has a place in the World to Come and who does not. Inasmuch as we determine that our fellow human being has no place with God, we can have no relation with our fellow human being. This applies particularly to ways of thinking that divide the world into the damned and the saved strictly on the basis of belief. Contrary to those traditions that declare theirs is the only path to God, the Talmud teaches that the non-Jew has a place in the World to Come, as does the Jew—indeed, even more readily than the Jew, since the Jew has a much greater responsibility to fulfill (see *Sanhedrin* 105a). The stranger has a place in the World to Come because he or she has a place in this world: since God's purpose in creation is to create a dwelling place for Himself, it is to create a dwelling place for one another, Jew and non-Jew alike.

Thus the gates to God's kingdom "are at all times open" to the stranger, as it is written in the midrash (*Shemot Rabbah* 19:4). Judaism does not paint itself into the theological corner of declaring that the path to God leads only through Judaism—*that* is why Judaism teaches that the relation to the stranger is like the relation to one of its own. To exclude the stranger from the World to Come on the basis of which creed he or she adopts is to exclude the stranger from this world; if the stranger has no place with God, *according to his or her deeds and his or her righteousness*, then the stranger can have no place with his or her fellow human being. Hence, Judaism realizes, if we say to the stranger, "Only through this path, only through this doctrine, can you come to God," then we can have no human-to-human relation with him or her. Judaism, therefore, *commands* a human-to-human relation with the stranger. Where the human-to-human relation is concerned, there is no distinction between a Jew's relation to an Israelite and to a non-Israelite.

"Beloved are the strangers," says the midrash, "for Scripture in every instance compares them to Israel" (*Bemidbar Rabbah* 8:2). Beloved by whom? Beloved by God, as taught in another midrash: "I have loved you" (Malachi 1:2) refers to the stranger (*Bemidbar Rabbah* 8:2). According to Jewish teaching, each time a Jew encounters a stranger, he or she encounters one of God's beloved, one of God's children, a concept that falls outside the consciousness of any tradition that does not view God as a Father. Because the Jews cry out to God, "Father!" they can cry out to strangers, "Brothers! Sisters!" Here we recall the teaching from the midrash that states, "If you will estrange those who are distant [the strangers], you will ultimately estrange those who are near [the Jews]" (*Bemidbar Rabbah* 8:4). This means: recognition of our essential connection to the most distant of human beings rests upon our realization of a connection to those who are nearest. And each connection is connected to the other.

Closing Thought

Just as God has blessed the Jews with 613 commandments, so He has blessed the non-Jews with 7 commandments.[4] Thus commanded by God, the stranger is connected to God. And, connected to God, he or she has an *indispensable* role in the redemption of creation. Jewish teachings concerning the stranger, then, place a certain responsibility upon the stranger. In this manner, God sanctifies the stranger: the greatest honor one can show toward another human being is through the testimony concerning the responsibility of each human being for all human beings.

Judaism has something to teach anyone who seeks to enter into a dialogue with people outside of one's own tradition. If we insist that one can have a place with God only by adopting a particular belief, then we place ourselves outside the framework of interfaith dialogue. Traditions such as Christianity and Islam, which at various times have divided the world into believers and nonbelievers, face certain challenges in interfaith dialogue that perhaps Jews do not (of course, Jews have other challenges).

Before anyone was chosen to be a Jew or a non-Jew, we have the tale of Cain and Abel. In that story, God puts to Cain two questions: "Where is your brother?" (Genesis 4:9) and "What have you done?" (Genesis 4:10). God is not interested in what Cain believes. And to answer one question is to answer the other: we declare our understanding of where our brother is—Israelite or *ger*—through what we have done, according to the divine commandment. *That* is the Jewish teaching on the stranger.

CONTRIBUTORS' QUESTIONS FOR DAVID PATTERSON

1. You speak of the human being as one "created in the divine image of the Infinite One," as one who has "infinite value." Human worth would thus appear to be *unconditional*. Yet with regard to strangers you cite what appear to be *conditions*. Strangers would seem to have to *earn* value. How can it be that there is a human being, created in the image of the *Infinite* One, who is *finite* to the point of being "utterly alien"? Does the Jewish tradition support a notion that one kind of stranger—at the extreme, the kind bent upon my extermination—has the power to exclude him- or herself, *on principle*, from that *infinite value* which accrues to the human qua human? Further, you note that this stranger-as-*zar* is "irredeemable." Is there no hope that those considered to be *zarim* can change their ways through repentance and become *gerim*?

2. Your essay cites the Jewish teaching that "a person does not have to be an adherent of Judaism to be counted among the righteous." Yet this nonexclusivist teaching appears to be undermined by your interpretation of the "chosenness" of the Jewish people. You characterize this chosenness as follows: Jews are to be distinguished from other peoples "in their singled-out mission to transmit certain teachings concerning, among other things, the treatment of the stranger"; they are to be distinguished from other peoples insofar as they are commanded to tell the world that "every human life has meaning and value." In a post-Holocaust world of intense and often violent conflict—some of which involves Jewish participants—how does this vision of the Jewish people square with "on the ground" realities? Does your understanding of Judaism's teaching concerning its mission to teach the rest of the

world about the sacredness of the stranger endanger a true pluralism of religions? Is there not an implied supremacism here?

RESPONSE BY DAVID PATTERSON

I am grateful to my friends and colleagues for their excellent questions. They are needful questions, as needful as the clarification they call for. Let me begin by clarifying the Jewish teaching concerning the holiness of every human being.

The infinite value of the human being lies in his or her infinite responsibility to and for the other human being; it is not a matter of being *entitled* to a special consideration—it is a matter of being *summoned* to a unique task. Hence the importance of *teshuvah*, which is a "response." Because the human being is holy, he or she can desecrate his or her own soul by becoming murderous to the point of becoming monstrous. By the same token, because he or she harbors a trace of the holy manifest as an infinite responsibility, the path to *teshuvah* always remains open, so that even the *zarim* can become *gerim*; the potential for one is tied to the other. The only thing that is given— that precedes every context—is the summons to respond to the outcry of my neighbor, a summons that *only I* can answer. Still, one can easily think of examples of human beings whose holiness is buried so deep that it appears to be beyond redemption in this realm. Nevertheless, in principle the movement of return and response remains a possibility for any human being.

The question of whether the stranger has to earn value is, in a sense, a non-question. Strangers do not have to earn value because they *already* have value, which means: they, like all human beings, are *already* responsible, so that it *already* matters how they act. Because of this *already*, the stranger's value is not earned—it is *imposed*, from on high. No human being can exclude him- or herself from this *already*; it underscores an absolute that is at work prior to and apart from all contexts. To exclude oneself from this absolute—to determine the value of a human being according to contingencies or accidents such as race, gender, or ethnicity—is to become *zar*.

With regard to the matter of exclusiveness in the Jewish teaching on chosenness, I repeat: Jews are chosen to announce the chosenness of every human, to declare that every life is summoned to a mission *indispensable* to all of creation. To say that the Jews are given this assignment is not exclusivist, since it is an assignment to announce the nonexclusiveness of humanity. An exclusivist position would be one that divides humanity into the saved and the damned according to the content of one's belief, rather than the righteousness of one's actions. The idea is that every person is singled out, every nation is a people apart, inasmuch as each one has a unique calling that no other can fulfill, a mission that can be fulfilled only by engaging in certain actions.

Because Judaism does not maintain that anyone who would enter the Kingdom must enter Judaism's fold, it adopts a pluralist position with regard to religion. It defends a "true pluralism" of religions, a concept that entails exercising good judgment about the qualities of religions. Thus the National Socialist Deutsche Christen was a religious sect unacceptable to Judaism, as is Aztec religion, which demanded the offering up of thousands of human beings on the altar. Indeed, all religions that "pass their children through fire" are unacceptable. A religious stance that allows for the "honor killing" of young women suspected of "lewd behavior" is regarded as inferior to one that does not. While there is an implied dimension of height here, there is no implied supremacism. To be sure, Judaism takes Christians and Muslims who are true to their calling to be higher than Jews who are not. The teaching that every soul is holy and that Jews are sent to transmit that teaching does not amount to saying Jews are better, even though it does maintain that Jews are different. Indeed, the trialogue in this volume proceeds from the premise that there are differences among Jews, Christians, and Muslims. But it does not adopt the premise that one is better than the other; such a premise would preclude trialogue.

If I understand it correctly, the question concerning "'on the ground' realities" seems to conflate policies of the Israeli government with the teachings of Judaism; if there is such an implication, it is an unjust one, and it implies an illegitimate double standard. Who, for example, would criticize Christian teaching because of the policies of the British government or Muslim teaching because of the policies of the Egyptian government? Only a state that makes religious law—halacha or shari'a—into state law is subject to such criticism. Nevertheless, I shall reply to the question, beginning with the matter of the "intense and violent conflict" in our post-Holocaust world.

If we take a measure of the world's intense and violent conflict in modern times, we find that it is rarely initiated by the Jews; it is certainly never glorified by the Jews and is often resisted by the Jews. Is it necessary to name the many regions of the world known for their intense and violent conflict? How many of the world's terrorist organizations call themselves

Jewish? How many call themselves Islamic? When the Jews kill their enemies, they do not hold public celebrations; their attitude, rather, is like the one expressed in a statement attributed to Golda Meir, in response to the Arab onslaught against Israel: "We can forgive you for attacking us. We can perhaps even forgive you for killing our children. But we will never forgive you for making our children kill your children." When one of Israel's cities takes more than four thousand rocket hits, the Israelis do not eliminate the problem, as they surely could, because it would involve too many civilian deaths for the "other." Instead, they take the hits, take the casualties even to their children, while trying to minimize the problem as best they can. What would the American reaction be if San Diego or Buffalo should take four thousand rocket hits from Mexico or Canada? What would be the world's reaction if Damascus should take four thousand rocket hits from Israel?

With regard to other "facts on the ground," I think that this question also lacks a certain legitimacy, inasmuch as I take it to be a question about Israeli government policy and not about what takes place, for example, in the Jewish communities of America. But if I must speak of facts on the ground and how they square with the Jewish stance toward the stranger, here are a few:

- Israel provides most of the advanced medical care for the Arabs of Israel and the Palestinian territories, as reported by the World Health Organization in May 2004.
- Since 1967, when the Jews regained control of Jerusalem, everyone who comes in peace is free to pray in the Holy City.
- Israel has contributed food and medical assistance to survivors of disasters throughout the world, including hurricane victims in Central America in 1998, Colombian earthquake victims in 1999, victims of drought in Georgia in 2001, and victims of the earthquakes in India in 2001 and in Haiti in 2010, to name just a few of the many examples.
- Israelis were among the first to send help to Cambodia and Rwanda in the aftermath of genocide, as well as among the few to receive Bosnian and Vietnamese refugees by the hundreds; they have taken in hundreds of Sudanese refugees as well, many of whom are Muslims.
- At least two dozen organizations are members of IsraAID, the Israel Forum for International Humanitarian Aid, including Save a Child's Heart, the Chembe AIDS Project of Malawi, and Israeli Friends of the Tibetan People.

- The humanitarian assistance that Israeli and non-Israeli Jews extend to the world is radically disproportionate to what is provided by other nations, when the size and population of the Jewish State and the Jewish people are compared to the size and population of, say, the Christian and Muslim lands.

While there are facts on the ground that may be a source of shame to the Jewish people, they are a source of shame precisely because of the Jewish teaching concerning the stranger. Without that teaching, there would be no reason for embarrassment. Without that teaching, there would be no facts on the ground such as the ones listed above. More than any argument, the actions outlined in these few examples demonstrate that, from the standpoint of Jewish teaching, the value of the stranger does not have to be earned, that the teaching is neither exclusivist nor supremacist, and that the Jewish people have a profound sense of mission to humanity. They are actions that declare to humanity, "*Hineni*! Here I am, for you!"

NOTES

Epigraph: Jonathan Sacks, *The Dignity of Difference: How to Avoid the Clash of Civilizations* (New York: Continuum, 2003), 59–60.

1   Emil L. Fackenheim, *Jewish Philosophers and Jewish Philosophy*, ed. Michael Morgan (Bloomington: Indiana University Press, 1996), 133.

2   Chaim Kaplan, *Scroll of Agony: The Warsaw Diary of Chaim A. Kaplan*, trans. Abraham I. Katch (Bloomington: Indiana University Press, 1999), 130.

3   See Nachmanides, *Commentary on the Torah*, trans. Charles B. Chavel (New York: Shilo, 1971), 1:112.

4   According to the Talmud (*Sanhedrin* 56a), the seven Noahide commandments are (1) establish courts of justice, (2) do not commit blasphemy, (3) do not commit idolatry, (4) do not commit adultery, (5) do not shed blood, (6) do not commit robbery, and (7) do not eat flesh of a living animal.

4

Canopies of Hospitality

Post-Shoah Christian Faith and Making Room for Others

HENRY F. KNIGHT

This goodly frame, the earth. *See*ms to me a sterile promon-
tory; this most excellent canopy, the air, look you, this brave
o'erhanging firmament, this majestical roof fretted with
golden fire, why, it appears no other thing to me than a foul
and pestilent congregation of vapours. What a piece of work is
a man! How noble in reason! How infinite in faculty! In form
and moving how express and admirable! In action how like an
angel! In apprehension how like a god!
            —*Hamlet*, Act II, Scene 2, lines 288–98

Hamlet's Anguish and a Shoah-Wounded World

"Look you," how Hamlet's commentary unfolds. His world is wounded
to the core. Hamlet declares the overarching expanse of creation's firmament, its "most excellent canopy," to be nothing more than "a foul and pestilent congregation of vapours." His father, the king of Denmark, is dead,
murdered by his mother and his uncle. Hamlet's knowledge of that act of
ultimate betrayal tore his world apart.

Hamlet's comments above capture the dilemma that post-Holocaust
Christians like me face when we ponder the crisis of faith occasioned by

the Shoah. Like Hamlet, we live in a wounded world. Ours is torn apart by the cries of murdered children. Irving Greenberg's criterion of the "burning children" of Auschwitz haunts our moral and spiritual landscape just as surely as the ghost of Hamlet's father haunted his. "No statement, theological or otherwise, should be made that would not be credible in the presence of the burning children."[1] The presence of those children, and others like them, changes the shape of our world for everyone in it even though the impact for some is more drastic than for others.

To be sure, the Shoah changed the shape of Jewish life thereafter. In various ways, every Jew, past and present—even future—was targeted by the Nazis for destruction. As Elie Wiesel has said, "Not all victims were Jews, but all Jews were victims."[2] But the Holocaust is not just a Jewish problem. Christianity also has a Holocaust problem that changes the shape of its world. That problem has several interrelated dimensions, among them a theological dilemma, one that Christianity shares with Judaism about the theological integrity of covenantal theism. This dilemma is compounded by issues surrounding the adequacy of Christianity's confessional language regarding the salvific role of suffering in God's providential care of creation. And as with Hamlet, Christianity faces the complicity of its own family in a crisis of moral integrity regarding Christian attitudes and behavior toward Jews before and during the Holocaust. Lingering supersessionism continues to influence Christian identity, which has developed historically at the expense of a discounted, signifying, Jewish Other.

The wounds are deep and unsettling. They make post-Shoah Christians face a radical vulnerability to human suffering, which challenges the core of the covenantal world and faith they share with Jews and produces a fundamental identity crisis rooted in a long and shameful legacy of contempt toward Christianity's Jewish Other. However, more than contempt is at stake in this relationship. It is entirely conceivable that through penitent soul-searching, Christians can free themselves from the extreme forms of disdain that are expressed in contempt regarding Jews. Yet the outcome of a more positive relationship with Jews could still express a logic of displacement that treats Jews in such a way that they remain constructs of the Christian imagination who are eventually superseded—and not *others* who matter in their own right in the Christian scheme of things. The deeper and subtler issues are whether supersessionism is essential for Christian identity and whether Christian identity is truly able to make room for the other as Other.

The Lingering Problem of Supersessionism

Supersessionism is a belief or attitude that one's truth or identity builds on and surpasses any claims and foundations shared with others. According to Regina M. Schwartz, the problem underlying supersessionism is a fundamental mind-set that Christianity shares with Judaism and Islam. In her book *The Curse of Cain*, Schwartz identifies two primary ways of construing the world, what she calls "logics" of interpretation. Each of the three monotheistic traditions of Abraham, she observes, tends toward the excluding logic of scarcity in contrast to a present, but often obscured, logic of plenitude.[3] Schwartz posits that a hermeneutic of scarcity is employed by each of the monotheistic traditions to protect fundamental truth claims. If God is one and Truth is one with God, then the revelation of that Truth should be one. The alternative lens, what she calls a logic of plenitude, is rooted in a sense of the richness of creation and its abundant gift of life. Accessible through practices such as midrash for Judaism, parables for Christianity, and Sufism for Islam, the logic of plenitude provides an alternative mind-set that may also be encountered in each of the traditions.[4] Of course, the power dynamics among the three and between Judaism and Christianity have made a frightening difference in how these choices have been made and embodied over the centuries. And in the secularized eyes of the Third Reich, supersessionism reappears in the guise of social Darwinism.

Any prolonged examination of the Shoah eventually comes face-to-face with a world deeply wounded by the evil of arrogant and narcissistic claims that separate life into those who count and those who do not. If we have the courage to follow the logic of scarcity unflinchingly into Auschwitz, we eventually come to the "selection" ramp, where those condemned to immediate execution are separated from those who are spared, if only for a while. Like it or not, whenever we stand in a place where we separate human beings who count from those who don't, we step into this domain. That ground is unholy and has been walked by more than Nazi doctors and Schutzstaffel (SS) officers. It has been trod by inquisitors and crusaders, priests and theologians, pundits and politicians. Almost always, those who walk this ground do so with the passionate conviction that they, and only they, are right.

We do not need to enter Auschwitz to confront the dark side of supersessionism's logic, but we should remember that such a God-forsaken place can be its final destination. Schwartz's analysis helps us see the other-denying logic that operates when one group builds its identity over against another. She argues that an inherent danger in the claim to be the one God's representative is the assumption that this identity must be equally singular.[5] Consequently, the identity of such a people often denies the credibility of any other who might make such a claim, declaring, as it were: Only my tent reflects God's ways with the world. With the Shoah, this canopy is torn asunder.

How then should we proceed? If post-Shoah Christians are going to face the wounded world they share with Jews, then they must turn to Jewish partners and confront that wounded world together. Moreover, if this critical dialogue is to come to terms with the deeper issues driving supersessionism, then that dialogue must eventually include more partners in the mending (and tending) of an even larger world. That is, this dialogue must expand to include Muslim partners as well as others in the care of our wounded world. And the issue of supersessionism and its logic of scarcity will remain central.

Wounded Faith for a Wounded World

As Johann Baptist Metz has courageously maintained, any mending of Christianity's sacred canopy occurs in dialogue with Jews—confronting their wounds and facing their world with respect and understanding.[6] Minimally, that relationship means that Christians need to read the works of post-Shoah Jewish thinkers and hear the testimonies of Jewish survivors. Christians should do this reading and listening without preconceptions about what they will discover. Indeed, this reading or listening, especially when survivor testimony is involved, can be likened to sitting shivah with Jewish friends. In the case of reading and attending to post-Shoah Jewish philosophers and theologians, many Christians seeking a post-Shoah religious hermeneutic will be helped by turning to thinkers such as Emil L. Fackenheim and Irving Greenberg.

Although Fackenheim primarily writes for Jews, he recognizes the theological dilemma that Christians face, particularly the problems the Shoah poses for reading and interpreting the biblical witness. Christian understanding can be helped by Fackenheim's midrashic, dialectical approach, which embraces the textual and experiential sources of covenanted identity while he holds himself unyieldingly accountable to the 1.5

million Jewish children who were murdered during the Shoah.[7] In similar fashion, the teaching of Rebbe Nachman of Bratslav, who urged that there is nothing as whole as a broken heart, informs Greenberg's helpful insights about a form of wounded trust that he calls "moment faith."[8]

Greenberg's "moment faith" means several things. First, moment faith is evoked and expressed in times when the covenantal wholeness of life is embodied and experienced. Yet those occasions are transitory and encountered in a broader context in which life does not always conform to relational wholeness and health. Indeed, there are moments in which evil prevails over good, as in the Shoah, confronting those who live in its aftermath with the need for a form of faith that does not fear confronting the dark side of the world. In this regard, the Shoah stands as an *unassimilated* event for even the most mature forms of faith. That is, even though faith addresses what happened, faith does not absorb or integrate it, at least not completely. The suffering remains "other" to the meaning that faith brings to such encounters. Faith addresses what happened and in its vulnerability to that reality is wounded by the suffering it faces. Wounded, moment faith calls us to face the murdered children at the same time as it provides us with a reason for letting ourselves be wounded by their suffering.

Such an approach will necessarily be an open-ended, unfinished venture that takes history with utmost seriousness, no matter how much confidence such moment faith expresses in the covenantal task that has been entrusted to human beings as partners in God's creation. Likewise, an ongoing encounter with the biblical witness will reflect the chastened interactions of wounded faithfulness. Fackenheim's midrashic proposal challenges that faithfulness to remain open and honest, steadfastly committed to suffering humanity at the same time as it is equally engaged with the witness of scripture and the root experiences that give the biblical text its life. As a Christian in respectful conversation with scholars like Fackenheim and Greenberg, I am able to incorporate their insights into my own Christian identity, as long as I am able to do so in the spirit of generosity and gratitude that is rooted in the logic of plenitude with which they write. What I cannot do is adopt their strategies in such a way that I usurp their voice or witness in the process—not to mention their place in God's house in which I am but a chastened guest. Therefore, the way forward for me is a wounded trek with these and other companions who know their way as the limping walk of Israel. And if Schwartz is right—and I believe she is—then the logic of plenitude opens up to the Muslim Other just as surely as it does to our Jewish brothers and sisters.

Mending a Torn Canopy—Tending a Wounded World

Both the biblical Noah and Shakespeare's Hamlet knew what it meant to live under a torn canopy. Like it or not, so do we, whether we understand that reality literally or figuratively. We know what it means to lose the transcendent canopy of meaning that shelters us from the storm. Unlike Hamlet, however, Noah also lived on the other side of a mended firmament, under its sign of the rainbow. A cosmic Band-Aid, as it were, the bow marked creation's canopy with a reminder of its rending as well as a sign of its diversity of life and shared responsibility for its care. In other words, the mended "roof" of creation—God's house—incorporated its wounds into its restored wholeness.

When we look closely at this fragile, covenantal canopy of ours, we recognize how extensively it has been torn and how we share responsibility with others for its tearing. Likewise, we confront our responsibility for its repair. The mending, however, is less a single act, or series of acts, than it is a way of tending our wounded condition and holding the story that serves as the narrative under and within which we live. How we relate to that canopy makes all the difference in the world.

Whatever else we face in the shadows of our fragile firmament, we know that we must tend the canopy itself—the way it frames our lives and the place it gives to others in its domain. That is, the problem is not simply violence or the underlying problem of supersessionism, or any specific combination of those factors—no matter how vexing or dangerous they may be. The framing logic of our ways of holding the world—our religious mind-sets—must be addressed. If not, the problems of supersessionism, exclusivism, and disdain for the Other will return in new forms.

Canopies of moment faith (wounded and mended) are discrete and limited. Like other forms of faith, they can be closed or open, erected and tended in hospitality, or set up and protected to guard those who gather within them. But moment faith, knowing what is at stake in its *after Auschwitz* modality, is in position to recognize and choose the creation-based wager for life that post-Shoah faithfulness calls forth. To be sure, a fundamental, *either-or* option remains, but not one that many might expect. The choice is either to embrace life in all its plenitude or to engage life solely in order to ward off that which would lead to its diminishment. Further, the choice is not between traditions per se. This choice can be made within them—a choice that mirrors God's wager of creation, a wager for life, for relationship. The choice is the one made in Noah's story, when God provides the mending of the rainbow in the face of humanity's still present violence toward the Other. Likewise, the choice is made in the biblical story of Job, when God makes room for adversarial otherness in God's domain of life.[9] It is the same choice that Moses put before his people at the threshold of the Promised Land. It is also the choice that Abraham made at Mamre just after he accepted the sign of circumcision and responsibility for living in covenant with the God of creation. The question for Christians, then, is whether Christianity with all its edifices can learn to pitch its tent with Abraham and Sarah, prepared to welcome the unexpected presence of God and God's ways in the approach of strangers from beyond Christianity's own limited domain.

According to Jewish legend, Abraham's tent was a canopy open on all sides, reflecting, as it were, God's canopy of heaven with its openness to others and the practice of hospitality within.[10] Abraham's canopy was limited, like the canopies of moment faith, but it reflected God's ways with any who ventured near. That was its secret. It remains the secret of the wedding canopy, the sukkah, and the Tent of Meeting. Likewise, if we look closely at Jesus' praxis of hospitality and the hermeneutic of plenitude embodied in his ministry, we see similar manifestations of meaning and action that we may view as his tents, which he pitched to challenge the logic of scarcity he met in the dynamics of Empire that oppressed his people and that were present, as well, in parts of his own tradition.

The choice Jesus offers post-Shoah Christians need not be the rejection of Judaism—his tradition—or the rejection of Christianity. Rather, it can be a choice about how one holds either tradition and honors the holy within it.[11] With Schwartz's help, I recognize that the parabolic imagination of Jesus, like the midrashic imagination of Judaism, operates with a logic of plenitude, or what we might dare suggest is the promise of creation as expressed through the human imagination. Similarly, I see the hospitality of Jesus, embodied in his table fellowship, teachings, and healing acts, to be one with the unfolding promise of creation. They are his "tents of meeting," relational gestalts of generosity, compassion, and hospitality. They are ways in which his ministry reflects God's ways with creation or, to use his language, announces the encounterable presence of the rule and realm of God in our midst.

As with its numerous counterparts, post-Shoah Christian identity is formed around the central figure of Jesus; however, in the light of supersessionism's confessional violence to Jewish others, we may distinguish between a Christomorphic identity and a Christocentric one. Both share the confessional centrality of the figure Jesus. Yet the former provides a way of holding the central confession of Christian identity without resorting to the hermeneutics of scarcity that can poison conventional perspectives of monotheistic faith.

In explaining why a post-Shoah Christian remains Christian and does not convert to Judaism (or, for that matter, Islam), the short answer is Jesus. Christian identity is formed in his image. The difference arises in what Christians claim about that formation process. Most typically, Christocentric identity is formed around a particular understanding of Jesus as the full embodiment of God in human history and with an equally significant role in the healing of sin and the breach in creation that is its fractious condition before God and every creature. A Christomorphic identity would also be formed around a particular understanding of Jesus as God's full expression in human history as well as the embodiment of creation's fundamental intentionality for life that Jesus articulated in his teaching and ministry. However, a Christomorphic faith would also seek to honor the Rule and Realm of God, which centered Jesus' life through recognition that it came from beyond himself and acknowledgment that the presence of God's Rule and Realm on earth depended on how he, Jesus, acted toward others. Jesus pitched his tent, as it were, with words and actions, welcoming others at table, in the temple, in fields, on the road. His world, his faith, was an act of the imagination (hermeneutics) that was at the same time a relational incarnation, that is, a specific instantiation, of the full promise of creation in the midst of human affairs. That gestalt of grace and hospitality is present, for example, when parents forgive children, when people share their food to feed the hungry, and when strangers are welcomed in acts of hospitality and generosity.

In these ways, Jesus remains the central figure in post-Shoah Christian confessional life. Furthermore, by acknowledging that his richly textured life centered in his understanding of God's ways with human beings, we are encouraged to move with and through him in more inclusive and representative ways. We may even claim that Jesus is uniquely transparent regarding the ways of God he represents, but such uniqueness need not obscure God's ways with others or cut others off from them if they do not see Jesus as we do—or even see him at all—in this gestalt of the fullness of life. The way of hospitality and generosity remains what it is—hospitality and generosity open to others.

Our work begins with our imaginations and how we hold our worlds. It includes attending to the way we use our language—for example, recognizing that this essay is itself a canopy of words. That is, we pitch our tents with our words and our imaginations as well as with our deeds. But the test remains the same. Do the words indicate and the deeds acknowledge that we know that there is only one fragile firmament that God provides and that the best we can do is to ask if, in their hospitality, our tents reflect God's more excellent canopy, providing room for the otherness of creation to bear its fruit and grow? The hermeneutics of plenitude and the praxis of hospitality may be the best way we can enact and honor Jewish and Christian notions that we are created in the image of God at the same time that we respect Muslim reserve regarding any language that speaks of God's image at all. In the end, as post-Shoah people of faith, we dwell under the limited canopies we construct, praying that they will truly reflect God's ways with the world.

CONTRIBUTORS' QUESTIONS FOR HENRY F. KNIGHT

1. Your essay speaks profoundly to the Christian obligation in a post-Shoah world. You make clear why the Shoah shreds Christianity's canopy of supersessionism, but does your outlook challenge Islam in similar ways? Is there, in fact, any significant way in which the Shoah speaks to Islam, as well as to Christianity? Further, in speaking to Christian obligations, might there also be a need for you, as a Christian advocating a logic of plenitude, to heed also the cries of the millions of innocent Muslims who have been casualties of wars in Afghanistan, Iraq, and other predominantly Muslim regions?

2. Your critique of scarcity thinking might be used to critique eschatology, which often rests on a distinction between the saved and the unsaved. Does your vision of the tent extend as well to your vision for "the world to come"? If so, what are some of the implications for authentic trialogue?

RESPONSE BY HENRY F. KNIGHT

The Shoah discloses the dark side of supersessionism to be a violent expression of its logic of scarcity, what I describe elsewhere as the funding logic of conquest.[12] By disclosing the potential in any faith tradition that operates with this logic, the Shoah stands as a warning to the excesses of supersessionism, especially when what David Novak calls soft supersessionism (displacement logic) shifts into hard supersessionism (replacement logic).[13] Perhaps the teaching case in this regard is what happened to Martin Luther when he slipped from a soft form of supersessionism, in which he hoped that Jews and Judaism would respond positively to his rediscovery of the good news of Christ's message to the world, to a harder, vitriolic one. When his hope for converting Jews did not materialize, Luther became more and more resentful, eventually reacting to the Jewish "no" in stronger and stronger expressions of condemnation and contempt. One need only follow the historic trajectory of his sermons to see that the difference between displacement thinking and replacement logic is one of degree, not kind. The consequences of this way of thinking are revealed once the sanctions against overt forms of violence are lifted. When that occurs, one who is displaceable can also be replaced.

As I sought to explain in my essay, any lessons applied to Islam must be drawn by Muslims. If Schwartz is correct, and she makes a convincing case, then the funding logics of scarcity and supersessionism are present in all three Abrahamic traditions—as are the contrasting hermeneutics of plenitude. Still, since I am a stranger to Islam even though I seek to understand and value it as a familial tradition, I hesitate to venture too far in suggesting how Muslim scholars should address the challenges of supersessionism they will undoubtedly face. Nevertheless, as an outsider to their tradition I wonder what prevents the supersessionism of "dhimmitude" from becoming violent in a pattern not unlike Luther's transition from positive regard for Jews in hopes of their conversion to resentment and vitriol in the face of their resistance to his version of the Christian Gospel. I offer that question to my Muslim colleagues knowing well the failure of Christian theology to grapple with this matter. My own contribution is reserved for a transparent description of my own struggle—a Christian jihad, if you will—asking what a similar task might be like for Muslims while pondering what I might learn from honoring their work as an expression of their faithfulness to the One God we each serve.

The suggestion that the hermeneutical distinctions I make between the logics of scarcity and plenitude might be utilized in looking at matters of eschatology is instructive. A quick but misleading response would be to suggest that most eschatological visions of the end of history are expressions of the logic of scarcity, especially those that focus on a final judgment. However, that would confuse the very distinctions I have sought to make about the role of the religious imagination in the way we hold our worlds and one another in them. Instead, recognizing that eschatological visions are in many ways the creation story in future tense, we should ask how our lenses of scarcity and plenitude might affect the way Christians ponder the world to come and the final outcome of history or the consummation of creation.

The logics of plenitude and scarcity refer to characteristics of the religious imagination. They are lenses through which we view the world. Consequently, the issue is how one perceives and speaks of the world to come. That is, the operating logic of the religious imagination is a present-tense phenomenon characterizing how one attends to all temporal matters. Even if the expectation is for a singular coming of God's intended domain, one can anticipate that singular reality in a way that reduces the coming world to one's own construction of it or limits what is being anticipated in ways that foreclose God's creative embrace of life that is being ventured and ultimately fulfilled. Just as important, one can attend to the lived moments of scarcity in which we find ourselves and yet have choices about how to dwell in those situations.

The categories of saved and unsaved carry the potential of being used by those who view the world through the logic of scarcity. But the logic of scarcity is not a necessary component of such a distinction. In the New Testament Gospel of Matthew, Jesus' version of the final judgment takes attitudes of dividing the world up into those who count and those who do not and turns them against themselves, exposing the fallacy of scarcity thinking and the danger that lurks in presuming an attitude that only God may exercise. Those who have previously divided the world into the saved and the damned are confronted with a different order of either-or logic. What "counts" is how human beings dwell in the world with others, how they treat one another. The logic of scarcity is dislodged, revealing a relational plenitude that must, nonetheless, be enacted to bear its own fruit.

One might also turn to John's apocalyptic vision in the New Testament and view that enigmatic text through the lenses of scarcity and plenitude.

Reading through the lens of scarcity, one is typically caught up in the matter of who counts and who does not, who is on the side of God and goodness and who is not. Utilizing this point of view, the reader seeks to find the key to the allegorical code of the vision John has recorded to determine one's place in God's coming domain. The message and its singular truth are embedded in the vision but must be extracted from it. The question "What does it mean?" is oriented to finding the correct interpretation with the expectation that there is a singular outcome that controls and guides the entire trajectory. In contrast, one can approach an apocalyptic text like John's Revelation cognizant of its dreamlike character and seek to enter its rich panoply of associations. As a participant in the drama, one is drawn toward the envisioned final marriage between heaven and earth. The canopy of heaven descends to embrace those canopies of covenantal regard that have reflected God's ways with the world. As the text points out (Revelation 21:22), a specific institution (the temple, or, for that matter, church or mosque) is not the final, superseding reality. Rather, covenantal union is celebrated without mediation.

As these examples show, *how* one anticipates the shape and character of the future matters significantly. Even the most dramatic scenarios of final judgment can function as expressions of plenitude or of scarcity thinking, depending upon the way they are approached and held. More generally, the mind-set of scarcity can lead to an ever-increasing need to control the open-ended character of the future, while the mind-set of plenitude rests more in the wager of the present embracing the unfolding character of life. The logic of plenitude recognizes that even in moments of true scarcity there are usually choices that transcend those presented by the circumstances at hand. With that said, the Shoah, especially with situations that Lawrence L. Langer has described as moments of "choiceless choice," stands as an extreme challenge to this observation and the natural unfolding of creation's logic of life.[14] Indeed, we could say that this feature of the Shoah undermines an essential aspect of human being and does fundamental violence to God's gift of life in creation. Such awareness underscores again that the role of the religious imagination is not an esoteric matter but one that is essential for determining how Jews, Christians, and Muslims dwell with one another and embody their responsibilities to care for the life entrusted to them.

NOTES

Epigraph: William Shakespeare, *Hamlet*, Shakespeare Online, http://www .shakespeare-online.com/plays/hamlet_2_2.html.

1   Irving Greenberg, "Cloud of Smoke, Pillar of Fire: Judaism, Christianity, and Modernity after the Holocaust," in *Auschwitz: Beginning of a New Era? Reflections on the Holocaust*, ed. Eva Fleischner (New York: KTAV, 1977), 23.

2   Elie Wiesel, acceptance speech at Congressional Gold Medal award ceremony, April 19, 1985. Available online at http://www.jewishvirtuallibrary.org/jsource /US-Israel/RR4_19_85.html.

3   Regina M. Schwartz, *The Curse of Cain: The Violent Legacy of Monotheism* (Chicago: University of Chicago Press, 1997), 1–13.

4   The interpretive role of these distinctive hermeneutical practices reflects my own reading of these rhetorical strategies. In various ways they express a logic of plenitude or abundance.

5   Jonathan Sacks develops a similar critique in his book *The Dignity of Difference: How to Avoid the Clash of Civilizations* (New York: Continuum, 2002), 45–66.

6   Johann Baptist Metz, "Christians and Jews after Auschwitz," in *The Emergent Church: The Future of Christianity in a Postbourgeois World* (New York: Crossroads, 1987), 19, 32.

7   Emil L. Fackenheim, *God's Presence in History: Jewish Affirmations and Philosophical Reflections* (New York: Harper Torchbooks, 1970), 3–34.

8   Greenberg introduced his notion of moment faith in his still evocative lecture given in 1974 and first published in 1977. See Greenberg, "Cloud of Smoke, Pillar of Fire," 27–34.

9   See my reflection, "Facing the Whirlwind Anew: Looking over Job's Shoulders from the Shadows of the Storm," in *Remembering for the Future: The Holocaust in an Age of Genocide*, ed. John K. Roth and Elisabeth Maxwell (London: Palgrave, 2001), 745–59.

10 Louis Ginzberg, *Legends of the Bible* (Philadelphia: Jewish Publication Society, 1956), 109–12.

11 This distinction is important, especially when we remember that Jesus called this way of holding his tradition a narrow way. The way of plenitude requires risk and vulnerability. The way of scarcity is itself not scarce, but common and well traveled. For example, Jesus follows his statement about God's house as a place in which there is room for many dwelling places (John 14:1–4) by stating, "I am the way, the truth, and the life. No one comes to the Father but through me" (John 14:6). If the axis on which his logic turns is an algebra that determines who is saved and who is not, then the logic remains an ultimate determination of who counts before God. That is the logic of scarcity. If the axis is the relational quality of creation and his logic is that of the plenitude of creation, then the admonition "No one comes to the Father but through me" is a demand to attend to the relational presence of Jesus before his disciples. It is a summons to full, covenantal presence before Jesus, a summons to relationship—a claim that ostensibly any child of God

can make in the presence of any other child of God: No one comes to the Father except by and through the other before you.

In other words, the narrow way of Jesus can be interpreted in more than one way. And that way depends upon the axis on which its logic turns. If the axis is that of determining who is saved and who is not, then the logic expresses a divine hermeneutic of scarcity. After Auschwitz, this way of thinking portrays God as a righteous Mengele. Can that oxymoron serve any moral good?

We may press the matter further. If the axis is purity, then the determination becomes who is pure and who is not. If power, then the question is about who has power and who does not. We are still trapped within the logic of scarcity. If, however, the narrow way is that of following the relational logic of creation, then the question may be posed simply by the presence of the other.

12 Henry F. Knight, "Beyond Conquest: Post-Shoah Christian Anguish and the Palestinian-Israeli Dilemma," in *Anguished Hope: Holocaust Scholars Confront the Palestinian-Israeli Conflict*, ed. Leonard Grob and John K. Roth (Grand Rapids, Mich.: Wm. B. Eerdmans, 2008), 176–90.

13 David Novak, "The Covenant in Rabbinic Thought," in *Two Faiths, One Covenant? Jewish and Christian Identity in the Presence of the Other*, ed. Eugene B. Korn and John T. Pawlikowski (Lanham, Md.: Rowman and Littlefield, 2005), 66–68, 71.

14 Lawrence L. Langer, "The Dilemma of Choice in the Deathcamps," in *Echoes from the Holocaust: Philosophical Reflections on a Dark Time*, ed. Alan Rosenberg and Gerald E. Meyers (Philadelphia: Temple University Press, 1988), 118–27. See also Lawrence L. Langer, "Ghetto Chronicles," in *Admitting the Holocaust: Collected Essays* (Oxford: Oxford University Press, 1995), 46.

5

The Place of Non-Muslims
in the Islamic Concept of the "Other"

The Need for Rethinking Islamic Tradition
in the Pursuit of Religious Pluralism

BASSAM TIBI

All religions have problems when they encounter the stranger. As a Muslim scholar, I argue that the ways in which Muslims have traditionally viewed non-Muslims are unacceptable in the twenty-first-century world. My inquiry explores how the concept of political pluralism might be applied to religions in their interactions with one another and, in particular, how such pluralism could become increasingly acceptable to contemporary Muslims in their interactions with people of other religious traditions, especially Jews and Christians.[1]

Within Islam, one way to approach such issues is scriptural. In this perspective, emphasis can be placed on Qur'anic verse 49:13: "Then, we have created you as divergent peoples and tribes in order to make you encounter one another." This statement underpins the claim that pluralism is a part of Islamic culture. In all honesty, however, one has to correct this view and say that pluralism is a concept of modernity that has not existed originally as such in any religion. In Islam—both in its religious thought and in its cultural history—only non-Muslim monotheists are granted tolerance. Islam, moreover, prescribes the tolerance of Jews and

Christians as *dhimmis*, those who are not considered equal to Muslims.[2]

All religions claim absoluteness for themselves, but Islam is unique in this regard because it considers itself the "final" religion, valid for all humankind; it thus asserts *siyadah* (its superiority). The Qur'an claims that Islam is the only *din* (religion) recognized by Allah (3:19). The Qur'an further states that the prophet Muhammad is the *khatem* (seal, finalization) of all religions (40:33). Of course, Islam maintains a basic differentiation among non-Muslim "others"—between *kuffar* (infidels, unbelievers) and *Ahl al-Kitab* (People of the Book, non-Muslim monotheists). But again, although Jews and Christians are respected by Muslims, the latter fail to see the former as equals.

A new reading of Islam is needed, one that fosters equality with other religions. In the early twenty-first century, however, one cannot expect an Islamic acceptance of equality with all religions and yet overlook the fact that even traditional Islamic standards are jeopardized by Islamism, as I shall call militant political Islam. In Islamism, the doctrinal differentiation between monotheists and infidels or unbelievers is completely abandoned. Proponents of Islamism, whom I shall call Islamists, indiscriminately view all non-Muslims, including monotheists, as infidels. In Islamist ideology, people of other faiths are addressed with contempt. Monotheists are viewed as allied with *al-yahud wa al-salibiyun* (Jews and crusaders); they are also put on equal footing with non-monotheists as *kuffar*. Certainly, the Islamist outlook is not in line with the Qur'an, and this potent contemporary perspective threatens the Muslim encounter with the stranger.

Despite these obstacles, a synthesis of Islam and pluralism is possible. Such a synthesis, however, requires an honest willingness to rethink some key Islamic concepts regarding the status of the non-Muslim other, a rethinking that extends beyond mere polemics. At the heart of the matter is the issue of whether Muslims can and will abandon their supremacist claims. Within Islam, resistance against such an abandonment is strong. One typical example comes from the Saudi scholars Ali M. Jarisha and Mohammed Sharif al-Zaibaq, both of whom reject trialogue with Judaism and Christianity on the grounds that it "could only take place at the expense of Islam, because Islam is the only true religion. . . . To abandon this claim is to do a great damage to Islam."[3] This rejection of trialogue illustrates Islam's predicament with regard to religious pluralism.

Islamists who envision an Islamic world order replacing the existing pluralistic one are not, as Abdulaziz Sachedina claims, "extremist groups abusing Islam" in a "misuse of religion by a vocal minority."[4] Such apologetics distract from reality. Trialogue requires a wholesale abandonment of Muslim supremacist attitudes and the worldview that underpins them. The same issue that occurs on a global scale applies to Islamic countries with non-Islamic minorities, for example, Indonesia, and to countries with Islamic minorities, for example, India. If Muslims fail to accept pluralist thinking regarding non-Muslims, there is not likely to be peace within such countries. Another aspect of this problem is illustrated by current conditions in Iraq, where Muslims (Sunni and Shia) frequently have killed one another. No "one Islam" exists, but when a pluralist culture is lacking, then one version of Islam may come to claim supremacy; violent sectarianism often erupts. There is need for a pluralism that promotes peace not only between Muslims and others, globally and locally, but also among Muslims, who are themselves a diverse people.

Islamic *da'wa* (proselytization) ignores the fact that non-Muslims throughout the world will not succumb to the claim of *siyadah* (supremacy) as articulated by universalist Islam, be it advanced by violent religionists or by those who utilize more peaceful means to promote their agenda. Muslims must abandon Islamic universalist claims in order to avoid a conflict with non-Muslim societies, as well as within those Islamic societies where non-Muslims live as minorities. Those who are poised to impose their sectarian vision on all of humanity are in conflict with those who subscribe to diversity and whose political system fosters pluralism. Support for the choice of pluralism is not an imposition placed upon Islam alone; rather, it is an argument for diversity that should be advanced among all faith traditions.

Useful trialogue among Jews, Christians, and Muslims requires support for pluralism. This aim would be in line not only with the Qur'an but also with the Hadith (oral traditions relating to the prophet Muhammad), which states that "al-ikhtilafi fi ummati rahm" (difference in my *umma* [community] is a sign of mercy). The normative quality of these provisions is useful for establishing the legitimacy of pluralism in Islam. However, advocacy for pluralism based on scripture or Hadith has never dominated Islam in reality—past or present. The promotion of pluralism within Islam will continue to be difficult.

An "Islamic state," rooted in shari'a (Islamic law) and serving as the nucleus of a new Islamic world order, is another concept at odds with pluralism. Well-educated Muslims will not find in the Qur'an or in the Hadith the term "order" (*nizam*) or any synonymous concept. Any talk of Islamic governance can refer only to an ethical vision, rather than to any particular system of government. The cultural acceptance of pluralism within Islamic societies—as well as an acceptance of pluralism by Muslims in international relations with non-Muslims—is an issue that has bearing on the success or failure of trialogue among the Abrahamic religions. What is required is an Islamic political ethics that accepts pluralism in ways reflecting the Qur'anic precept "Lakum dinakum wa liya di" (You have your religion and I have mine [109:6]). This ethical norm should determine Muslim behavior in politics and society; it should serve as the point of departure for interreligious and intercultural dialogue and trialogue.

To promote pluralism that abandons supremacist claims and thus helps prevent a "clash of civilizations," I argue for the growth of a civil Islam. I find support for these views in Islam's heritage of Hellenized rationalism, especially as that outlook is reflected in the political philosophy of Abu Nasr al-Farabi (ca. 870–950). Al-Farabi's view of the perfect state is an especially excellent model for a civil Islam in the twenty-first century.[5]

In interreligious trialogue, communication with the stranger requires shared knowledge of all cultures involved. The Islamic tradition of adopting the legacy of the Hellenistic culture provides a model for establishing a common discourse across cultures. The Hellenization of Islam contributed not only to the flourishing of its civilization but also to an Islamic embrace of rationalism, which was shared by Muslim and Jewish philosophers.[6] Muslim philosophers in the classical age of Islam had positive attitudes toward the Greek tradition. At that time, open-minded Muslim philosophers called Aristotle the *Mu'allim al-Awwal* (First Master), while al-Farabi, the most significant Muslim philosopher during this period, was ranked as *al-Mu'allim al-Thani* (second to Aristotle). In giving a top ranking to a non-Muslim thinker, Islamic rationalists exhibited a high degree of open-mindedness in their encounter with the stranger. In their cultural borrowings, classical Muslim rationalists established legitimacy for their adoption of ideas from non-Muslims. In a similar vein, I argue that Islam today needs to embrace democratic pluralism. This movement is in harmony with the mind-set of the Prophet, who once said, "Utlubu al-Ilm wa law fi al-sei" (Seek for knowledge even in China), knowing that China was not a Muslim country. Learning from others can be done in the spirit of an open Islam, which seeks knowledge within the framework of a reason-based universal discourse.

Classical Islam embraced Greek philosophy with minimal difficulty. What prevents contemporary Muslims from acting in the same way to infuse pluralist democratic values into Islam? Contemporary Muslims must challenge themselves to accept that they belong to one humanity (*al-nas*), which is not identical with the Islamic *umma*. The realities of the world-at-large belie this monolithic Islamist concept of one *umma*, a concept embraced in contrast to *al-nas*. Acceptance of pluralism is essential both for world peace and for inner peace within Islamic civilization itself.

Importantly, the pluralism necessary for serious trialogue depends on cross-cultural consensus regarding a common core of ethical values. The envisioned consensus can unite humanity and advance democratic peace. But, as we have seen, it remains true that democratic pluralism is in conflict with any concept of an Islamist peace, a peace rooted in the belief of a utopia that unites humanity and encompasses the globe under the banner of Islam, *dar al-Islam* (House of Islam).

In this debate, it is important to reiterate my view that, like it or not, democracy and pluralism lack religious roots—Islamic, Christian, or any other. The idea of religious pluralism is a modern secular concept. The Muslim scholar Hamid Enayat has rightly argued that Islamic awareness of this innovative line of thought continues to be weak and blurred.[7] Muslims in early modern times first encountered the concept of pluralism and democratic rule through their exposure to "cultural modernity" as elites in their societies became better educated. For example, Rifaʿa Rafiʿ al-Tahtawi, the first Muslim imam (leader) who traveled to Europe and became a student there, expressed a deep admiration for the French culture of democracy. He witnessed the July 1830 revolution in Paris and was impressed to see that representatives of the toppled regime were granted basic human rights. For Imam Tahtawi, this outcome was evidence—as he said—"for how civilized the French are and how their state is bound to justice."[8] Subsequent to the work of Tahtawi, early Muslim modernists and reformists were more critical of Europe, owing to its colonialism in Islamic lands. Some Muslim liberals continued efforts to reconcile Islam with modernity, but even they evaded basic issues and did not venture into a fundamental rethinking of Islam.[9]

For contemporary Islamists, "authenticity" counts more than learning from others. A revival of Islam's rationalist legacy from both Hellenistic and early modern times would help reverse recent developments and could promote the Islamic adoption of pluralism and democracy. Of course, there needs to be a balance between one's particular identity and openness to others. Historical references show how Muslim rationalists in the past were able to achieve that balance. Today, the search for authenticity emphasizes exclusiveness.[10] Acceptance of an alien impact on oneself is not allowed. This closedness impedes democratic pluralism and makes it very difficult for Islam to encounter the other in creative and peaceful ways. A civil Islam that accommodates pluralism and the idea of democratic peace is the alternative to militant political Islam.

Without the legitimization of pluralism in Islam, there can be no political, religious, or cultural underpinnings that would allow Muslims to embrace world peace based on democratic principles. For this reason, the rejection of democracy by political Islamists is to be taken most seriously in order to avert destructive consequences. In contrast to an acceptance of the concept of popular sovereignty, Islamists apply God's sovereignty to politics. The model they present as an alternative to democracy is *Hakimiyyat Allah* (God's rule).

It would be self-deception to overlook the power of militant political Islam while arguing for democratic pluralism. Nevertheless, the effort pursued in this chapter to establish an Islamic worldview based on democratic pluralism is not wishful thinking. What action is needed under these conditions? The answer is education in democratic pluralism, along with the needed religious reforms and cultural innovations. Among these reforms—arguably foremost among them—is the need for seeking the separation of religion and politics.[11]

In my view, Islam's embrace of pluralism is a prerequisite for religious reform. Fortunately, the spirit of classical Islamic ethics is in line with the pursuit of a cross-cultural morality that embraces pluralism. I agree with Enayat that it is "neither . . . inordinately difficult nor illegitimate to derive a list of democratic rights and liberties" from Islamic sources in the spirit of an "open Islam."[12] However, to go beyond scriptural confines, a rethinking of Islamic concepts must be undertaken. Only then can full legitimacy for pluralism and democracy in Islam be achieved.

These initiatives are important for the success of any trialogical endeavor, but they run counter to the fundamentalist agenda oriented toward establishing *Hakimiyyat Allah*. Even though *Hakimiyyat Allah* is not an authentic Islamic concept, but rather an interpretation that has no grounds either in the Qur'an or in the Hadith, it has become a popular public choice. On the basis of the Qur'an and the Hadith (the only two authoritative sources in Islamic faith), the politics of "shari'atization" embraced by political Islam can be dismissed. What is at issue, however, is not primarily a scriptural matter. Islam's predicament with modernity—with the latter's pluralistic outlook—is rooted neither in problems of a scriptural nature nor in issues relating to academic matters.[13] The real issue is that culture makes a difference and that, as a result, we have seen a "religionization" of politics and a politicization of religion. Shari'atization of Islam entails these developments, which are stumbling blocks for Islam's inclusion in fruitful dialogue and trialogue. As I have argued above, Islamist calls for an "Islamic state," presented as an alternative to a democratic state based on pluralism, create an impasse for Muslim societies and impede Islam's participation in needed trialogue.

The same is true regarding calls for *tatbiq al-shari'a* (implementation of Islamic law) pursued as a shari'atization of politics. In the Qur'an, shari'a is not fundamentally "law," but rather a set of interpretative divine provisions based primarily on the ethics of *al-amr bi alma'ruf wa al-nahi an all munkar* (to enjoin the good and forbid the evil). In the course of history, shari'a developed into a legal system restricted to civil and penal law. Shari'a is characterized by four (diverse) Sunni schools of law, each with its own tradition of civil, rather than state, lawmaking; it should be noted that I do not here mention Shi'i varieties of law. Furthermore, Islamic law has been primarily the civil law for the divergent Hanafi, Shafi'i, Hanbali, and Maliki religious communities, not a comprehensive legal system or a state law. In Islamic history, shari'a was never directly attached to *siyasa* (the authority of the head of state to act in legal matters). Joseph Schacht's authoritative study of Islamic law rightly shows that shari'a and *siyasa* were separate realms.[14] Enayat persuasively argues that shari'a "was never implemented as an integral system, and the bulk of its provisions remained as legal fictions."[15] In other words, the claim of *tatbiq al-shari'a* advanced by the exponents of militant political Islam is similarly constructed on a fiction.

As practiced in Iran, and earlier in Afghanistan under the Taliban, *tatbiq al-shari'a* supports authoritarian nondemocratic rule. Faced by the need for good governance and the political culture of an open society, Muslims are challenged to establish political legitimacy for an Islam imbued with the values of democratic pluralism. As a Muslim scholar, I acknowledge the existing tensions burdening this pursuit; I reiterate that the search for a synthesis between Islam and democracy cannot be done successfully without dealing in candor with these tensions. In this regard,

I again agree with Enayat when he states: "If Islam comes into conflict with certain postulates of democracy it is because of its general character as a religion. . . . An intrinsic concomitant of democracy . . . involves a challenge to many a sacred axiom."[16]

Muslims of the twenty-first century should not repeat the mistake of early Muslim reformers, who failed because they clearly evaded hot-button issues. A necessary rethinking of Islam requires a subjection of religious doctrine to reason. At the same time, the search for an opening for democratic pluralism and good governance in Islam requires religious underpinning provided by the Qur'an. As we have seen, the Qur'an embodies the spirit of an ethical embrace of democracy, but not explicit rules of governance. Hitherto, most approaches to reform in Islam have been both selective and limited in scope; they have evaded dealing with a secularization of politics. This secularization of politics is, however, a basic requirement for resolving the conflict between Islam and democracy. To avoid a common misunderstanding, I emphasize that by secular democracy I mean a system of governance separated from religion but not from religious ethics. Islamic ethics can help underpin democracy. Yet, as we have seen, Islamic ethics is not to be equated with a notion of "Islamic democracy," since democracy is based on popular sovereignty, a universal principle unrelated to any specific religious precepts.

Authentic trialogue is actually practiced only among equals. If a religion denies others equality, then no dialogue or trialogue can ever be successful. Thus pluralism is among the basic elements required to establish a truly equitable encounter with the other. That said, one of the major dilemmas noted in this chapter is contemporary Islam's clash with modernity and the political culture of pluralism that emanates from it. As we have observed, that which is based on the concept of *umma* presupposes cohesion rather than diversity and thus falls outside of a culture of pluralism.

To introduce the idea of a trialogue based on pluralism, a cultural underpinning within Islam is needed to legitimate this interaction. As we have seen, Islam in the twenty-first century stands in need of a culture of pluralism to address issues that arise in both sectarian and multireligious societies. In most Islamic countries, this culture of pluralism is not in place. Such a culture cannot be imposed from the outside; rather, it must arise within the world of Islam itself. Muslims need to learn respect for ethnic and religious differences, including the culture of religious minorities living within Islamic societies.

CONTRIBUTORS' QUESTIONS FOR BASSAM TIBI

1. An Islam that espouses pluralism, you say, cannot be based solely on scripture or religious ethics, though both can provide support for a pluralistic philosophy. You say that within Islam there must be a commitment to democratic pluralism and the separation of religion and the state. Will this commitment not have theological implications? Would not a civil Islam inevitably influence (however subtly) Islamic theology? In actual practice, can a Muslim be both religiously conservative and politically liberal—"liberal" understood as characterizing one who embraces democratic pluralism?

2. You describe a nearly insoluble dilemma regarding Muslim attitudes toward the non-Muslim. On the one hand, you point out that Islam persistently maintains an attitude of superiority toward non-Muslims even when providing for their safety and well-being. On the other hand, you identify an internal need in Islam for the practice of respect toward the stranger and the cultivation of faith-friendly political pluralism. For its own well-being, you contend, authentic Muslim identity depends upon developing a capacity to embrace pluralism. You point to the model of Muslim openness toward Greek rationalist inquiry during the Middle Ages as an example of what might be possible. What in Muslim tradition grounded this willingness to engage boldly the insights of non-Muslim thinkers such as Aristotle? How might this period be instructive in developing an openness to life, particularly in a world that continues to feel the effects of events such as the Holocaust, twenty-first-century terrorism, and violent responses that implicate all three Abrahamic traditions? What in Muslim tradition might challenge the openness that blossomed during the Middle Ages?

RESPONSE BY BASSAM TIBI

I have indeed argued that an espousal of a political culture of religious pluralism by Islam cannot be based solely on religious ethics and that within Islam there must be a commitment both to democratic pluralism and to the separation of religion and state. I am now asked about the theological implications of such a reformist commitment. I understand the question well and share its concern fully. I think, however, that the question may be based on a misunderstanding of an argument in my essay, an argument perhaps not presented as clearly as I intended. Of course, a Muslim cannot be Salafist (an adherent of a highly conservative Sunni movement) and liberal at the same time. A commitment to religious reform and cultural change is a requirement for establishing a position within Islam that views the stranger as a full partner in dialogue/trialogue. This is what pluralism is all about.

As a reformist Muslim, I am familiar with the procedure of *tafsir* (exegesis) in Islam. Most Muslims believe that *tafsir* will come to terms with the challenges I have noted, without a fundamental rethinking of the doctrine of supremacy with regard to the other of a different faith tradition. I argue that this procedure cannot work in the way it is intended. Any textual reinterpretation devoid of critical reasoning is insufficient to establish religious pluralism. Institutional safeguards, paired with liberal secular perspectives, are required for such fundamental attitudinal changes to take hold.

The second question asks what needs to be done to establish openness in interreligious dialogue/trialogue in a post-Holocaust world. After spending a term studying Islamist varieties of antisemitism at the Center for Advanced Holocaust Studies at the United States Holocaust Memorial Museum in Washington, D.C., I feel confident addressing a question concerning regard for the religious other in a world that continues to feel the effects of the Holocaust and current acts of terrorism that implicate the Abrahamic traditions. Indeed, I can speak to a matter I have encountered in my studies: Islamist antisemitism that evokes memory of a time preceding the Holocaust. As a liberal Muslim, I am shocked to the bone by what is said about Jews in the writings of Islamists. There is a conflict within Islam not only between liberals and conservatives; there is also a conflict between a humanist Islam and a jihadist-xenophobic Islam.

The value of a revival of the buried Islamic tradition of rationalism in medieval Islam lies in large measure in that tradition's openness toward non-Muslims. As I have noted in my essay, our Prophet himself asked believers "to seek knowledge, even in China." In this spirit, Muslim medieval philosophers read the legacy of Hellenism and embraced it. In contrast, contemporary Islamists—in the name of *asalah* (authenticity)—develop a mind-set of purification that establishes a fault line between what is considered to be "Islamic" and what is not, a fault line that also lies between the Islamist self and the religious other. In order to embrace Plato's views on the *madina al-fadila* (the perfect polity), al-Farabi separated the state from religion. Continuing in this line of thinking two centuries later, Ibn Rushd (Averroes), established the concept of *al-haqiqa al-muzdawaj* (double truth): revelation and reason lie in separate realms. Contemporary Muslims need to accept this distinction if they are to embrace a pluralism of religious traditions.

In view of the strength of political Islam/Islamism in the contemporary world, many Westerners have adopted an accommodationist position, overlooking an Islamist worldview rooted in a notion of supremacy. The supremacy of Islam propounded by Islamism constitutes the basic obstacle to the pluralism of cultures and religions of which I have spoken. New forms of antisemitism have emerged from contemporary Islamism, a movement lacking authentic roots in Islam. Only a liberal Islam committed to pluralism is in a position to counter Islamism effectively.

NOTES

1   On the concept of pluralism. *See* John Kekes, *The Morality of Pluralism* (Princeton, N.J.: Princeton University Press, 1993). On democratic peace that also applies to religions. *See* the seminal work by Bruce M. Russett, *Grasping the Democratic Peace: Principles for a Post–Cold War World* (Princeton, N.J.: Princeton University Press, 1993); and the reader edited by Michael E. Brown, Sean M. Lynn-Jones, and Steven E. Miller, *Debating the Democratic Peace* (Cambridge, Mass.: MIT Press, 1996).

2   See the Jewish complaint by Bat Ye'or, *Islam and Dhimmitude: Where Civilizations Collide* (Madison, N.J.: Fairleigh Dickinson University Press, 2002).

3   Ali M. Jarisha and Mohammed Sharif al-Zaibaq, *Asalib al-Ghazu al-fikri li al-'alam al- Islami* [Methods of Intellectual Invasion of the Muslim World] (Cairo: Dar al-I'tisan, 1978), 202.

4   Abdulaziz Sachedina, *The Islamic Roots of Democratic Pluralism* (New York: Oxford University Press, 2001), 6n4.

5   The relevant writings by al-Farabi are available in an English translation. See Richard Walzer, ed., *Al-Farabi on the Perfect State* (Oxford: Clarendon Press, 1985). On the related Islamic heritage. *See* Franz Rosenthal, *The Classical Heritage in Islam* (London: Routledge, 1975). See also the chapter on al-Farabi in Peter Adamson and Richard C. Taylor, eds., *The Cambridge Companion to Arabic Philosophy* (Cambridge: Cambridge University Press, 2005), 52–71. For information on the first and second waves of Hellenization in medieval Islam. *See* W. Montgomery Watt, *Islamic Philosophy and Theology*, 2nd ed. (Edinburgh: Edinburgh University Press, 1995). The magnitude of intellectual indebtedness of Islamic philosophy to Hellenism is shown in Charles Butterworth, ed., *The Political Aspects of Islamic Philosophy: Essays in Honor of Muhsin S. Mahdi* (Cambridge, Mass.: Harvard University Press, 1992).

6 An example is the common discourse shared by Ibn Rushd (Averroes) (1126–1198) and Moses Maimonides (1135–1204). See the chapter by Steven Harvey, "Jewish and Islamic Philosophy," in Adamson and Taylor, eds., *The Cambridge Companion to Arabic Philosophy*, 349–69.

7 See Hamid Enayat, *Modern Islamic Political Thought* (Austin: University of Texas Press, 1982).

8 Rifaʻa Rafiʻ al-Tahtawi, *Takhlis al-ibriz ila talkis Paris* [Paris Diary] (Cairo, 1834; repr., Beirut, n.d.). See the excellent German translation of Tahtawi's Paris diary, edited and with an introduction, by Karl Stowasser, *Ein Muslim entdeckt Europa* [A Muslim Discovers Europe] (Munich: C. H. Beck, 1989), 223.

9 On this issue. *See* Nadav Safran, *Egypt in Search of Political Community: An Analysis of the Intellectual and Political Evolution of Egypt* (Cambridge, Mass.: Harvard University Press, 1961), in particular 85, 96–120, 179.

10 See Robert Lee, *Overcoming Tradition and Modernity: The Search for Islamic Authenticity* (Boulder, Colo.: Westview Press, 1997).

11 For amplification of these points. *See* Bassam Tibi, *Islam between Culture and Politics*, updated ed. (2001; New York: Palgrave Macmillan, 2005), 148–66. My argument is in continuity with Ali ʻAbdelraziq, *Al-Islam wa usul al-hukm* [Islam and the Patterns of Government] (Cairo, 1925; repr., Beirut: Maktabat al-Hayat, 1966). On Islam as ethics. *See* Sohail H. Hashmi, ed., *Islamic Political Ethics: Civil Society, Pluralism, and Conflict* (Princeton, N.J.: Princeton University Press, 2002), and, in particular, Bassam Tibi, "Peace and War in Islam," 175–93.

12 Enayat, *Modern Islamic Political Thought*, 131.

13 See Tibi, *Islam between Culture and Politics*, 4–6.

14 See, for example, Joseph Schacht, *An Introduction to Islamic Law* (Oxford: Clarendon Press, 1982).

15 Enayat, *Modern Islamic Political Thought*, 131.

16 Ibid., 126.

6

The Jewish Roots of Emmanuel Levinas's Metaphysics of Welcome

LEONARD GROB

Any human face is a claim on you . . .
—Marilynne Robinson, *Gilead*

In his essay titled "Religion and Tolerance," the twentieth-century French philosopher Emmanuel Levinas speaks of Judaism as a "religion of tolerance" at its core. Such tolerance, for Levinas, is not to be understood in its customary sense as open-mindedness before the doctrines of those who are strangers to Judaism: "Before appearing to the Jews as a fellow creature with convictions to be recognized or opposed, the Stranger is one towards whom one is obligated."[1] I, as a Jew, am thus not merely to be broad-minded with regard to the religious views of the stranger. Before any intellectual exchange of religious views—before dialogue—the stranger-as-Other is one who demands of me as a Jew nothing short of radical hospitality.[2] Responding to the command to welcome the Other invests a Jewish life with ethical import.

In his philosophical writings, Levinas takes these claims about the stranger yet further, making explicit that which he believes is implicit within Judaism. Indeed, "to be obligated" to the stranger is not a demand placed before Jews alone. To be obligated is the very definition of what it means to be human! For René Descartes's *Cogito, ergo sum* (I think, therefore I am), Levinas substitutes *Obligo, ergo sum* (I am obligated, therefore I am). Levinas goes so far as to depict the nature of this obligation as the need to give the stranger "the bread out of one's own mouth and the coat from one's shoulders."[3] He thus gives metaphysical import to the act of hospitality, an import that distinguishes the welcome of the stranger from any conventional understanding of hospitality as the product of some moral calculus. Levinas contends that it is not merely "a good choice" that I host the stranger: the act of welcome is constitutive of my very humanity-as-ethical.

Drawing on Jewish sources, Levinas thus formulates a "metaphysics of welcome." Indeed, in his view Judaism remains a particular tradition that aspires to universality: it announces to all of humankind the fundamental role that an ethics of welcome plays in constituting us as genuinely human. Such chosenness-of-mission, however, is not to be misconstrued as sectarian spiritual arrogance: Judaism's teaching—its injunction to offer hospitality to the stranger—"does not turn into an imperialist expansion. . . . It burns inwards, as an infinite demand made on oneself, an infinite responsibility."[4] The Hebrew Bible speaks of Judaism's occupying a "position outside nations," but this position "is a moral category rather than a historical fact to do with Israel and its particularism. It is a particularism that conditions universalism."[5] It is the purpose of this chapter to elucidate this "metaphysics of welcome"; in it I endeavor to articulate a vision of primordial hospitality, which, according to Levinas, has its origins within Judaism.

Such a vision of hospitality extended to the stranger/Other is not altogether new in the history of religious thought. Adumbrations of the command that the stranger be shown hospitality are found in many religious writings throughout the ages. Yet Levinas argues that religio-philosophical thought in the West has most often remained impervious to a notion of the other-as-truly-Other. Within a universe of discourse in which self-interest is the supreme law, someone other than me cannot, on principle, present me with a genuine moral challenge. Others cannot challenge me to proffer true hospitality, since these others exist solely within my individual ego's sphere of meaning-giving powers. Indeed, the very nature of their being is understood as determined by the interests of my egoist existence. Within these traditional systems, I habitually objectify others: others are "for me." I classify others, give them a role, a set of attributes. And it is not only *human* others who are subject to my categorizing ego. "*Everything* is at my disposal," Levinas proclaims, "even the stars, if I but reckon them."[6] Most religio-philosophical teachings in the history of Western thought have thus been little other than "egologies."

If others in these teachings have challenged me at all, Levinas argues, the challenge has been directed at the *extent* of my ego's powers, rather than the *right* I have to exercise them. Indeed, I am always being contested by others in a battle of self-interested wills. As the French existentialist philosopher Jean-Paul Sartre has argued, others try to objectify me even as I attempt to objectify them.[7] All interhuman relations are characterized by a struggle for power. For Levinas, the challenge posed by the Other (within a Judaism rightly understood) is radically different. The Other contests not the *adequacy* of my powers but rather the *arbitrary* character of my egoist ambitions as a meaning-giving subject. I must be taught by the Other not what I *cannot* do but what, in an ethical sense, I *must* not do. What is challenged is not my *ability* to appropriate the world through my categorizing ego but rather my *right* to do so! What I hear from the other-qua-Other, Levinas claims, are the words "Thou shalt not kill." Harkening to this injunction constitutes my inaugural act as an ethical being. In Levinas's words, "Morality begins when freedom . . . feels itself to be arbitrary and violent."[8]

Thus I am not myself, I am not at home, until the welcome has occurred. For Levinas, I am estranged from myself, never self-identical. Indeed, I only become who I am insofar as I extend hospitality to the stranger who teaches me to be responsible, and thus "to be" in the only sense that matters. Levinas argues that "the humanity of man, subjectivity, is a responsibility for Others. . . . He is stitched of responsibilities."[9] Playing on the double meaning of the French word *hôte*, connoting both host and guest, Levinas reminds us that within the alleged safety of what we may believe is our true home, we are really in a fundamental exilic state: we are more guest than host. Until I welcome the Other, I am, paradoxically, a stranger in my own home! A home only becomes an authentic home—a home worthy of its name—at the moment when I open it to the Other who calls me to account and thus invests my being with ethical import. I come to realize that I am *infinitely* more than a self-interested being, infinitely more than an ego giving meaning to all that surrounds me. Indeed, I have encountered one who is truly Other, one whom I cannot incorporate into my own systems of thought, and thus one who can challenge a freedom arbitrarily exercised. Before the welcome, my home is only a "pagan" site, a dwelling without the dimension of transcendence that appears with the birth of ethics.

Further, although moral concerns have always played a significant role in Western religious and philosophical systems, Levinas argues that ethics, understood in its conventional sense, must be radically called into question in a post-Holocaust world. Western teachings failed to prevent the Nazi slaughter. Levinas contends that attending to Judaism's core teachings concerning the stranger can help heal our wounded world, a world "of which Judaism is not only the conscience, but also the testimony . . . ; the cruelty where the burning of *my* suffering and the anguish of *my* death were able to be transfigured into the dread and concern for the *other man*."[10] If it remains faithful to its core—if it recalls that "the welcome given to the Stranger which the Bible tirelessly asks of us does not constitute a corollary of Judaism . . . but . . . is the very content of faith"—Judaism can teach us a fundamental reverence for the stranger/Other so often lacking in philosophic and religious systems.[11] Hospitality is not just "some region of ethics" but rather, as the contemporary French philosopher Jacques Derrida notes in his discussion of Levinas, "ethicity itself."[12]

For Levinas, then, Judaism teaches that I, in the most meaningful sense of "I," must invert a fear of death—the essence of egoism—into a fear of committing murder. As a Jew, I learn "that there is something more important than my own life and that is the life of the Other."[13] In contrast to the ethos of the perpetrators of the Holocaust and its silent bystanders, Judaism emphasizes the "Hineni" (Here I am!) of the Hebrew Bible as the mark of the human qua human. The only authentic meaning of "I" is the "I" embedded in the word *Hineni*. Citing Genesis 18:2, Levinas notes that Abraham's utterance, "Hineni," to the three strangers who approach his tent at Mamre is embodied in his act of *running* to serve his guests. For Levinas, I cannot approach the Other quickly enough, since it is the call to responsibility by the Other/stranger that makes me who I am. Playing on the word *host*, Levinas terms the "host" at bottom a "hostage," one "besieged" by the Other's command that I be hospitable. Like Abraham, I do not merely come within reach of the Other like one who has weighed the matter and decided to perform a conventional act of welcome. Rather, in *running* toward the Other, I am someone drawn obsessively to him or her, someone who is *beset* by the desire to welcome the Other, someone who is unremittingly "obliged."

If I as host am also hostage, in what sense can it be said that I have any choice as to whether or not I welcome the Other? Levinas was often asked if it is possible to recognize the absolute commandment "Thou shalt not kill" in the face of the Other and to disobey it despite that recognition. Levinas claims that this is indeed the case. There is always the possibility of "injustice and radical egoism, the possibility of accepting the rules of the game, but cheating."[14] Yet, although I am free to objectify others—even to the point of murder—I cannot succeed in killing *the Other*. As announced by both the Hebrew Bible and the Talmud, the face of that Other stands constant, calling me to responsibility, calling me to be hospitable. Even if I were to murder a fellow human being, the Other would not disappear.

Abraham's welcome of the strangers at Mamre is but one of numerous instances when the God of the Bible enjoins hospitality upon the Hebrews. The command "Thou shalt love the stranger" is uttered thirty-six times within the Hebrew Bible. In Exodus and Leviticus this command to welcome the stranger is often accompanied by the reminder that the Hebrews were once themselves strangers in Egypt.[15] But we are reminded to exercise caution lest we misconstrue the injunction to mean that we should open ourselves to the stranger *only because* we, too, know the anguish of exile. For Levinas, the emphasis is not on welcoming the stranger because we ourselves, having been mistreated, do not wish others to suffer in the same way. We are cautioned not to understand the biblical passage as rooted in a moral calculus by means of which I would never want done to another what has been done to me.[16] Such a misreading is rooted in the notion that there is already a fully formed "I" who consciously weighs whether or not to perpetuate a cycle of pain. For Levinas, "There is, as it were, an exile more original than the historical crisis of being cast out from a homeland, the exile of self-estrangement."[17] I cannot exist in any meaningful (moral) sense until I have encountered the face of the Other.

As the responsible human being I have become, I am only now ready to engage in any dialogical/trialogical exchange worthy of its name. Interreligious discourse—a key theme of this volume—is thus derivative of a more fundamental mode of discourse: welcoming the call of the Other that challenges the ego's arbitrary assumption of power. Although this inaugural ethical act embodies a dimension of transcendence—and is thus ahistorical—it is a precondition for historical acts such as those of interreligious dialogue/trialogue.

It is telling that many of the words used by Levinas to refer to my being called to responsibility by the stranger—words such as "provocation," "accusation," and "persecution"—are the very terms that so often denote interreligious *strife*. But in the Levinasian sense, these terms refer to my being shaken from my egoist existence and called to responsibility by the Other. The Other, as it were, hunts me down. He or she "accuses" me of an amoral, arbitrary appropriation of power; "persecutes" me in the sense that my ego is stripped of its pride without having made a calculated decision to allow this to occur; and "provokes" me to become responsible beyond any deliberation on my part. I, as an individual, can refuse the call, but in doing so I fail to realize my humanity. Only as a responsible "I" can I enter into what can be called interreligious discourse—indeed, any discourse worthy of the name.

Yet one must be constantly vigilant to root the call to dialogue in the metaphysics of welcome discussed above. Without a grounding in what Levinas terms the "optics" of ethics, dialogue may, paradoxically, give way to violence:

> There are oppositions . . . that, at first blush. *Seem* . . . to do no more than give rise to reflection and discussions, call for committees, conferences . . . to dispel violence. One soon perceives that all the difficulties they contain can in fact be overcome. All but one. And that last difficulty remains insoluble and annoying because, without realizing it and out of patience, the minds dealing with it turn toward violence and guile, speak of conversion and expulsion, of using force and driving into the sea. . . . One must refuse to be caught up in the tangle of abstractions . . . whose dialectic, be it ever so rigorous, is murderous and criminal.[18]

Jewish-Christian relations are a case in point. Jewish-Christian dialogue calls for "a new attitude . . . the search for a proximity that lasts even after dialogue has become impossible" (87). What is called for, Levinas argues, is "maturity and patience for insoluble problems . . . the presence of persons in the full force of their inevitable responsibility . . . to recognize and name those insoluble substances and keep them from exploding in violence, guile or politics" (87). This endeavor, Levinas adds, consists of "attention and vigilance: not to sleep until the end of time, perhaps . . . the difficult working on oneself: to go toward the other where he is truly Other, in the radical contradiction of their alterity" (87–88). And although Levinas speaks less frequently about Judaism's relation to Islam, we can assume that the principle articulated above holds in this instance as well: Jews and non-Jews must "keep watch" together, must be twin "insomniacs" working to avoid interreligious violence, honoring the essence of the call to responsibility.[19]

Judaism's charge to welcome the Other does not assume a homogeneous world: "I am always alone in being able to answer the call."[20] Levinas contends that Judaism works for a peace that understands difference; it strives to honor the sacredness of each individual of each faith tradition in the endeavor to overcome the urge toward domination. Judaism thus "affirms the possibility of that ultimate intimacy, beyond the dogma affirmed by the one or the other."[21] Judaism, for Levinas, does not condemn alien doctrines; it condemns only that which "can disfigure the human face of my neighbour."[22]

CONTRIBUTORS' QUESTIONS FOR LEONARD GROB

1. In light of the Holocaust and ongoing genocidal and terrorist actions—some of which implicate the monotheistic traditions—is the philosophy of Emmanuel Levinas adequate as a framework for trialogue? Levinas's thinking makes moral obligation toward the other central in the human encounter. But trialogue asks us to radically respect not (only or in the first place) the identity of the other as a human person in general but the other as a *believing* person in particular. Is it not the case that participants in trialogue require more than respect for their otherness? Are they not asking that the other understand and even appreciate their religious particularity? Is Levinas's philosophy adequate to deal with dimensions of trialogue such as understanding, appreciation, empathy, and love? Is interreligious dialogue not an act of love? May it not be said to constitute a religious experience?

2. "I am obligated, therefore I am." By what or by whom am I obligated? If being obligated is only a matter of a moral calculus and not something that arises from the Commanding Voice of God, as depicted in Jewish thought, is Levinas's contention not reducible to just another "egology"? Is not such a concept of obligation merely one moral principle among others within a Western philosophical tradition? What would situate Levinas's thinking within that specifically *Jewish* tradition that calls for obligation to God as an absolute? How does Levinas's thinking fit into the context of a post-Holocaust Christian, Muslim, *Jewish* trialogue?

RESPONSE BY LEONARD GROB

I am asked first to reflect on the adequacy of Levinas's philosophy as a framework for trialogue in a post-Holocaust and still genocidal world. Levinas's work is haunted by the Holocaust. His writings—and, notably, his reflections on interreligious dialogue—are an attempt to rethink a Western tradition of ethical and religious thought that has failed, and continues to fail, to come to grips with the genocides of our time. In Levinas's analysis, traditional ethico-religious thought is rooted in philosophical thought that has most often viewed the ego as constituting *the* point of departure for an understanding of the human condition: I come into the world as an ego seeking gratification. Self-interest reigns supreme. Peaceful regard for the other person will only be undertaken insofar as that person is seen primarily as one who serves my needs. Any notion of a transcendent call to honor the humanity of the other person is deemed at best derivative, at worst illusory. Thus, in Levinas's view, the Western ethico-religious tradition may well have provided some of the fertile ground upon which the Holocaust and more recent genocides have taken place.

In contrast to this tradition, Levinas's philosophy is rooted in the call to ethical responsibility for the other person. I become who I truly am—a moral being—only when I am summoned to responsibility by the Other. The defining moment of my existence as a human individual is my encounter with that Other whom I cannot comprehend in my own terms, an Other to whom I must be hospitable, an Other from whom I learn the ultimate moral lesson, "Thou shalt not kill." This Other lies outside the sphere of all my attempts to categorize, to label, and to comprehend him or her. I am called to responsibility by a face that opens me to the realm of the transcendent: the Other comes from a place radically alien to the self-interested ego, a place Levinas terms "outside of being." Rather than "facing being"—my usual mode of concern for how I appropriate the world around me—Levinas celebrates the primordial act of "being faced."[23]

What bearing does this thought have on interreligious dialogue in a genocidal world? Levinas's privileging of ethics as the foundation for all philosophical and religious thought represents a breakthrough in the Western tradition. In declaring ethics, rather than ontology, "first philosophy," Levinas celebrates the sacredness of the Other whom I may not kill. As a framework for trialogue among the Abrahamic religions, Levinas's philosophy would undermine any endeavor to encompass the other of a different faith tradition *within the terms* of a tradition that is my own. In being taught what I must not do, the stage is set for trialogue in a fundamentally new vein. Being taught responsibility for the Other is a precondition for all meaningful trialogue. Authentic trialogue occurs with "the presence of persons in the full force of their inevitable responsibility," when the parties to trialogue recognize insoluble problems and "keep them from exploding in violence," when these parties "keep watch where conflicts tend to break out," creating "a new religiosity and solidarity."[24] In a post-Holocaust genocidal world—a world where hatred of the religious other has contributed and continues to contribute to ongoing violence, including genocide—Levinas's philosophy provides a new paradigm for interreligious peacemaking.

What I have written above also speaks to the next questions I am asked: How does a Levinasian respect for the Other assist me in encountering the *believing* other who engages me in interreligious dialogue? Does Levinas's framework of thought enable me to appreciate the Other's "religious particularity"? Can Levinas speak to dimensions of trialogue that incorporate "understanding, appreciation, empathy, and love"? Can trialogue constitute a religious experience? For Levinas, encountering the Otherness of the Other *implies* respect for his or her "religious particularity." I welcome the alterity of the Other in all his or her dimensions, including the Other's religious particularity. Further, I cannot genuinely "understand, appreciate, or empathize" with others in trialogue *until* my encounter with the Other. It is not until I have been awakened, ethically, by the face of the Other that I become a being able to undertake each of these actions in an authentic sense. And Levinas speaks of the ethical moment in terms of that "love" which my interlocutors want included in interreligious dialogue: "Ontology as a state of affairs can afford sleep. But love cannot sleep. . . . Love is the incessant watching over of the other."[25] Finally, interreligious dialogue is rooted in an encounter with the transcendent, which can indeed be termed a "religious experience": "I will say," Levinas proclaims, "that the subject who says 'here I am' [in the presence of the Other] testifies to the Infinite. It is through this testimony . . . that the revelation of the Infinite occurs."[26]

A final set of questions is posed to me: "By what or by whom am I obligated?" If being obligated is just one moral obligation among others, is it not reducible to just another act of the ego? Am I not obligated to God? For Levinas, God is indeed the source of my obligation. But Levinas is careful not to take the name of God in vain! That name, according to Levinas, has been "subject to abuse"; faith must be "purged of myths," specifically, the myth that God remains *part of* rather than *beyond* being.[27] Further, obligation is not reduced to merely one ethical command among others, to be obeyed—or not—according to some moral calculus. "Being faced" is the *inaugural* act of ethics itself. Unlike most ethical thinkers, Levinas is concerned neither with any list of moral obligations nor with the principles upon which they might be based. His is a metaethics, a way of being in the world in which I am invested with the infinite task of being responsible to the Other.

I am asked if the ethical act is indeed a response to *an Other who is Absolute*. For Levinas, the ethical act is a *living absolute*; he is unwilling to posit yet one more static truth in a history of ideas concerning the nature of "the Absolute." The Other is more "call" than theoretical construct. He or she is to be encountered, rather than posited. More verb than noun, more vocative than indicative, the Absolute is to-be-enacted.

My critics imply that God is missing from my account of the ethical act; the implication here is that religion has been reduced to ethics. Such a reduction could not be further from Levinas's mind: God's trace is witnessed in every encounter with the Other. Yet we must be wary of any theology that would posit God as a static being. God is often spoken of by Levinas as *a-Dieu* (to-God), rather than *Dieu*. Although explicit God-talk may be missing from my chapter, *implicitly* the God who is wholly Other is invoked throughout the course of my essay, as God is invoked throughout Levinas's corpus: "The subject of our enquiry," he argues, "is the very fact of revelation. . . . Ethics provides the model worthy of transcendence and it is as an ethical kerygma that the Bible is Revelation."[28]

This contention that the (Hebrew) Bible is Revelation brings to mind a response to the last question posed to me: How is Levinas's philosophic framework for trialogue *Jewish*? I contend that Levinas's so-called philosophical works and his Jewish works are interdependent. Indeed, Levinas articulates his aim to translate Hebrew, the language of biblical religion, into Greek, the language of philosophy. In his emphasis on "bringing the meaning of each and every experience back to the ethical experience between men," Levinas comes to view Judaism as an experiment for discovering what is humanly possible.[29] He argues, further, that our understanding of responsibility has been "historically conditioned" by Jewish sources. Abraham's welcoming of the strangers in Genesis is just one case in point. We cannot separate Levinas's philosophical articulation of radical hospitality from the teachings of Judaism. As one Levinas scholar puts it, "Ethics needs Jewish thought in the sense that it requires a true infinite, a radically transcendent God."[30] For instruction as to how to invest trialogue with ethical import, we can do no better than to turn to Levinas's *Jewish*/philosophical celebration of the call of the Other.

NOTES

Epigraph: Marilynne Robinson, *Gilead* (New York: Farrar, Straus and Giroux, 2004), 66.

1 Emmanuel Levinas, "Religion and Tolerance," in *Difficult Freedom: Essays on Judaism*, trans. Sean Hand (Baltimore, Md.: Johns Hopkins University Press, 1990), 173 (italics are mine).

2 Following the practice of many Levinasian scholars who write in English, I capitalize the word *Other* (Levinas's *autrui*) to denote one whose alterity is not reconcilable with my egoist desires. When addressing those who remain, potentially or actually, within my sphere of meaning-giving activities, I write the first letter of *other* (Levinas's *autre*) in lowercase. This distinction is further clarified in the discussion that follows.

3 Emmanuel Levinas, *Otherwise than Being or Beyond Essence*, trans. Alphonso Lingis (Pittsburgh: Duquesne University Press, 1998), 55.

4 Levinas, "Religion and Tolerance," 174.

5 Levinas, "A Religion for Adults," in *Difficult Freedom*, 22. It should be noted that in his essay titled "Monotheism and Language," to be found in the same volume, Levinas speaks of all three Abrahamic traditions as teaching "universalism to the world, even if they did not always agree on matters of pedagogy" (178).

6 Emmanuel Levinas, *Totality and Infinity: An Essay on Exteriority*, trans. Alphonso Lingis (Pittsburgh: Duquesne University Press, 1969), 37 (emphasis is mine).

7 See Sartre's discussion of the "look" of the Other in *Being and Nothingness*, trans. Hazel Barnes (New York: Pocket Books, 1956), pt. 3, "Being-for-Others," chap. 1, sec. 4.

8 Levinas, *Totality and Infinity*, 84.

9 Ibid., 67.

10 Emmanuel Levinas, "Demanding Judaism," in *Beyond the Verse: Talmudic Readings and Lectures*, trans. Gary D. Mole (Bloomington: Indiana University Press, 1994), 4.

11 Levinas, "Religion and Tolerance," 173.

12 Jacques Derrida, "A Word of Welcome," in *Adieu to Emmanuel Levinas*, trans. Pascale-Anne Brault and Michael Naas (Stanford, Calif.: Stanford University Press, 1999), 50.

13 Emmanuel Levinas, "The Paradox of Morality: An Interview with Emmanuel Levinas," trans. Andrew Benjamin and Tamara Wright, in *The Provocation of*

Levinas: Rethinking the Other, ed. Robert Bernasconi and David Wood (London: Routledge and Kegan Paul, 1988), 172.

14 Levinas, *Totality and Infinity*, 173.

15 See Exodus 22:21; Exodus 23:9; Leviticus 19:33–34.

16 I extend gratitude for this insight to Christina M. Smerick, Shapiro Chair of Jewish-Christian Studies at Greenville College. Her unpublished manuscript "Responsibility for the Stranger: Jewish Perspectives on Hospitality" has influenced my thinking in this chapter.

17 R. Clifton Spargo, *Vigilant Memory: Emmanuel Levinas, the Holocaust, and the Unjust Death* (Baltimore, Md.: Johns Hopkins University Press, 2006), 188.

18 Emmanuel Levinas, "Beyond Dialogue," in *Alterity and Transcendence*, trans. Michael B. Smith (New York: Columbia University Press, 1999), 86, 88.

19 On Judaism's relation to Islam. *See*, for example, Levinas, "Monotheism and Language," 179. Here Levinas celebrates "the memory of a common contribution [by Jews and Muslims] to European civilization in the course of the Middle Ages."

20 Levinas, "Israel and Universalism," in *Difficult Freedom*, 177.

21 Ibid., 176.

22 Levinas, "Religion and Tolerance," 174.

23 For an extensive discussion of this juxtaposition of terms. *See* Terry A. Veling, "In the Name of Who? Levinas and the Other Side of Theology," in *Pacifica: Australasian Theological Studies* 12, no. 3 (October 1999): 283–86.

24 Levinas, "Beyond Dialogue," 87–88.

25 "Dialogue with Emmanuel Levinas," in *Face to Face with Levinas*, ed. Richard A. Cohen (Albany: State University of New York Press, 1986), 30.

26 Emmanuel Levinas, *Ethics and Infinity: Conversations with Philippe Nemo*, trans. Richard A. Cohen (Pittsburgh: Duquesne University Press, 1991), 106.

27 Emmanuel Levinas, *Nine Talmudic Readings*, trans. Annette Aronowicz (Bloomington: Indiana University Press, 1990), 14; Levinas, *Totality and Infinity*, 77.

28 Levinas, "Revelation in the Jewish Tradition," in *Beyond the Verse*, 148.

29 Levinas, "Jewish Thought Today," in *Difficult Freedom*, 159.

30 Robert Gibbs, "Height and Nearness: Jewish Dimensions of Radical Ethics," in *Ethics as First Philosophy: The Significance of Emmanuel Levinas for Philosophy, Literature, and Religion*, ed. Adriaan T. Peperzak (New York: Routledge, 1995), 23.

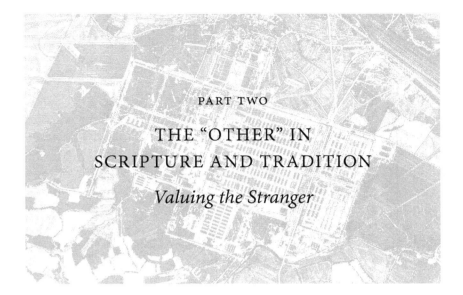

THE "OTHER" IN SCRIPTURE AND TRADITION

Valuing the Stranger

W hile exploring the permanent exhibition at the United States Holocaust Memorial Museum (USHMM) in the autumn of 2007, sixteen of the contributors to *Encountering the Stranger* stood before the remnants of a Torah ark from the synagogue in the German town of Nentershausen. Desecrated but not destroyed completely in the November 1938 pogroms collectively called *Kristallnacht*, this Torah ark is honored within the museum, which is appropriate because the *Aron ha-Kodesh* (the Holy Ark), as it is called in Hebrew, occupies a special, sacred space in every synagogue.[1] It does so because the ark houses scrolls, precious possessions for each and every Jewish community, that contain inscriptions of the Pentateuch, the Five Books of Moses—Genesis, Exodus, Leviticus, Numbers, and Deuteronomy—the most important parts of the Hebrew Bible (Tanakh).

Visitors to USHMM are not told what happened to the Torah scrolls that were once safely kept in the ark of the Nentershausen synagogue. It is not far-fetched, however, to think that those scrolls, like so many others during the years of the Holocaust, were mutilated and burned. So, as one stands before the Torah ark at USHMM, an absence can be felt. Disrespect for and defacing of the Other, as the scarred and empty Torah ark suggests, would silence—if it could—scripture that proclaims one God to be the creator of the world and human life (Genesis 1–2); tells the story of Abraham, whose faith gave birth to Judaism, Christianity, and Islam

(Genesis 11–25); and affirms that "you shall love your neighbor as yourself" (Leviticus 19:18).

Absence and silence can be intensified as one stands before the Nentershausen Torah ark at USHMM because, while the Torah scrolls from the Nentershausen ark are missing, Hebrew writing on its lintel, a supporting beam or mantel above the ark's doors, is not. Like many Torah arks, the one at Nentershausen had an inscription taken from the Talmud (*Berachot* 28b), the authoritative rabbinical commentary on the Torah: *Da lifnei mi attah omeyd*—Know before Whom you stand. These words, which call one to attention and accountability, to reverence and awe before God, the source and sustainer of life, did not escape the notice of those who plundered the Nentershausen synagogue in November 1938, for an unknown assailant attacked them in a violent attempt to silence their voice, erase their authority, and eradicate their credibility. Their scarred condition bears witness to shameless arrogance even as the wounded words provide a fragile and poignant, if not forlorn, judgment against the hubris and hatred that divide humankind.[2]

When contributors to this book reconvened for discussion after exploring USHMM's permanent exhibition, the trialogue concentrated for a time on the Torah ark from Nentershausen. We came to feel that the ark had addressed us through the words on its lintel: Know before Whom you stand. Differences in our religious traditions meant that our experiences were not identical during and after the time when we faced those words, but all of us agreed that the encounter with the desecrated Torah ark and its scarred inscription made us deeply aware of concerns we shared. Whether our identities were Jewish, Christian, or Muslim, we all could feel the loss, including the denial of freedom to practice one's religion, that would be ours if places and writings sacred in our own traditions were so horrifically disrespected and profaned. We could also feel abhorrence for any person or community identified with our own tradition that would stoop to such atrocity, an experience that made us mindful of our accountability and responsibility for the traditions that are ours.

As we took stock at USHMM in October 2007, focusing our attention and trialogue on renewed and deepened awareness that we stand responsible before God, our coreligionists, and those who profess faiths related to but different from our own, we were well aware that our work was taking place in a post-9/11 world, one in which al-Qaeda's attacks on New York's World Trade Center and the Pentagon in Washington, D.C., six years earlier had exacerbated suspicion about Islam and hostility toward Muslims. We scarcely could have anticipated, however, the upsurge of such suspicion and hostility that erupted in the summer and autumn of 2010, when plans for the construction of an Islamic community center near Ground Zero in New York City became so highly charged and volatile that the answer to the question "Is America Islamophobic?"—the cover of *Time* magazine raised it explicitly on August 30, 2010—apparently was yes.[3]

At the time of this writing in late 2011, it is still too early to tell how those contentious events will play out. But it can be said that if genuine trialogue among Jews, Christians, and Muslims was not conspicuous by its absence during the summer and autumn of 2010, too often its place was replaced by strident, intolerant, religiously and politically partisan, and belligerent voices, which were epitomized by that of Terry Jones, an obscure Christian pastor from Gainesville, Florida. His "Burn a Koran Day" campaign was thwarted only after American political and military leaders intervened with warnings that Jones's plans would seriously inflame much of the Muslim world. Even that intervention, however, was insufficient to deter Jones completely. On March 20, 2011, he publicly burned the Qur'an. Within days, news of that provocation swept through Afghanistan, leading to demonstrations and violence that left more than 20 people dead, including several United Nations employees, and about 150 wounded.

More quietly but with increasing timeliness and urgency, work on this volume continued, and while that process was too far along for the contributors to address explicitly the controversy surrounding the Islamic community center near Ground Zero, the chapters in this part—along with all the others in the book—bear on those disputes, which, unfortunately, are not likely to end with the controversies that swirled about Islam in 2010 and 2011. In particular, the chapters in Part Two are relevant because they concentrate on texts and text-related traditions that are sacred to Jews, Christians, and Muslims. More specifically, they explore how scripture and interpretation of it in those traditions have emphasized—but also, at times, failed to observe—the value of the stranger, the one who is different from us, the Other who might seem threatening and sometimes actually be that way but who could also become and be the one(s) before whom we stand in accountability and responsibility and who do so for us as well.

The Jewish scholar Peter J. Haas begins Part Two by concentrating on the ways in which classic rabbinic Judaism has understood encounters with the stranger. Judaism, Christianity, and Islam all have their roots in convictions that revelation of God has taken place and that truth about such revelation is found in scripture. In addition, each of these traditions affirms that covenants exist between God and humankind. These covenants, similar but not identical, emphasize Divine-human obligations and responsibilities, which also prescribe and proscribe how individuals and communities should relate to one another. Along with their merits, such outlooks carry with them the temptation to think that one of the Abrahamic traditions is superior to the other two, which invites exclusivism.

Haas argues that while signs of that temptation can be found from time to time in Judaism's history, the normative tradition of classic rabbinic Judaism has resisted it and valued the stranger by making inclusive room for all those who honor the Divine and the human, even if their religious ways of doing so differ from those of Judaism. "A long-standing and sustained strand within rabbinic Judaism," says Haas, "emphasizes that religions other than Judaism have a legitimate relationship with the Divine, even if their relationships differ from the Mosaic covenant. The persistence of this view even among the most conservative and inward-directed elements of the Jewish community indicates that inclusivism is an essential part of the Judaic understanding of the other."

Noting that "Jewish and Christian monotheism makes empathy with strangers mandatory," Margaret Brearley's chapter uses scripture and practices in medieval Christianity to illustrate and illuminate what should and should not be meant by valuing the stranger. "Like rabbinic Judaism," she indicates, "medieval Christianity developed specific institutions for welcoming and caring for strangers." These institutions often provided very practical hospitality—food and shelter, clothing and health care— for those, including the destitute among them, who received a welcome. According to Brearley, however, the problem was that medieval Christian hospitality to strangers, "while universal in theory . . . was selective in practice and restrictive. . . . In the Christian hierarchy of dangerous and hated strangers, Jews were paramount and more threatening than Muslims." But medieval Christians often took Muslims to be extremely threatening too.

What about the situation today? As for valuing the stranger, Brearley senses that interreligiously mixed signals remain, but her chapter includes a compelling image for what might yet unfold in the future, an image full of challenges because it thinks of trialogue in ways that invoke visions of what she calls "an open home," which involves much more than words alone. As Brearley suggests, fully valuing the stranger requires open homes that reflect "an open heart": "A meal shared—appropriate to religious dietary requirements—affirms shared humanity and true neighborliness."

Continuing the exploration of interreligious history to probe what valuing the stranger ought and ought not to entail, Rochelle L. Millen turns to developments in her Jewish tradition. She indicates that her chapter concentrates on two questions: "Must religious truth be absolute? Can there be a religious community—and religious individuals—whose belief structures about transcendence leave room for theological convictions other than their own?" Her response pivots around a Jewish tradition that wonders why God created Adam, the first human being, who turned out to be so frail, fallible, and flawed. *Midrash Rabbah*, a collection of interpretations of the creation narrative in Genesis, suggests that God knew there would be a difference, including disagreement, between God's truth, which is absolute, and humanity's apprehension of that truth, which would have to be hard-won through earthly and even earthy experience. "Human truth," as Millen puts the point, "even when derived from texts considered divinely inspired, is thus, by definition, partial, fragmented, and both created through and limited by history."

Within Judaism, this understanding is supported by the Noahide commandments (Genesis 9), seven imperatives that are taken to be binding on all humanity. In Millen's words they are "the prohibitions against idolatry, blasphemy, murder, immorality (adultery and incest), theft, and the consumption of animal flesh from a live animal. This last prohibition is understood to limit animal pain, even when humanity is permitted (Genesis 9:3) to be carnivorous, and to restrain cruelty. In addition to these six prohibitions, the establishment of courts of justice is required to enforce the prohibitions and to promulgate any other laws deemed useful or necessary."

Millen argues that the Noahide commandments not only establish the grounding for civilization but also create a "foundation for pluralism" because they entail the possibility that multiple religious understandings may be consistent with them. The Noahide tradition is ethically and religiously demanding, but within it a home for the flourishing of Judaism, Christianity, and Islam can be found. The truth that each tradition contains is not to be confused let alone equated with God's truth, but at their best each of the Abrahamic traditions can approach the Divine in mutually insightful and supportive ways. When that happens, the stranger—no longer seen to be so "strange"—comes closer to being truly valued.

Turning attention to current events, Riffat Hassan's chapter underscores that much needs to be done before those who are strangers to us are truly valued rather than being seen as threatening others. "Is it possible," she asks, "to 'depolarize' the world and to build a bridge between 'the West' and 'the world of Islam' in the aftermath of 9/11?"—a question made all the more relevant by the renewed hostility in 2010. Hassan argues that two shortcomings must be overcome for interreligious engagement to prove helpful in that depolarization. First, movement must take place beyond "inadequate distinctions . . . between the fundamental teachings of a religion and the cultural practices of its adherents; second, invidious comparisons [should not be] made between the highest ideals and best practices of one's own religion and the worst features of another religion." Hassan takes corrective steps in those directions by concentrating on the Qur'an's teachings about ethical and religious pluralism. Her approach provides a corrective for Muslims and non-Muslims alike, because it emphasizes the Qur'an's normative status, which includes multiple injunctions that give priority to valuing strangers through acts that furnish hospitality and encourage mutual esteem and friendship.

Bülent Şenay, Hassan's coreligionist, amplifies what valuing the stranger entails by exploring the Qur'an's understanding of "the ethics of *tawallî*" (friendship). The Qur'an makes clear that friendship involves moral conditions. Friendship is deplored with those who are unjust, who do not treat people with respect, and who do not honor what is sacred and holy, for such persons are not worthy of what friendship entails. But the goal should be for strangers to value one another so that friendship rightly results. Şenay emphasizes that the odds in favor of that outcome are enhanced to the degree that "reflexive listening" takes place. Such listening goes beyond hearing what another has to say. Reflexive listening takes in what is heard and brings that content to bear on one's own awareness. When reflexive listening takes place in the context of authentic religious trialogue, the presence of the Other—the stranger—adds value because it shows how difference can be complementary and how it can deepen insight about oneself and others as we strive in and through our traditions to discern together what is true, right, and good.

A reminder from Hubert G. Locke brings Part Two to a close: where relations among Jews, Christians, and Muslims are concerned, it is crucial that people speak to one another with candor. Politeness, courtesy, and civility are immensely important, but if Jews, Christians, and Muslims truly value one another, no substitute exists for honest questioning, candid discussion of differences, and forthright explorations that can only go beyond disagreement if they confront it openly. As Locke sees the situation, "Islam, Judaism, and Christianity confront and engage one another across a geographical and cultural divide that events of the past several decades have only served to heighten. Placing these events and their participants in an appropriate analytic framework and perspective is one of the several, foundational tasks we face."

Locke's inquiry about that framework identifies three impulses—theocratic, fundamentalist, and majoritarian—that need to be confronted in Jewish-Christian-Muslim relations. At various times, these impulses have characterized all of the Abrahamic traditions, although one must always remember than none of those traditions is monolithic. Great variety and diversity exist in them all. Nevertheless, wherever the theocratic impulse is at work, using "the mechanisms and instruments of the state to advance religious ideals and convictions," the other tends to be disrespected. The same is true of the fundamentalist impulse, which takes itself to possess "the correct or valid expression of [a] tradition, with either the implicit or explicit understanding that all other beliefs and practices are incorrect or false." Likewise, the majoritarian impulse, which assumes that the majority view is just and right, is tempted to deny value to those in the minority. Absent honest debate and criticism when these impulses assert themselves, the value of people in different traditions will be compromised and so will the integrity of our own.

Know before Whom you stand. That imperative from the Torah ark of the Nentershausen synagogue is a uniting theme throughout *Encountering the Stranger* and especially in Part Two. The One before whom Jews, Christians, and Muslims stand makes room for those traditions, affirming in the process that they and their adherents should act to enhance the value of all. In the troubled twenty-first century, no task for Jews, Christians, and Muslims is likely to be more important than that.

NOTES

1   Authorized and incited by Nazi leaders when a minor German official died after an assassination attempt by a young Jew named Herschel Grynszpan, the antisemitic riots of *Kristallnacht* (crystal night) targeted Jewish communities throughout Germany and Austria on November 9–10, 1938. Sometimes these November pogroms are referred to as the "Night of Broken Glass" because the wreckage

included so many smashed windows that the replacement value reached more than $2 million in the cash equivalent at the time. The onslaught was far more devastating than that. A great many Germans, their religious heritage and identity overwhelmingly Christian, were involved and implicated in the widespread carnage. While their friends and neighbors watched, the perpetrators looted and wrecked Jewish homes and businesses, torched hundreds of synagogues while inactive fire brigades stood by, desecrated cemeteries, killed scores of Jews, and terrorized virtually every Jew in the Third Reich. In the aftermath, some thirty thousand Jewish men were arrested and sent to concentration camps at Dachau, Buchenwald, and Sachsenhausen. The November pogroms of 1938 showed that no Jew could ever expect to live a normal life in Nazi Germany.

2   For insightful discussion of the significance of the Torah ark at USHMM, one that helped inform the reflections here. *See* Henry F. Knight, "Before Whom Do We Stand?" *Shofar* 28, no. 3 (Spring 2010): 116–34. One of the contributors to this volume, Knight in particular called attention to the Torah ark at USHMM when our trialogue took place there.

3   For a summary of the construction controversy. *See* Spencer C. Tucker, "Ground Zero Mosque Controversy," in *The 9/11 Encyclopedia*, 2nd ed., ed. Stephen E. Atkins (Santa Barbara, Calif.: ABC-CLIO, 2011), 1:221–24.

7

Encountering the Stranger
in Classic Rabbinic Judaism

PETER J. HAAS

Judaism, the religion of the Jewish people, understands itself to be based on a revelation from heaven. Like the other Abrahamic faiths, it is covenantal, but in distinctive ways. According to both the biblical story and later rabbinic teaching, the Israelites were chosen from among all other peoples to become "a kingdom of priests and a holy people" (Exodus 19:5–6). Much of the Torah (or Pentateuch) describes both the giving of this special covenant through Moses at Mount Sinai during the exodus from Egypt and the demands it confers. The holy Temple in Jerusalem, with its attendant priesthood and its particular sacrificial rites, stood at the very center of the covenant's fulfillment. Much of the Jewish scripture chronicles the historical ups and downs of the Israelite community as it adhered to, or strayed from, this priestly system. Profoundly affecting relationships, including trialogue, among Jews, Christians, and Muslims, major historical issues have swirled around the roles this cultic center might play in the lives of other peoples and religions. As this chapter aims to demonstrate, inclusivism and universality are emphasized in Judaism's biblical and rabbinic traditions.

Concern for the inclusion of others is present at the very beginning of the Temple's history. According to 1 Kings 8:41–43, King Solomon's prayer at the dedication of the "First Temple" included these words: "Or if a foreigner who is not of Your people Israel comes from a distant land for the sake of Your name—for they shall hear about Your great name and Your mighty hand and Your outstretched arm—when he comes to pray toward this House, oh hear in Your heavenly abode and grant all that the foreigner asks You for, as does Your people Israel; and they will recognize that Your name is attached to this House that I have built."[1] Note that what is important here is not "race" or tribal affiliation but the willingness to worship the one Deity acknowledged by Abraham. In other words, all monotheists who recognize the Abrahamic covenant could make use of the Temple, and their worship was regarded as fully valid.

This much is held in common by all the Western Abrahamic traditions. The particular rabbinic appropriation of this biblical tradition took form during the early centuries of the first millennium of the Common Era. It grew in response to the destruction of the Jerusalem Temple by the Romans and was meant to fashion a mode of maintaining the Hebrew covenant in the absence of the Temple with its priesthood and sacrifices. The rabbinic interpretation of the scriptural legacy was based on the assumption that one could still live within the bounds of the Sinaitic covenant by conducting one's personal life in ways that were guided by the principles laid down in the original revelation. The holiness of the Temple could be transferred to the home, and the holiness of the priesthood could be taken up, albeit in symbolic fashion, by the Jewish people at large. In other words, the early rabbis declared that Jews were called upon to live *as though* the Temple and its holiness still functioned in the diverse villages, communities, and households of the dispersed House of Israel. Discussions and rules for doing so dominate all subsequent rabbinic literature, including the Talmud, the midrash, and the prayer book.

In making this transfer, the Talmud also continued to recognize the validity of non-Jewish worship directed toward the Abrahamic Deity. One example is a discussion in the Babylonian Talmud, *Menahot* 73b, which revolves around the question as to how rabbinic law should deal with sacrifices brought to the Jerusalem Temple by a non-Jew. In this discussion, both major authorities, Rabbi Akiba ben Joseph and Rabbi Yose the Galilean, accepted as a matter of course that non-Jews could bring, or have sent, offerings to the Temple.[2] At issue between them, and later discussants who invoke them, is the secondary question of what sacrificial accompaniments (such as the wine offering), if any, were ineligible to be brought. What such discussions show is that the classical rabbis never regarded non-

Jews as such as being excluded from the Temple worship of the Divine. The House of Israel had special duties and obligations, but this did not mean that Jews had exclusive access to holiness, Truth, or salvation.

Over the centuries, this openness to the inherent worth of non-Jewish religions and cultures is reflected in numerous rabbinic discussions. Some discussions revolved around the status that should be accorded to extra-biblical knowledge. Could rabbis, for example, draw on the "pagan" scientific knowledge of the day or on popular concepts to produce appropriate interpretations of biblical texts? The answer here was generally that such outside knowledge was perfectly admissible. Another question often taken up dealt with the nature of rabbinic authority. In general, the rabbinate evolved as an intellectual elite that required logic and reasoning—not personal charisma or private revelation—to validate interpretation.[3] Given these priorities, it might seem that rabbinic interpretation, standing in tight logical continuity with the Sinaitic revelation, would be privileged in contrast to the teachings of other Judaic groups, let alone those of the early Church or, later, Islam.[4] Yet the rabbis were well aware of the limits of their own mental abilities when it came to understanding the intent or will of the Divine, and so they left many questions unanswered, or only tentatively answered, until "the coming of Elijah." In the end, rabbinic Judaism was able to establish itself as the normative form of post-Temple Judaism because it maintained that its interpretations of the scripture were based on the publicly verifiable application of science and logic. Non-Jews could participate in and contribute to these discussions.

The Hebrew Bible itself justified the rabbis' respect for non-Judaic sources of knowledge. It makes clear that the Deity who gave the revelation to Moses at Sinai is also the Creator, the One who brought all peoples into existence. The prophet Amos, for example, offers a prime example of this biblical perspective, comparing the kingdom of Judah to the other peoples in the region and taking the Judeans to task for assuming that they enjoy superior status or special divine protection. The rabbis understood such scripture to mean that all of Creation, including all human beings, falls under the concern and rule of the Divine. Indeed, the rabbinic tradition holds that God established a series of covenants, including but not necessarily limited to those made with Adam, Noah, Abraham, and Moses. While they might be logically inferior to the Judaism being fashioned by the rabbis, other monotheisms were still regarded as enjoying a covenantal relation with the Divine.

There was, of course, an alternate view. A more exclusivistic outlook emerged from the prophets active in the period from the destruction of Solomon's Jerusalem in 587 or 586 BCE to the building of the Second Temple in the late sixth and early fifth centuries BCE. These latter biblical writers and prophets regarded the rebuilding of the Jerusalem Temple as a cosmic event that reflected a kind of apocalyptic struggle between Good and Evil. On this view, the Jews did indeed have a distinct role to play in the triumph of Good. This Manichaean view persisted into the Greco-Roman period (we find it, for example, in the "War Scroll" of the Dead Sea Scrolls) when the Hebrew Bible was given more or less the form in which we now have it. It is important to note, however, that when Jewish scripture was given its final redaction, the earlier, more inclusivistic views were not excluded or suppressed. The first century BCE Book of Jubilees, for example, illustrates the perseverance of the earlier inclusivism by specifically noting that a covenant with all humankind was made with all the descendants of Noah after the Flood.

In fact, the tradition of such a "Noahide" covenant was taken up by the early rabbis, and a reference to it can be found already in the *Tosefta* (*Avodah Zarah* 8:4) from the middle to late third century of the Common Era. It is discussed, for example, in the Babylonian Talmud (*Sanhedrin* 56a), which lays out the seven rules that make up this covenant. The pertinent passage begins as follows: "Our Rabbis taught: seven precepts were the sons of Noah commanded: [the establishment of] civil society, blessing of the divine, [and prohibitions against] idolatry, adultery, bloodshed, robbery, and the eating of flesh cut from a living animal."[5] The Talmudic text then proceeds with a lengthy discussion of whether these seven laws are the only ones binding on "the Children of Noah" (i.e., his descendents) and how they were derived. The importance of this passage and others related to it includes the fact that the rabbis simply took it as a matter of course that all people were included in the divine plan and expected to follow basic laws of morality. According to the classical rabbis, then, any non-Jew who obeyed the basic moral rules encoded in the Noahide covenant was a "righteous gentile" and was able as such to enter "the World to Come" (i.e., Paradise) just as any obedient Jew was. The Mosaic covenant may have been more stringent, but it was hardly exclusive in its promise of a blessed afterlife.

This more inclusive attitude was carried forward into the medieval Jewish law codes as well. In his influential medieval code of Jewish law (the

Mishneh Torah), Moses Maimonides (1135–1204) explicitly notes that the "righteous of the nations of the world" share a portion of the world to come without the need to become Jews. The relevant passage in Laws of Kings and War 8:10 reads as follows:

> Moses our Rabbi bequeathed the Torah and the commandments only to Israel, as it is said [in Deuteronomy 33:4], "an inheritance [for the] congregation of Jacob," and to whoever wants to convert [to Judaism] from among the other peoples, as it is said [in Numbers 15:15, "there should be an eternal law for all your generations,] alike for you; alike for the gentile." But as to one who does not wish to convert [to Judaism], they may not force him to receive the Torah and the commandments. Likewise Moses our rabbi commanded us through the words of the Great One, to force all those in the world to accept the commandments that were commanded to Noah, and all who do not accept them may be killed, but one who does accept them, is called a "ger toshav" in all instances.[6]

While Maimonides is more tolerant of "non-Judaisms" than many other writers of the time are, the fact remains that he is a major figure in medieval Judaism and his attitude has continued to be highly influential. It is thus no surprise that a relatively tolerant and open position toward Islam and Christianity continued to find voice throughout the medieval period, despite the often difficult relationships that obtained between actual Christian and Islamic communities. Thus, for example, the poet Yehuda Ha-Levi (ca. 1075–1141), in his "Apologia" for Judaism, titled *Treatise in Defense of a Despised Tradition* (usually known as the *Kuzari*), depicted all three Western monotheistic religions as worthy, even as he regarded Judaism as the "heart" (*Kuzari* 2:36–44) as compared to the other parts of the body. In one passage he states: "The Rabbi said, 'Similarly, the Divinity in relation to us is like the soul in relation to the heart [just as the soul first connects to the heart and then spreads to the rest of the body, so does God's influence in the world connect first to Israel and then spread to the rest of the world]. . . . Just as the heart's inherent equilibrium and pure makeup allows the soul to attach to it, so, too, does the Divinity attach Itself to Israel because of their inherent nature.'"[7] Elsewhere, he depicted all three religions as sharing the same roots, with Judaism being the generative seed (*Kuzari* 4:23).

Another example of this cautiously inclusivistic view is a ruling in the *Shulkhan Arukh*, the great sixteenth-century law code, concerning whether one is required to say "amen" after hearing a prayer. In *Orekh Chayyim* 215:2, the *Shulkhan Arukh* notes that one should say "amen" after the prayer of any other adult Jews, even if one has not heard the prayer itself from beginning to end. The assumption is that the hearer can rest assured that the person saying the blessing is saying appropriate words. If a non-Jew, an apostate, or a minor is saying the blessing, or if the wording is changed, then one is not required (or permitted?) to respond. After this clause there is a comment by Moses Isserles (1520–1572), a central European rabbi who glossed the code with standards prevailing in Europe, which states that a Jew does in fact answer "amen" after the blessing of a non-Jew if the wording of the entire prayer has been heard (and found acceptable).

Although the *Shulkhan Arukh* and other medieval sources rarely refer to Christianity or Islam by name, the intent is usually clear since they were the most significant non-Jewish religions in the relevant context. As one moves into the modern period, however, the sources become more explicit. One good example is the case of Rabbi Yaakov Emden (1697–1776), a traditional Talmudist who served the Jewish community in Hamburg, Germany, from 1733 until his death. While Emden was both unquestionably traditionalist in his religious practice, and in fact is regarded even today as an exemplary Orthodox intellectual leader, it is also clear that he was already being influenced by the Enlightenment. Thus Emden argued for mutual toleration between Judaism and Christianity. In his essay "Seder Olam Rabbah VeZuta," he writes to Christians, "You, members of the Christian faith, how good and pleasant it might be if you will observe that which was commanded to you by your first teachers; how wonderful is your share if you will assist the Jews in the observance of their Torah."[8] On the other hand, in addressing himself to a Jewish readership, he argued, "We should consider Christians and Moslems as instruments for the fulfillment of the prophecy that the knowledge of God will one day spread throughout the earth" (Commentary to *Pirke Avot*, 4:13). As can be adduced from this passage and others, Emden understood Christianity and Islam to be offshoots of Judaism, designated by the Divine to help spread knowledge of the true Creator.

Although the Orthodox Jewish world has somewhat stepped back from Emden's outlook, an inclusivistic model has persisted in non-Orthodox Judaisms down to the present time. A representative statement can be found in the "Pittsburgh Platform" adopted by American Reform Jewish rabbis in 1885. Its sixth point states:

> We recognize in Judaism a progressive religion, ever striving to be in accord with the postulates of reason. We are convinced of the utmost necessity of preserving the historical identity with our great past. Christianity and Islam, being daughter religions of Judaism, we appreciate their providential mission, to aid in the spreading of monotheistic and moral truth. We acknowledge that the spirit of broad humanity of our age is our ally in the fulfillment of our mission, and therefore we extend the hand of fellowship to all who cooperate with us in the establishment of the reign of truth and righteousness among men.[9]

Ultra-Orthodox Jews are ambivalent about such outlooks, but few express disagreement as strongly as Rabbi Saadya Grama. In his 2003 book, for example, he writes: "The difference between the people of Israel and the nations of the world is an essential one. The Jew by his source and in his very essence is entirely good. The *goy* [i.e., non-Jew], by his source and in his very essence is completely evil. This is not simply a matter of religious distinction, but rather of two completely different species."[10] Significantly, this book was condemned by numerous North American Orthodox and Ultra-Orthodox rabbis.

Despite occasional outbursts such as Grama's, a long-standing and sustained strand within rabbinic Judaism emphasizes that religions other than Judaism have a legitimate relationship with the Divine, even if their relationships differ from the Mosaic covenant. The persistence of this view even among the most conservative and inward-directed elements of the Jewish community indicates that inclusivism is an essential part of the Judaic understanding of the other.

CONTRIBUTORS' QUESTIONS FOR PETER J. HAAS

1. Within Judaism, you identify two traditional attitudes toward the stranger. In an older inclusivistic orientation, with roots in the practices of the First Temple, Jewish identity has no monopoly on the holy or access to it—or to the world to come. In this tradition, Jews were set apart to bear witness to a universal summons to covenantal worship and responsibility. You cite another, more exclusive tradition with ori-

gins probably traceable to the prophetic traditions of the Second Commonwealth. Those traditions persisted as parallel, though competitive, strands within Jewish history. The task is to recognize the presence of both and the options they represent for Jews in the present. How then do these choices between inclusivism and exclusivism configure and present themselves in a post-Holocaust world still plagued by traditional forms of antisemitism and beset by a "new antisemitism," some of it clearly manifest in the Muslim world?

2. You conclude by saying that "a long-standing and sustained strand within rabbinic Judaism emphasizes that religions other than Judaism have a legitimate relationship with the Divine." Yet it would seem that the parts of other religions that Judaism sees as having legitimate relationships with the Divine are parts that approximate the Jewish experience. Judaism appreciates the monotheism of Christianity and Islam, but does it not see the adherents of these faiths as *mis-taking* revelation, misunderstanding what God wants of them? If the idea/belief is that Christianity and Islam are the "offshoots" of the "generative seed" (Judaism) and that they are recognized as having a covenantal relation with the Divine, what does that say about the fundamental truth claims of the non-Judaisms?

RESPONSE BY PETER J. HAAS

The notions of inclusivism and exclusivism each carry two different meanings in the context of the questions raised about my essay. On the one hand, these terms can refer to the social attitudes of Jews toward non-Jews. On the other hand, they can refer to a theological orientation as to whether non-Jews can be in a covenantal relationship with the Deity or, in the more specific Judaic formulation, if they too have access to "the world to come."

As regards the social level, unquestionably the post-Shoah world with its rising "new" antisemitism is having a significant impact on Jewish attitudes toward others. The Shoah severely undermined the Jewish community's confidence in modernity and in political liberalism. More particularly, the trust Western Jews used to have in the reliability and goodwill of non-Jewish neighbors and friends is now more in question. Implicitly or explicitly, unconsciously or consciously, a deep-seated sense exists that in the end the Jews can rely only on themselves. This alienation from the outside world has not prevented (and perhaps has subtly encouraged) growing assimilation among Jews and an increasing rate of intermarriage. Nonetheless, a psychological distance from non-Jews lurks in Jewish life in the West and in Israel in a way that does not appear to have been the case before the Shoah. This social distancing surfaces in a number of ways, including an increasing sense of ethnic identity, the adoption of traditional practices and prayers even among the more liberal elements of the Jewish religious community, and sometimes an unexpected and visceral sensitivity about any criticism of the State of Israel by "outsiders."

This social hesitancy, however, should be distinguished from the theological issue of whether non-Jews as individuals have a place in the world to come or whether other religions have a covenantal relationship with the Deity. The relationship between social connections and theological assumptions is, of course, quite complicated. The two streams of thought I described in the Jewish tradition have waxed and waned throughout the centuries, depending on the relationships Jews have had with their host cultures. At times of oppression and persecution, Jews tended to have a dimmer view of non-Jews and felt that only the exceptional ones might be "righteous gentiles" and so have a place in the world to come. When relationships were better, the notion that there could be other valid religions became more acceptable. Furthermore, just as it is possible to regard Judaism as the only true religion and yet recognize that there are occasional "righteous among the nations," so too it is possible to hold that Christianity or Islam does bear a relationship with the Divine while still feeling that some (or even most) people who claim to be Christians or Muslims are not righteous. In short, a complex mixture of inclusivism and exclusivism can be found among Jews. Probably the most accurate description is to say that any particular Jew's attitudes toward Christianity and Islam are largely a function of how that person perceives, or has had experiences with, particular Christians and Muslims.

This entire question of Judaism's relationship to the world's religions has become much more complicated in the past several decades as Jews have come into closer contact with religions other than Christianity and Islam. Jews, for example, have been increasingly drawn to some of the spiritual exercises of Buddhism and Hinduism. While it is not a particular theological problem from within Judaism to hold that certain righteous Hindus or Buddhists might have a place in the "world to come," it is harder to think of them as being in a covenantal relationship with the Abrahamic Deity, since they do not acknowledge that Deity. Thus in these cases, Judaism might turn out to be more inclusivistic as regards individual Buddhists and Hindus, but exclusivistic as regards Buddhism and Hinduism.

Both Christianity and Islam see themselves as "completions" or "restorations" of Judaism. That is, both see themselves as at some level having emerged from Judaism, and so both have built-in perceptions of Judaism. These perceptions usually regard Judaism as being incomplete or garbled. From the point of view of Judaism, however, matters are quite different. Judaism does not have any foundational theological category in which it places Christianity or Islam. This situation is reflected in the fact that within the formative texts of Judaism neither of these religious traditions is explicitly discussed or even acknowledged. There are, of course, halachic (legal) texts that address various practical issues regarding relationships with Christians and Muslims (e.g., should one regard as "idolatrous" loaves of bread baked by a Christian in anticipation of Easter?). But only in rare cases do these matters involve taking the other religions seriously as theological systems with which Judaism needs to come to some understanding.

The point is that from the classical Jewish perspective, neither Christianity nor Islam is seen as an "offshoot" or "sister religion." When they are alluded to at all, those religions are simply regarded as "other." That is to say, Christianity and Islam are no different from all other religions; though in and of themselves theologically immaterial to Judaism, these religions are capable of yielding up righteous individuals ("righteous of the nations of the world"). A Christian or Muslim who abides by the basic moral laws of the "Noahide code" is thus assured a place in the world to come just as is any other human being who abides by those laws. This place in the afterlife is completely independent of whether or not the person is a Christian, a Muslim, or even an outright pagan.

Not until the Middle Ages did Jewish thinkers explicitly engage Christianity and Islam as religious systems. This engagement largely consisted of the impressive scholarly interchanges that took place among Jewish, Christian, and Muslims intellectuals who found, among other things, that they had common ground in the texts of Aristotle. Thinkers in all three traditions had to confront the place of the other in the grand scheme of things and to enunciate attitudes toward communities that were different but still claimed relationship to the Deity and Hebrew scripture. Jewish thinkers took different positions in these circumstances. Some regarded both Christianity and Islam as kin to Judaism insofar as they all shared monotheism. Others regarded these religions as little more than apostasies, idolatries, or paganisms. More positive attitudes emerged toward Christianity only in the nineteenth and early twentieth centuries because of the Enlightenment and the social rights granted to Jewish citizens. Modern Jewish encounters with Islam—more recent and intimately bound up with Zionism and the State of Israel—have been more ambivalent. In all of these cases, however, it is often hard to distinguish between attitudes toward Christians and Muslims in general and Jewish perspectives about the nature of Christianity and Islam.

The silence of most Jewish texts regarding a specifically theological characterization of Christianity or Islam allows for diverse claims to be made. One claim has been that only one Torah exists, vouchsafed to the Jewish community; other religions are simply not part of that covenant, even though they might be close to it Another claim is that although the Torah-covenant is exclusive to Judaism, nothing precludes the Deity from giving other people their own covenant and mission in the world. Franz Rosenzweig (1887–1929) forged a middle path by saying that while Judaism was the one true star of redemption, other monotheistic religions such as Christianity and Islam were the rays conveying the truth of Judaism to other benighted people and so were in their own ways fulfilling a divine function. In this sense, Christians and Muslims, as Christians or Muslims, would be seen to be part of the divine covenant, albeit playing a secondary or derived role. In contrast, Martin Buber (1878–1965) seemed to think that, at the end of the day, the differences among all religions fall away as one enters an authentic "I-Thou" relationship with the Divine. In opposition to Rosenzweig and Buber would be neo-Orthodox Jewish thinkers such as Isaac Breuer (1883–1946), who barely regarded Christianity as a religion at all and never even mentioned Islam.

In sum, two basic attitudes run through the Jewish tradition. One regards the Torah as the one and only covenant made between the Deity and humankind and sees other religions as essentially existing outside that covenant to a greater (Breuer) or lesser (Rosenzweig) extent. The other and more modern attitude, exemplified by Buber, regards the Torah as revealing true religion but one that is available to all and not to Jews exclusively.

NOTES

1. Translation from *Tanakh: The Holy Scriptures; The New JPS Translation according to the Traditional Hebrew Text* (Philadelphia: Jewish Publication Society, 1985). All quotations from scripture in this chapter are from this translation.

2. These discussions, of course, were of only theoretical interest since by the time these two authorities were rendering their opinions the Temple had already been destroyed. The various rules that emerge from the Talmudic discussions are set forth in Maimonides' *Mishneh Torah*, Laws of the Making of Offerings, Chapter 3.

3. See, for example, the debate between rabbis Joshua and Eliezer in the Babylonian Talmud (*Baba Metzia* 59b), in which an argument by Rabbi Eliezer was rejected because he could not prove it to the satisfaction of other scholars, despite his being able to invoke miracles and even a voice from heaven attesting to the truth of his position.

4. The Babylonian Talmud is generally held to have reached its present form by the middle of the seventh century (CE) at the latest and thus before the full development of Islam in the Arabian Peninsula.

5. I have added the words in brackets to clarify the translation. The word translated here as "civil society" is *denim*, roughly meaning civil law.

6. A "ger toshav" is literally a "resident alien" in the biblical community, but Maimonides uses it as equivalent to the rabbinic "righteous gentile."

7. From *The Kuzari: In Defense of the Despised Faith*, trans. and annotated by N. Daniel Korobkin (Lanham, Md.: Jason Aronson, 2004), 91–92.

8. See Harvey Falk's translation of Emden's essay, which is available online at http://www.auburn.edu/~allenkc/falk1a.html.

9. The complete text of the Pittsburgh Platform can be found at the Jewish Virtual Library, http://www.jewishvirtuallibrary.org/jsource/Judaism/pittsburgh_program.html. For a more detailed analysis of Jewish "inclusivism." *See* Alan Brill's 2004 essay "Judaism and Other Religions: An Orthodox Perspective," which is available online at http://www.bc.edu/dam/files/research_sites/cjl/texts/cjrelations/resources/articles/Brill.htm.

10. Self-published in Hebrew under the title *Romemut Yisrael Ufarashat Hagalut* (Lakewood, N.J.: Beth Medrash Govoha, 2003). The book's title can be translated into English in several ways, including *The Grandeur of Israel and the Issue of Exile* and *Jewish Superiority and the Question of Exile*. For additional detail. *See* Allan Nadler, "Charedi Rabbis Rush to Disavow Anti-Gentile Book," *Jewish Daily Forward*, December 19, 2003, http://www.forward.com/articles/7311. The quoted passage appears in Nadler's article.

8

Encountering the Stranger

Aspects of Medieval Christianity

MARGARET BREARLEY

Judeo-Christian monotheism teaches radical identification with strangers. Jews are to recall their past exile in Egypt: "I have been a stranger in a strange land" (Exodus 2:22); gentile Christians, although now "of the [Jewish] household of God," are to recall that their ancestors include pagan "strangers and foreigners" (Ephesians 2:19). Although Hebrew scripture warned that intimacy with strangers brought specific dangers—"strange wives" were associated with idolatry, "strange women" with prostitution—biblical injunctions on kindness to strangers reflected God's own accessibility to strangers. Solomon, dedicating the Temple, urged God to hear the stranger's prayer and "do according to all that the stranger calleth to thee for" (1 Kings 8:43). Abraham's hospitality to strangers (Genesis 18:1–16) became exemplary since strangers could potentially embody an invisible divine presence. As a text from the Christian New Testament puts that point: "Be not forgetful to entertain strangers: for thereby some have entertained angels unawares" (Hebrews 13:2).

Jewish and Christian monotheism makes empathy with strangers mandatory: "Ye know the heart of a stranger. *Seeing* ye were strangers in the land of Egypt" (Exodus 23:9). Whereas, according to Joseph H. Hertz, pagan "love of the alien is something unknown in ancient times," the Torah explicitly teaches love of the stranger: "The Lord your God . . . loveth the stranger. . . . Love ye therefore the stranger: for ye were strangers in the land of Egypt" (Deuteronomy 10:17–19).[1] Oppression of strangers is forbidden: "Thou shalt neither vex a stranger, nor oppress him" (Exodus 22:21). Full justice and provision for strangers are imperative (Exodus 12:49; Deuteronomy 26:13).

Within the covenantal bond with God, however, the stranger's identity is complex, for "the Bible makes the experience of marginality normative for the people of God."[2] When blessing God, David affirmed, "We are strangers before thee, and sojourners" (1 Chronicles 29:15; cf. Leviticus 25:23), while a New Testament epistle, 1 Peter, refers to Christian believers as "strangers and pilgrims" (2:11). This theme was especially persistent in medieval theology; Saint Francis of Assisi (ca. 1181/82–1226), for example, typically described friars as "pilgrims and strangers in the world." Estrangement from this world and the search for "a better country . . . a heavenly one" (Hebrews 11:16) rendered Christians dependent on God's "hospitality," which the New Testament exemplifies in a parable of Jesus when the father eagerly runs to embrace the prodigal son (Luke 15:11–32). Practical hospitality toward strangers was thus also *imitatio dei*, commanded by Jesus (Matthew 25:35) and in New Testament writings such as 1 Timothy 5:10, and it symbolized spiritual hospitality toward Christ himself.

Like rabbinic Judaism, medieval Christianity developed specific institutions for welcoming and caring for strangers, including hospices and hospitals on the model from late antiquity of *pandocheion* hostels "accepting all comers."[3] The sixth-century *Rule of St. Benedict* institutionalized monastic hospitality: "Let all guests be received like Christ."[4] In typical medieval monasteries, all travelers were received by the guest-master, a monk with a dedicated budget for the guest house and entrusted with unquestioning care for traveling strangers and pilgrims, with whose needs he was required to show empathy. Monastic hospitality to strangers was a profound spiritual duty, considered to multiply friendship and lessen enmity and to honor God, increase charity, and secure heavenly reward.[5] Hospitality extended partially to certain strangers cast out from society; some medieval monasteries created leper hospitals and hospices to shelter single mothers and reformed prostitutes. Monasteries defaulting on debts occasionally hosted Jewish creditors demanding repayment and exercising squatters' rights.

Secular laws, like the Magna Carta (1215), protected traveling strangers;

ecclesiastical canon law protected travelers, pilgrims, and outlaws seeking asylum in churches. Medieval courtly romances offered important vernacular role models for the laity regarding how to encounter and relieve the distressed stranger. The norm was to offer a warm greeting, a meal, a night's lodging, and, if necessary, fresh clothing and the tending of any wounds.

Meanwhile, in addition to welcoming the stranger, voluntary self-estrangement, temporary or permanent, became a Christian ideal. Long-distance pilgrimage, including by women, was commonplace. Abandonment of class, status, and society was a mark of penitence and sanctity; Saint Benedict (480–543), dressed in skins, was mistaken by shepherds for a beast. Saints were often "socially amphibious";[6] occasionally, newly religious nobility voluntarily undertook menial work. Solitaries estranged themselves permanently from home, town, and community to worship God in marginal locations, forest or wilderness. Some gave spiritual and practical guidance to strangers as anchorites in walled-up cells or as hermits; others acted as ferrymen or prayed for wayfarers in bridge chapels.

More problematic, involuntary estrangement occurred within medieval marriage. In addition to ecclesiastical reforms under Pope Gregory VII (1073–1085) that required parish priests to renounce concubines, new emphasis on clerical celibacy led indirectly to intrusive legislation for married laity, forbidding intimate relations on numerous holy days and during the forty-day periods before Christmas and Easter. Such bans constituted nothing less than forcible estrangement for much of the year.[7]

While universal in theory, medieval hospitality to strangers was selective in practice and restrictive even within Christian society; it certainly embraced little of Emmanuel Levinas's "infinite enlargement of responsibility."[8] Although exceptions could be found, certain categories of people, including actors, prostitutes, and vagabonds, were usually regarded with hostility and treated as estranged marginal groups. Of particular importance for the focus of this book, "heretics" were actively persecuted. Heresy, which involved alleged or actual estrangement from aspects of ecclesiastical doctrine and practice—and thus, in ecclesiastical eyes, from both Church and God—was regarded as contagious sickness. An eleventh-century monk called heresy "depravity," "poison," "madness and devilish error."[9] Following the late eleventh-century Gregorian reform movement designed to empower the papacy and to centralize ecclesiastical power in Rome, growing religious dissent and heresy were fought bitterly by the increasingly authoritarian Church. The Crusades, instigated initially to regain access to Christian holy sites in Jerusalem from Muslim control, inadvertently brought "renewed contact with Eastern heresy."[10] Eventually, during Pope Innocent III's papacy (1198–1216), brutal massacres occurred during the 1209 Albigensian Crusade against Cathar heretics in Languedoc. The Franciscan and Dominican mendicant missionary orders, founded respectively in 1209 and 1216, were dedicated to preaching against theological "strangers" (heretics, pagans, Jews, and Muslims). In 1231, Pope Gregory IX (1145–1241) gave them full powers of inquisition and tools of repression to stamp out real or imagined theological dissidents. Two leading German inquisitors soon "claimed to be able to detect a heretic by his or her appearance."[11]

Medieval Christian attitudes toward "paganism" showed coexistent respect and cruelty. Vernacular courtly literature contained occasional examples of idealized pagans, notably, Feirefiz in Wolfram von Eschenbach's *Parzival* (ca. 1200–1210), a knightly hero capable of virtue and love. Medieval historical chroniclers acknowledged the valor and heroism of contemporary Baltic pagans. Yet in practice, treatment of them could be merciless. Slavs were captured in vast numbers, transported by Christian and Jewish merchants and sold within Muslim regions as slaves and for harems. The quasi-monastic military Order of German Teutonic Knights committed terrible atrocities against northern pagans in Baltic lands during the Northern Crusades, initiated by papal decree in 1171 and lasting into the fifteenth century.[12]

Virtually unknown north of Spain and yet omnipresent in the Christian imagination, Muslims were strangers in absentia. Long demonized as infidels, Muslims were nevertheless alluringly exotic to Western minds nourished on Pliny's accounts of fabulous Oriental beings. Islam was little understood but greatly feared, its violent jihad an ever-present military threat to the eastern and southern borders of a Christendom already shrunk by past Islamic military conquest and economic blocking of key Mediterranean trade routes by Saracen corsairs and pirates. From the eleventh century onward, Muslim hegemony in southern Spain and Turkish military conquest of Asia Minor brought new perceived dangers, as Christians were attracted in Spain to Islamic high culture, in Anatolia to widespread conversion.

Ignorance of Islam—the Qur'an, translated into Latin for Peter the Venerable of Cluny (1092–1156) only in the 1140s, remained little known—

led to Muslims being characterized as "pagans" both in Latin chronicles and in vernacular oral epics; *pagan* and *Saracen* became virtually synonymous terms. In the twelfth-century *Chanson de Roland*, the fictional Charlemagne asserted to the Muslim emir Baligant, "Never to Paynims [pagans] may I show love or peace."[13] Love of God and fellow Christians was a crucial factor both within the twelfth-century spiritual renewal and within the "sanctified violence" of crusades. As Jonathan Riley-Smith has shown, although theologians such as Peter Lombard (ca. 1100–1160) "emphasized that enemies must be included in our love for all men," in the realities of war love was never extended to the enemy, whose alterity was stressed: "Crusading literature and propaganda played on the existing xenophobia by the use of emotive terms—enemies of God, servants of the Devil, servants of the Anti-Christ—to describe the Muslims."[14] The influential Cistercian Bernard of Clairvaux (1090–1153) understood the Templars' warfare against Islam as radical eradication of evil.

Contemporary crusading propaganda, directed at Christian audiences who were typically attached to relics and images, commonly portrayed Muslim Saracens as idol worshipers belonging to an Oriental pagan cult. As John V. Tolan has noted: "The idolatrous other is an essential foil for Christian virtue. . . . The image of idolatry . . . perhaps . . . stems from a projection of *Christian* practice onto the imagined enemy."[15] In a reverse mirroring, Christian preoccupation with sexual purity led Peter the Venerable to characterize Islam as a religion "of the lascivious."[16]

Both in Mozarabic Spain and in western Christendom, some contemporary theologians who polemicized against Islam in defense of Christian orthodoxy were more nuanced though no less hostile. They saw Islam neither as idolatrous nor as "a separate religion, distinct from other spiritual rivals," but as "a variant, heretical version of Christianity."[17] Muhammad was portrayed as a deceptive Oriental heresiarch, given to mixing truth and error, and prey to carnal power and sexuality. Thirteenth-century Dominican theologians dedicated to mission wrote more knowledgeable treatises on Islam, designed primarily to refute for Christian audiences Muslim objections to Church doctrine.

Yet during periods of peace in the twelfth-century Kingdom of Jerusalem, Frankish Christians and Muslims developed mutual bonds of respect, even friendship, to an extent that shocked European newcomers. Many Franks adopted Oriental dress or learned Arabic, a few read Arabic literature, and Frankish and Muslim lords hunted together. From the late twelfth century, vernacular literature commonly portrayed the Islamic hero Saladin (1138–1193) as generous and valiant and other Muslim fictional heroes as noble Christian knights in all but religion, even as the embodiment of Christian love. In thirteenth-century western Europe, Muslim philosophy increasingly influenced Christian thought, and, even a century earlier, Peter the Venerable emphasized "the rationality and learning of his Muslim audience," despite his conviction that, because of their domination of Asia, Africa, and parts of Spain, Muslims were the "worst adversaries" of the Church.[18] He contrasted Muslim rationality and learning with the perceived irrationality of Jews, whom he regarded as "animal-like beings . . . less than human."[19]

In the Christian hierarchy of dangerous and hated strangers, Jews were paramount and more threatening than Muslims. Intensifying preexisting Judeophobia among some ancient Egyptian, Greek, and Roman writers, "most Christian writers of the first seven centuries wrote against the Jews."[20] Influential Church fathers demonized Jews as utterly estranged from God, humanity, and goodness. In the words of Saint Gregory of Nyssa (d. 385/86), Jews were "murderers of the Lord . . . enemies and slanderers of God . . . advocates of the devil, progeny of poison snakes." They were "criminals, degenerates, . . . enemies of all that is decent and beautiful."[21] Canon laws and secular laws passed from the fourth to the seventh centuries forbade inter alia intermarriage, Jews' holding public office, and all social and religious relations with Christians. Jews were thus forcibly segregated from Christian society. Throughout the Middle Ages and beyond, sermons, creeds, and the Easter Week liturgy fostered hatred of Jews. The Church employed all medieval forms of mass communication—homilies, church windows, statuary, paintings, and drama—to demonize Jews and estrange them from their Christian neighbors. Minor clerics and popular mendicant preachers were the main instigators of blood libels, desecration of the Host libels, and some pogroms and massacres. Some popes and bishops sought to mitigate Christian violence toward Jews, but Church teaching itself enflamed it.

Commentators have noted many causes of Christian Judeophobia including theological motives such as supersessionism, greed, clerical resentment of royal protection of Jews (Jews were the king's lucrative "slaves"), and increasing ecclesiastical obsession with sexuality, demonology, and heresy. Most important, from the eleventh century, "the concern with external and internal enemies posed serious dangers to the Jewish minority."[22] Internal enemies especially included real or alleged Christian "Judaizers." The Church feared social relations between Jews and Christians, often warm at the grassroots level and attested to from the fourth to the twelfth centuries. Notable clerical converts from conviction included even a bishop and court chaplains.[23] From Saint John Chrysostom (ca. 347–407) to Martin Luther (1483–1546), some of the most vitriolic preachers against Jews intended to destroy existing philosemitism within their Christian audience. If salvation lay exclusively within Church sacraments and doctrines, then for Christians to consort with Jews endangered both their souls and the Church's unique, supreme authority.

Christianity's chief external enemy was Islam. Displaced anger and vengeance against distant Muslim violence against Christians were channeled against neighboring Jews. In 1009, Caliph Mansur al-Hakim (985–1021) destroyed the Church of the Holy Sepulchre in Jerusalem and by 1014, thirty thousand other churches; many Christians forcibly adopted Islam. Thereupon in France and the Rhineland, Jewish communities were forcibly expelled in revenge. "God wills it," the cry of Pope Urban II (ca. 1035–1099) rallied the First Crusade against Islam (1095–1099), triggering massacres of thousands of Jews along the Rhine and elsewhere in 1096. As James Carroll notes, in "Christian millennial fantasy, Jews . . . joined, or even replaced, Muslims as the defiling enemy."[24] Massacres occurred again in 1146 before the Second Crusade. Peter the Venerable demanded of King Louis VII of France (1120–1180): "What would be the profit if the Saracens, the enemy in distant lands were conquered, while the Jewish blasphemers, far worse enemies of Christians than Saracens, were allowed in our very midst."[25] The Third Crusade (1189–1192) unleashed further massacres of Jews in England.

Following the western conquest of Byzantine Constantinople during the Fourth Crusade (1202–1204) and consequent Latin jurisdiction for the first time over large Muslim populations, Pope Innocent III (ca. 1161–1216) passed a canon law at the Fourth Lateran Council (1215) to distinguish Christians outwardly from non-Christian strangers. Intended partly to protect "the physical and spiritual purity of Christians," mandatory patterns of hallmarking Saracens and Jews (through dress, color, badges, or hats) were virtually unprecedented within Christendom.[26] Yet, ironically, they in fact introduced into Europe exclusionary Islamic laws codified under the seventh- or eighth-century "Covenant of Omar." These Islamic measures were used somewhat haphazardly to distinguish in appearance, humiliatingly, second-class or so-called *dhimmi* citizens, mainly Christians and Jews, from Muslims.[27]

In Christian hands within western Europe, such legislation intensified existing oppression of Jews. Former neighbors were visibly made into strangers, segregated by ghettos (from 1220 onward), and persecuted by clerical propaganda, increasing massacres, expropriations, and permanent forcible expulsions. Thus Christians, the original guests in the Jewish household of God, ousted the Jewish hosts; the gentile prodigal son ejected the Jewish elder brother; the medieval Church, so hospitable toward orthodox western Christians, ensured for Jews the dire fulfillment of Lamentations 5:2: "Our inheritance is turned to strangers, our houses to aliens."

When theology ploughs the dragon's teeth of hatred, ruthless warriors eventually spring forth.

CONTRIBUTORS' QUESTIONS FOR MARGARET BREARLEY

1. You write that Jews and Christians are fundamentally called to an empathy with strangers rooted in remembering the historic welcome previously extended to them—for Christians by Jews, and for Jews by God. Then you recount an ironic history of hospitality's institutionalization, especially within the Christian Church: a tradition rooted in hospitality toward the other, you contend, eventually came to practice hostility and disdain toward its historic host. Moreover, you demonstrate a similar orientation of the Church vis-à-vis Muslims, treating them as enemies when they are a threat, appreciatively when their traditions serve the greater good of Christianity. Your essay concludes that this movement of theological control is a domestication of hospitality toward the stranger, transforming its openness and risk into safe, controllable relationships with the Other. What are the possibilities of creating new forms of Muslim, Christian, Jewish dialogue/trialogue that may begin to undo such a domestication and institutionalization of hospitality?

2. You close your essay with the words: "When theology ploughs the dragon's teeth of hatred, ruthless warriors eventually spring forth." Yet you claim that the welcoming of the stranger is a central precept of Judeo-Christian monotheism. You also note that during the medieval period, protection for the stranger, "while universal in theory, was selective in practice." The medieval Christian path you describe took the believer

from a position of respecting the other to a demonization that often resulted in murderous acts in the name of the faith. Is this path one that could have been predicted by a reading of essential tenets of Christian theology (as your final quotation seems to imply)? Or might it be the case that historical circumstances determined the movement within Christianity from the embrace of strangers to their frequent exclusion from a moral universe? What are the implications of your response given the fact that we live in a post-Holocaust world in which religious violence is on the increase?

RESPONSE BY MARGARET BREARLEY

Historical circumstances can encourage, but rarely determine, movements within Christianity, since theology can respond to historical circumstances in simultaneously contrary ways, as the multiple Western medieval responses to expansionist military jihad, which I briefly adumbrated, clearly indicate. Indeed, precisely because, paradoxically, historical catastrophes can trigger creative as well as negative theological responses, many new forms of Christian, Jewish, and Muslim dialogue and trialogue already exist. The encounter with National Socialist antisemitism led to the Reverend James Parkes's pioneering study of historical Christian anti-Judaism in the 1930s and to the foundation of the Council of Christians and Jews (CCJ) in 1942. The post-Holocaust theology of writers such as Karl Barth, John T. Pawlikowski, Roy Eckardt, Franklin Littell, and Paul van Buren rejected Christian supersessionism, affirmed rabbinic Judaism, and explored the Jewishness of Jesus. The Second Vatican Council (1962–1965) initiated in its 1965 "Declaration on the Relation of the Church to Non-Christian Religions" a new era of interreligious dialogue with both Jews and Muslims. The 9/11 attack itself gave added impetus to long-established trialogues and Muslim/Christian academic centers. Indeed, so urgent is the perceived need to engage creatively with Islam that important initiatives in Christian-Muslim dialogue have been established since 9/11 within both the Roman Catholic Church (especially since 2006) and the Anglican Church.[28] Although in the current climate, Christian-Jewish dialogue—in Britain, at least—seems less well funded and weaker than trialogue and Christian-Muslim dialogue, there seems on the surface little need for even newer forms of dialogue or trialogue.

Yet the questions themselves suggest possible new responses. The first appears to denigrate both "a domestication and institutionalization of hospitality." But hospitality arguably *needs* to be domesticated and institutionalized. Only then can it fully embrace the stranger with radical openness. Christians still have much to learn about the practice of domestic hospitality within the home, even toward fellow Christians, let alone toward non-Christian neighbors and strangers. An open home reflects an open heart; a meal shared—appropriate to religious dietary requirements—affirms shared humanity and true neighborliness. As for institutional changes, many have been necessary and welcome; for example, the Western Churches abandoned formal cursing of "heretics, Jews, and infidels" (the so-called comminations) during the 1960s; many Church schools admit pupils of other faiths; and the Hope 2008 initiative encouraged British churches to undertake "a million hours of kindness" within their local wider communities during Whitsun. More institutional changes may be necessary and possible. Yet, while boundless hospitality can be practiced in homes and church halls, churches as sacred spaces consecrated to the God of Abraham, Isaac, and Jacob will have inevitable boundaries; spiritualities that practice the invocation of other deities are commonly excluded, and—because of its theological and, above all, political ramifications—I am among those critical of Dutch bishop Martinus Muskens's August 2007 proposal on Radio Netherlands that, for the sake of communal harmony, Dutch Christians should pray to Allah.[29]

The second question asks whether the path of demonization and murderous acts "could have been predicted by a reading of essential tenets of Christian theology." A theologian or church historian would answer this query far better than I can. But I would argue a negative response. True, certain medieval theologians and churchmen reprehensibly taught hatred. It can be said that from the mid-twelfth century, "organized, institutionalized hatred and intolerance were directed against Jews, Moslems, heretics, schismatic Greeks, homosexuals, lepers, and, later, witches and Gypsies."[30] Yet hatred most certainly was not and is not a tenet of Christian theology. On the contrary, Christianity, like its matrix, Judaism, is grounded in the absolute certainty of God's profound love for humankind and of the need to respond by loving God and one's fellow human beings. And yet . . . certain traditional modes of biblical exegesis—above all, decontextualized literal interpretation of single verses such as Jesus' saying, "Ye are of your father the devil" (John 8:44)—could (and occasionally still can) be exploited to foster rejection and demonization, especially of Jews and of Judaism, but also of Roma/Gypsies, people of color, and those deemed Other. Given that racism, largely discredited immediately following World War II, has reappeared in a variety of guises, a theology that values each human being as of infinite worth is urgently necessary.[31]

One implication of this outlook is that I have come to agree with Rabbi Abraham Joshua Heschel's suggestion that "Christian renewal should imply confrontation with Judaism out of which it emerged."[32] I believe that Christianity would be enriched by rediscovering certain aspects of Judaism and Jewish biblical exegesis, since, in the words of philosopher Franz Rosenzweig, "before God, . . . Jew and Christian labor at the same task. He cannot dispense with either."[33] The Orthodox Jewish conviction that the Torah has seventy faces, for example, demonstrates a complex awareness of the multifaceted nature of God's word and of truth, reflected in the multiple voices of Talmudic Bible interpretation: "Each page of the Talmud is an argument, a debate. Not a single page contains just one person's view."[34] This polychrome reveling in diverse opinions, complementing and conflicting with one another, has a converse side: an exalted view of each unique human voice, each human face. As Byron L. Sherwin has noted: "For the Jewish mystics, the divine may become incarnated in *each* human person. . . . Each human being, through the performance of sacred deeds, can incarnate the divine within themselves. . . . Each person is an envelope bearing a divine message, a divine presence."[35] *Each* person, note, and not through his or her ethnicity or belief or words but through his or her God-given capacity for sacred deeds—each person bears a divine stamp and should be regarded as inviolable, sacred. Each person, moreover, bears awesome responsibility since his or her daily actions have an effect on the well-being of the entire world.[36]

Our post-Holocaust world, in which religious violence flourishes, in which people are killed because of doctrinal or other differences, needs religions to desist from internal violence and oppression, as Sherwin noted: "Religions cannot expect to be credible in their opposition to strife unless they first eliminate triumphalism, strife and injustice within and among themselves."[37] Religions themselves need the generous optimism of Heschel, who was convinced that "in our age religious pluralism is the will of God. . . . Religions, true to their own convictions, disagree profoundly and are in opposition to one another on matters of doctrine. . . . [But] the voice of God reaches the spirit of man in a variety of ways, in a multiplicity of languages."[38] An optimistic hope lies, too, in the rabbinic view that the world can exist only because "the meritorious deeds of one or a few righteous individuals . . . counterbalance the wicked acts of the majority," or even because of one righteous man, and that "because of thirty righteous gentiles do the nations of the world exist."[39] The world needs not religious zealots, who can be ruthless, fanatical, and violent, but righteous people of faith serving their own communities and reaching out to others in love and with what the novelist Eva Hoffman calls "alert inquisitiveness," which is open to true encounter.[40]

Sacred deeds cannot deflect violence. Righteousness often ends in apparent failure; holiness can lead to martyrdom and death. But righteous individuals are messengers of goodness. Their words, deeds, and intercession on behalf of others bring blessing and alleviate suffering. Their encounter with the presence of the holy God mediates, in their encounter with strangers, God's gifts of peace, mercy, and irrevocable love.

NOTES

1   Joseph H. Hertz, *Affirmations of Judaism* (London: Humphrey Milford; Oxford: Oxford University Press, 1927), 138.

2   Christine D. Pohl, *Making Room: Recovering Hospitality as a Christian Tradition* (Grand Rapids, Mich.: Wm. B. Eerdmans, 1999), 105.

3   Olivia Remie Constable, *Housing the Stranger in the Mediterranean World: Lodging, Trade, and Travel in Late Antiquity and the Middle Ages* (Cambridge: Cambridge University Press, 2003), 1.

4   *The Rule of St. Benedict* (New York: Random House, 1981), chap. 53.

5   Cardinal Gasquet, *English Monastic Life* (1904; repr., London: Methuen, 1919), 98–99.

6   Alexander Murray, *Reason and Society in the Middle Ages* (Oxford: Clarendon Press, 1985), 402.

7   Cf. Uta Ranke-Heinemann, *Eunuchs for the Sake of Heaven: Women, Sexuality, and the Catholic Church* (New York: Doubleday, 1990); and Dyan Elliott, *Spiritual Marriage: Sexual Abstinence in Medieval Wedlock* (Princeton, N.J.: Princeton University Press, 1993).

8   Thomas W. Ogletree, *Hospitality to the Stranger: Dimensions of Moral Understanding* (Philadelphia: Fortress Press, 1985), 56.

9   Malcolm Lambert, *Medieval Heresy: Popular Movements from the Gregorian Reform to the Reformation* (Oxford: Blackwell, 2002), 18.

10   Ibid., 47.

11   Norman Cohn, *Europe's Inner Demons: The Demonisation of Christians in Medieval Christendom* (London: Pimlico, 2005), 45.

12   Cf. Eric Christiansen, *The Northern Crusades* (London: Penguin, 1997), 96.

13 *The Song of Roland*, trans. Dorothy L. Sayers (London: Penguin Classics, 1957), l.3596.

14 Jonathan Riley-Smith, "Crusading as an Act of Love," in *Medieval Religion: New Approaches*, ed. Constance Hoffman Berman (New York: Routledge, 2005), 56.

15 John V. Tolan, *Saracens: Islam in the Medieval European Imagination* (New York: Columbia University Press, 2002), 129.

16 Dominique Iogna-Prat, "The Creation of a Christian Armory against Islam," in Berman, ed., *Medieval Religion*, 342.

17 Tolan, *Saracens*, 134.

18 Ibid., 159.

19 Anna Sapir Abulafia, "Bodies in the Jewish-Christian Debate," in Berman, ed., *Medieval Religion*, 352.

20 Robert Michael, "Antisemitism and the Church Fathers," in *Jewish-Christian Encounters over the Centuries: Symbiosis, Prejudice, Holocaust, Dialogue*, ed. Marvin Perry and Frederick M. Schweitzer (New York: Peter Lang, 1994), 110. Cf. Peter Schaefer, *Judeophobia: Attitudes towards the Jews in the Ancient World* (Cambridge, Mass.: Harvard University Press, 1997).

21 Quoted in Michael, "Antisemitism and the Church Fathers," 109.

22 Robert Chazan, *The Jews of Medieval Western Christendom, 1000–1500* (Cambridge: Cambridge University Press, 2006), 241.

23 Richard Fletcher, *The Conversion of Europe: From Paganism to Christianity, 371–1386 AD* (London: Fontana Press, 1997), chap. 9.

24 James Carroll, *Constantine's Sword: The Church and the Jews* (New York: Houghton Mifflin, 2001), 253.

25 Quoted in J. A. Watt, "The Crusades and the Persecution of the Jews," in *The Medieval World*, ed. Peter Linehan and Janet L. Nelson (New York: Routledge, 2001), 154.

26 Tolan, *Saracens*, 196.

27 See Andrew G. Bostom, ed., *The Legacy of Jihad: Islamic Holy War and the Fate of Non-Muslims* (New York: Prometheus Books, 2005), 174–81.

28 In January 2002, the Anglican Church launched a series of major annual international seminars of Christian and Muslim scholars. Proceedings are edited by Canon Michael Ipgrave and published by Church House Publishing, London.

29 "Pray to Allah, Dutch Bishop Proposes," CathNews, August 13, 2007, http://www.cathnews.com/article.aspx?aeid=5904.

30 Frederick M. Schweitzer, "Medieval Perceptions of Jews and Judaism," in Perry and Schweitzer, eds., *Jewish-Christian Encounters over the Centuries*, 158–59.

31 Marek Kohn, *The Race Gallery: The Return of Racial Science* (London: Jonathan Cape, 1995).

32 Abraham Joshua Heschel, *Moral Grandeur and Spiritual Audacity* (New York: Farrar, Straus and Giroux, 1996), 272.

33 Franz Rosenzweig, *The Star of Redemption*, trans. William W. Hallo (New York: Holt, Rinehart and Winston, 1970), 415.

34 Daniel Gordis, *Does the World Need the Jews? Rethinking Chosenness and American*

Jewish Identity (New York: Scribner, 1997), 165. On the seventy faces of the Torah. *See Midrash Bamidbar Rabbah* 13:15. Cf. Rabbi Dovid Rosenfeld, "The 48 Ways," 2006, Torah.org, http://www.torah.org/learning/pirkei-avos/chapter6-624.html.

35 Byron L. Sherwin, *Studies in Jewish Theology: Reflections in the Mirror of Tradition* (Portland, Ore.: Vallentine Mitchell, 2007), 181.

36 Samuel Belkin, *In His Image: The Jewish Philosophy of Man as Expressed in Rabbinic Tradition* (New York: Abelard-Schuman, 1960), 137.

37 Sherwin, *Studies in Jewish Theology*, 171.

38 Heschel, *Moral Grandeur*, 272, 245, quoted in Sherwin, *Studies in Jewish Theology*, 194.

39 Belkin, *In His Image*, 138, 137; Babylonian Talmud, *Hullin* 92a, quoted in Belkin, 138.

40 Eva Hoffman, *Illuminations* (London: Harvill Secker, 2008), 33.

9

Noah and Others

Pluralism in Ancient and Modern Judaism

ROCHELLE L. MILLEN

In the concrete language characteristic of midrash, the *Midrash Rabbah* on Genesis struggles with the theological question of why God decided to create a creature as imperfect as the human being. The words of the midrashic text illuminate abstract concepts regarding human nature and political theory and point to a central issue of this chapter: Must religious truth be absolute? Can there be a religious community—and religious individuals—whose belief structures about transcendence leave room for theological convictions other than their own? Here is what the midrash states:

> R. Simon said: When the Holy One, blessed be He, came to create Adam, the ministering angels formed themselves into groups and actions, some saying, "Let the human being be created," while others urged, "Let this creature not be created." Thus it is written (in Psalms 85:11): "Loving-kindness and Truth fought together, Righteousness and Peace were in conflict." Loving-kindness [*chesed*] said, "Create, for the human being does acts of loving-kindness," while Truth said, "Don't create, for the human being is compounded of falsehood." Righteousness said, "Let the person be created, for he or she does acts of righteousness, while Peace urged, "Let the human creature not be created, for he or she is full of strife." What did God do? God took Truth and cast it to the ground.

The ministering angels said before the Holy One, "Master of the Universe, why do you despise your seal [of truth]?"[1] "Let Truth arise from the earth!" As it is written (Psalms 85:12), "Let truth spring up from the earth."[2]

Although it is not clear from the text whether God or the angels uttered, "Let Truth arise from the earth!" the straightforward explanation is that God responded with this declaration to the complaint of the angels, as if to say: "I am not despising my Truth, which is absolute. Human truth must be hammered and shaped in the crucible of history. The task of finding and defining that truth is one I give to human beings."[3] To state this declaration from another perspective, if Truth remains in heaven—the purview of God and thus absolute—creation cannot occur. Only God possesses absolute, objective Truth. The creation of the world, and of human beings designed to be partners with God in that creation, results in truth that of necessity includes subjective elements. Human truth, even when derived from texts considered divinely inspired, is thus, by definition, partial, fragmented, and both created through and limited by history.

An underlying assumption of this text is that human, historical truth is not monolithic; universal truths take many forms. As interpretations of the Torah are multiple (the Talmud states that "there are seventy faces to Torah"[4]), the subjective, contextual elements of human truths lead to diverse manifestations. This is another way of saying that the embeddedness of absolute principles in the nitty-gritty of practical life leads inevitably to distinct approaches for attaining similar ends.

The Noahide commandments, which are central to rabbinic literature, constitute a theological foundation for pluralism in Judaism, a pluralism in which Judaism is not seen to be the source of absolute religious truth in the world and salvation is not limited to Jews. These commandments, derived from Genesis 9, convey a universal eschatology founded upon basic ethical and practical components.[5] In that sense, they are part of the absolute Truth that God cast into human hands and minds to struggle with, formulate, and act upon. This chapter analyzes how the Noahide commandments have been applied to Jewish-gentile relations in medieval, early modern, and modern times.

The Noahide Commandments in Medieval History

The seven Noahide laws establish the grounding of civilized societies. In political theory, they may be seen as the foundation of all communities. They are the prohibitions against idolatry, blasphemy, murder, immorality (adultery and incest), theft, and the consumption of animal flesh from a live animal. This last prohibition is understood to limit animal pain, even when humanity is permitted (Genesis 9:3) to be carnivorous, and to restrain cruelty. In addition to these six prohibitions, the establishment of courts of justice is required to enforce the prohibitions and to promulgate any other laws deemed useful or necessary. In the Mishnah, the Noahide laws apply to all peoples of the world, and those who follow them are "eligible for the world to come."[6] That is, salvation is dependent not on belief in specific doctrines but on practicing essential ethical actions and restraints. The determining factor for individual redemption is moral behavior, which, at a minimum, safeguards the body, property, and family of each person, allowing for the cultivation of respect for all life.

But the Talmud also juxtaposes the people of Israel, pure monotheists committed to the Torah, with "the nations of the world," a phrase usually understood as referring to pagans and idol worshipers. The Talmud includes a body of precepts designed to regulate the contact of Jews and gentiles, its aim being to keep Jews away from idolaters and the support of idolatry. These limitations on Jewish-gentile interactions were followed, with some variation, during Talmudic times. Interestingly, some sources maintain that the early Church fathers used similar measures for the regulation of conduct between Christians and non-converted gentiles.[7] In the time of the Talmud, Jewish communities were usually large, and gentiles were pagans. But in the German- and French-speaking lands of Christian Europe, the Jewish communities were small and interaction with gentiles, that is, Christians, was necessary for the economies of these communities. The legal decisors (halachists, or specialists in Jewish law) began a process of redefinition of "idolaters." Their work planted the seeds of a "theory of tolerance."[8] By the fourteenth century, Christians were regarded as people of faith on philosophical and theological grounds, although some Jewish interpreters considered Christian monotheism not as pure as that of Judaism because of the doctrine of the Trinity.

The medieval disputations, forced upon the Jewish communities of Paris (1241) and Barcelona (1263) by the Dominicans and Franciscans, served a perhaps unintended purpose of compelling Jewish leaders to explore, examine, and clarify further the position and status of Jews in the gentile/Christian world.[9] Indeed, it can be said that the decrees of the Fourth Lateran Council convened by Pope Innocent III in 1215—decrees that, among other things, established the Franciscan and Dominican orders with the aim of diminishing heresy—led to increased scrutiny, censure, and harassment of Jews in Christian Europe. In this context, two important interpretations developed regarding the Noahide commandments and their implications: those of Moses Maimonides (1135–1204) and Rabbi Menachem Ha-Meiri (1249–ca. 1310).

When Maimonides wrote his renowned *Mishneh Torah*, he codified the Noahide commandments as they are stated in his Laws of Kings 8:11. Maimonides writes:

> One who accepts the seven Noahide commandments and is careful to
> follow them—such a person is regarded as one of the righteous of the
> nations of the world and has a share in the World to Come. This person
> is one who accepts and follows them because they were commanded
> by God in the Torah and because Moses our teacher taught that they
> were followed by the descendants of Noah in the past. But if one follows
> these commandments because they are rational, such a person . . . is not
> regarded among the righteous of the nations of the world or among their
> wise. (My translation)

The controversies regarding this text are many.[10] A primary question deriving from it is, How can Maimonides seemingly dismiss the wise of the world as not being wise if monotheism is not included as a foundation of their ethics? And second, must one believe in revelation and monotheism in order to be eligible for salvation? Would this not undermine the seeming universalism of the first part of Maimonides' formulation, which in turn is based on the Talmudic text?[11]

The first issue is clarified by analysis of the text itself. According to most scholars, the last line of the above text is based on an incorrect manuscript. Instead of reading "or among their wise," it should read "but from their wise."[12] This latter reading, which involves a reversal of two Hebrew letters, accords (theological/philosophical) wisdom—but not immortality—to those outside of Judaism. It acknowledges that fundamental ethical principles can be arrived at through rational means, an obvious conclusion from formulations of natural law and social contract theory. It affirms that those who live according to autonomously accepted morality are "wise" and that theological and philosophical wisdom is found among all peoples, even those with no religious beliefs or commitments. This view supports the notion that the Noahide commandment prohibiting blasphemy does not entail a belief in God. Rather, the commandment requires that one refrain from idolatrous practice as well as from any act that undermines belief in God. While tolerance within Judaism is broad, it excludes those who reject the moral restraints of Noahide law.

Such an understanding of tolerance rests on the legitimation of theological wisdom, universally construed. Noahide law is understood as a universal code of ethics. Judaism validates all knowledge of God's creation as worthy of understanding and mastery; all striving to relate to God and make meaning is seen as legitimate. Jewish religious integrity requires acknowledgment of the theological/philosophical wisdom of all peoples.[13]

This analysis leads to the second question: Is belief in the divine grounding of Noahide ethics requisite for "a share in the world to come"? Exploring this issue requires, first, an examination of the views of the significant late medieval thinker and decisor Rabbi Menachem Ha-Meiri. Ha-Meiri belonged to a group of rationalists in Provence. In the Maimonidean controversies that raged after Maimonides' publication of *Guide for the Perplexed*, Ha-Meiri defended philosophy, and this defense influenced his view of other religions. Ha-Meiri held that Christians and Muslims are not within the category of the idolatrous. By using positive language to articulate this notion, Ha-Meiri affirmed the status of these other monotheistic faiths. For instance, he writes:

> It has already been stated that these things [early Talmudic restrictions on social interactions with gentiles] were said concerning periods when there existed nations of idolaters, and they were contaminated in their deeds and tainted in their dispositions . . . but other nations, which are restricted by the ways of religion and which are free from such blemishes of character—on the contrary they even punish such deeds—are without doubt exempt from this prohibition. . . . But in so far as we have to deal with nations which are restricted by the ways of religion and which believe in the Godhead . . . it is not only permitted, but even meritorious to do so.[14]

Ha-Meiri is unusual among medieval thinkers in ascribing to religions outside Judaism the status of "founding religions," which use philosophical reasoning to determine doctrine and practical politics to formulate institutions and laws. He held in high esteem the functioning of legal institutions and maintenance of moral standards in society. Christians were to be classed with Jews and not with idolaters; by implication, this concept included Muslims. The social and intellectual interaction between learned Jews and Christians brought about an identification or sense of association. The assumption was that Jews and other nations share basic beliefs and tenets, indicating a basis for religious tolerance.

How do these insights apply to the question concerning whether a theory of universal salvation requires acceptance of an ethics founded on divine legislation? Some commentaries on Maimonides' text state that if people follow Noahide law and say that "we do so because it was commanded by our father, Noah, who received it from God [*mepi hagevurah*], then they merit 'a share in the world to come.'" If, however, they accept Noahide law because they heard about it from someone, or derived it from their own rational conclusions, their reward is only in this world.[15] However, other interpretations of Maimonides—for example, that those who accept purpose in the world rather than complete randomness and arbitrariness are included among "the righteous"—have led to a broad understanding of Maimonides' dictum. Thus Rabbi Abraham Isaac Kook (1865–1935), the great mystic, social activist, and first Ashkenazi chief rabbi in Palestine, argued that if one observes the Noahide commandments based on Mosaic revelation, one is counted among "the righteous of the nations of the world," as stated by Maimonides in the first sentence quoted above.

Somewhat paradoxically, this same Rabbi Kook maintained that the "wise" person, one whose rationality leads him or her to follow the seven commandments, is on a higher spiritual level than the "righteous" person. But this interpretation is consistent with Maimonides' emphasis on the rationality of all commandments.[16] Thus Jacob Katz argues that gentiles "are not commanded to believe in absolute monotheism," and Mary C. Boys writes, "Following Maimonides and subsequent rabbinic thought, 'the pious of all the nations of the world have a place in the world to come.'"[17] With these formulations in mind, it can be argued that Judaism offers a philosophical foundation for not regarding the stranger as other.[18] Even those who live by Noahide laws unreflectively—perhaps because such behavior prevails within a particular society—can be included under its broad rubric.

Early Modern and Enlightenment Concepts

While medieval halachists averred that Christians were not idolaters, certain seventeenth-century scholars developed a similar line of reasoning, extending the conceptual underpinnings of the Noahide doctrines in Jewish thought. The Lithuanian halachist Moses Rivkes, for instance, declared that Christians share Jewish beliefs in prophecy, revelation, and the truths of the Bible. Thus he maintained that Judaism and Christianity participate in a common heritage. As Katz states, however, such concepts remained "abstract" for these early modern halachists.[19] They lived in post-Reformation Christian Europe, a society segregated socially and physically by religion. Perhaps their immersion in Jewish society and religious life allowed them to develop a concept of tolerance, but that concept was more ideational than operative. In any case, the early modern halachists did not advocate blurring the boundaries between the communities in any but the most practical ways. And from a purely functional perspective, more friendly relations with those who held political power over an often unwanted minority group was simply realistic, much as Jeremiah's guidance was during the Babylonian exile: "Seek the welfare of the city where I have caused you to be captive and pray to God for it, for in its peace you shall have peace" (29:7). A conceptual framework that reduced tensions and articulated commonalities made sense when contact between the groups was necessary.

The Enlightenment and the Emergence of Modernity

While tolerance of the religious other has early roots in Jewish texts, the citizenship given to Jews by the French Assembly in 1791 encouraged further development of that idea, which was spurred by Enlightenment trends that lifted social restrictions on individuals, groups, and classes. With the slow disintegration of the ghettos, Jews no longer had a compulsory attachment to other Jews. An individual could be viewed as a human being quite apart from his or her religious and cultural background. Connections with the other no longer required reference to one's Jewishness. The separation of church and state advocated by Spinoza and defended by Moses Mendelssohn, Pierre Bayle, and John Locke was becoming a reality, although the process was slow and incremental;[20] it would not occur in France, for example, until the early twentieth century and was directly related to the conflagrations of the Dreyfus affair. In a society structured according to this ideal separation, the mutual relations of Christians, Jews, and Muslims would be unaffected by their faith; religious affiliation would affect only one's religion. It is clear, however, even now in the twentieth-first century, that "one's religion" can be construed more broadly than these early thinkers envisioned. It is also apparent, in this post-Holocaust era, that the optimism intrinsic to rationalism was an illusion. Hence the issues with which this volume deals.

The new era of legal equality moved the Jewish community from the margins of society toward the mainstream. Although sometimes accompanied by advocacy to "become one of us," that is, to convert to Christianity, the granting of civil rights to Jews was to have a profound effect upon Jews and Judaism. Nineteenth- and twentieth-century Jewish leaders followed the traditions of rationalism and the Enlightenment by emphasizing the common humanity of Jews and non-Jews, the equality of all persons and all peoples. Some maintained, with justification, that Jewish concepts of how to treat the other—even outside the social-political framework developed as a result of increased individual rights in Western culture—find their ultimate source not in the Mishnah or Maimonides' *Mishneh Torah* but in Hebrew scriptures. The renowned biblical scholar Moshe Greenberg clearly demonstrates how the biblical concepts of the sanctity of each person and God as creator of the world—and therefore of human diversity—lead to "the potentiality and the obligation of harmony among humans. Human differences are esteemed as testimonies to the creative greatness of God."[21] Greenberg shows how "even when intercommunal hostility alienated Jews from Gentiles, Jewish thinkers and legists [*sic*] applied the grand principles of sanctification of God's name, imitation of God, and harmony among men to create unilateral Obligations toward the Gentiles—obligations that did not depend upon reciprocity."[22] Greenberg correctly maintains that classical "Hebrew thought affirmed the basic unity of humankind in its creation myth, and complemented that myth with its messianic vision of a united humanity under God."[23] Only Jews were—and are—bound by the covenant described in the Torah, but Judaism affirms access to God, salvation, and ethics outside of its own community. Thus the necessity of welcoming the stranger is an essential aspect of biblical, rabbinic, and modern Jewish thought.

The contemporary Jewish thinker David Hartman accounts for the other by maintaining the view that revelation is not necessarily a source of absolute and eternal truth. Rather, it is a moment of God's speaking within a particular human history and in a particular language. Revelation indicates God's willingness to meet human beings, with all our limitations, and, according to Hartman, is therefore "always fragmentary and incomplete."[24] Articulating its meanings in history requires constant interpretation. Once the particularity of revelation is acknowledged, the need for universalizing one's faith evaporates. Each revelation of transcendence, each distinct spiritual path, becomes a testimony to the complexity and fullness and unending richness of Divine reality. The principle of creation with which Hebrew scriptures begin universalizes the sanctity of life, extending it therefore beyond any particular revelation.[25]

In this outlook, the seven Noahide commandments become a vehicle for each distinct faith community to actualize a life of morality and ethics. Indeed, the very existence of a plurality of religious communities testifies to the rich tapestry of practices and perspectives inspired by the human quest for God and transcendence in history. The lengthy disputes and commentaries in Judaism on the Noahide commandments indicate the seriousness in the tradition regarding how to encounter the other, how to view and understand those whose faith commitments differ from one's own. They prompt one to reflect as to how a specific vision can encompass the broader dimensions of unlimited truth.

And so it is, then, as the midrash indicated, that God threw Truth to the ground, entrusting human beings as partners in the uncovering, revealing, and creation of the plurality of truths that constitute Divinity.

CONTRIBUTORS' QUESTIONS FOR ROCHELLE L. MILLEN

1. You argue that the Noahide laws promote pluralism. Yet Jews have 613 commandments; gentiles have only seven. Will an authentic pluralism allow for such a hierarchy of responsibilities? Does this uneven distribution of responsibilities *connote* condescension on the part of the Jewish tradition? Might it be the case that this attitude fosters religious *tolerance* rather than religious *pluralism*? If so, does it not constitute a form of inclusivist thinking? Further, if the Noahide code is that to which everyone must adhere in order to achieve life in the world

to come, how are we to reconcile the apparently universalist claims implied by the positing of such a code with the emphasis on a plurality of truths in the *Midrash Rabbah* on Genesis?

2. You say that "the seven Noahide laws establish the grounding of civilized societies." You go on to argue that "the Noahide commandments become a vehicle for each distinct faith community to actualize a life of morality and ethics." This defense of the Noahide laws seems to suggest that a belief in monotheism is a crucial element in creating what we have come to know as civilized society, society rooted in moral imperatives. How does this outlook fit with the fact that monotheism often aids and abets massive violence, including, some would argue, the Holocaust, twenty-first-century terrorism, and violent responses to the latter? Does your view imply that polytheist or atheist traditions do not per se give rise to those moral imperatives so critical to the existence of civilization as we know it?

RESPONSE BY ROCHELLE L. MILLEN

> Law may be viewed as a system of tension or a bridge linking a
> concept of reality to an imagined alternative.
> —Robert Cover, "Nomos and Narrative"

These two questions require that I fine-tune, sharpen, distill, and clarify significant implications of the ideas presented in my essay. I am happy to have the opportunity to do so, as the Noahide commandments are an important aspect of interfaith discussion.

The first part of the initial question is based on the assumption that greater responsibilities in a delimited area both connote and denote a hierarchy of responsibilities that is undergirded by an axiology. That is, the more responsibilities given an individual or group, the higher the value of the person or collectivity. This notion recalls the many discussions in both Germany and France during the Enlightenment about the civic emancipation of the Jews. Christian thinkers and political leaders, from Christian Wilhelm von Dohm and Joseph II to Napoleon wanted Jews to become more like them.[26] Jews would be accepted if they were less Jewish in their dress, behavior, and culture. Acceptance was predicated on sameness.

Such an equivalence—in order to be valued as I am, we must be the same—is explicitly addressed in the Mishnah, which states:

[And a single person only, Adam, was first created] for the sake of peace in the human race, that no person might say to another, "My ancestor was greater than your ancestor," and that the heretics should not say, "There are many powers in heaven and [only one] human being was first created to proclaim the greatness of the Holy One, blessed be He, for a human being stamps many coins with one die and they are all alike, but the King of kings . . . has stamped all humanity with the die of the first human and yet not one of them is like his fellow. Therefore everyone is duty bound to say, 'For my sake was the universe created.'" [27]

This text from the Mishnah expresses the greatness of God in creating a diverse world. Each subset is different: individuals, nations, cultures, and religions. But in the large scheme, each is equally significant in the configuration of the whole. In contradistinction to Enlightenment thinkers, rabbinic Judaism accords equal worth to dissimilarity. Thus I would not agree that the seven Noahide commandments connote "an attitude of condescension." Rather, their existence indicates the embrace of that which is distinct from oneself in that its value is equal. One does not "put up with" or merely tolerate those whose historical journey is different from one's own—which indeed would be inclusivist—but rather fosters a "live and let live" attitude; I have my story and you have yours.

The incisive second part of this first question goes to the heart of the conceptual parameters of the Noahide code. The midrashic text acknowledges the diversity of human truths, which continues to develop within history; it recognizes the fluidity between revelation (divine) and tradition (historical) as components of religion.[28] But such variation requires a common basis, the fundamental conditions without which history falls apart and is relegated to the realm of evil. An example is what is sometimes designated as the golden era in Spain. For a period of approximately three hundred years, before Christian hegemony slowly moved down the Iberian Peninsula, Jews, Muslims, and Christians lived together in a mostly stable society. Although Jews and Christians were *dhimmis*, or of secondary status under Muslim rule, they were protected minorities. Thus history, culture, and religious life flourished. The Jewish community produced astronomers, mathematicians, poets, grammarians, and biblical commentators. When one's body, property, and family are not in danger, spiritual and intellectual pursuits can proceed unimpeded.

The Noahide code is inclusive just as the midrashic text affirms a plurality of truths. How that code, a foundation for civilization, can nonetheless spawn monotheisms characterized by violence, terror, and atrocity is a weighty question. How can this be, if the code's aim is to create a society rooted in moral imperatives?[29] The answer is that even the foundation of human history—the striving for peace and safety and harmony—remains an ideal. One can profess to believe in God and misuse that belief as a tool of terror. Such misuse recognizes holiness only in those like oneself and is animated by power, absolutism, and triumph rather than respect, humility, and seeing God in the face of the other. Adultery, theft, and murder are prohibited in the Noahide code because of the human propensities for immorality, greed, and violence. No society has yet attained the best balance of human inclination and justice; we are all—individually, nationally, religiously, and culturally—works in progress. Redemption can be reached, but we are not yet there.

For these reasons, I find the Noahide code in Judaism significant, even inspiring. For the code recognizes and accepts as legitimate and of equal axiological value paths to the transcendent other than its own. It declares that while Jews have their story and their covenant, others have different stories and relationships with the Divine. And each is true in its own way, as long as it preserves the bases of the code, understood as a sine qua non for the journey toward the ultimate redemption. This is so even when a story or tradition is not strictly monotheistic, as in Buddhism or atheism. Nonetheless, in these cases a component is lacking. For the Noahide laws are not natural law in the sense that "all that is required of the nations is that they obey the moral law as dictated by human reason."[30] As Michael Wyschogrod indicates, such a view would imply that God's relationship is only with Israel; other nations would not be permitted their own covenantal relationship with God. In Wyschogrod's words: "This, however, is a biblical theology altogether unacceptable. It ignores the promise to Abraham that through his election the nations, too, will be blessed; it further ignores the covenant with Noah, which is not natural law but a covenant in its own right. . . . To be commanded by God is to be addressed by him, and it is therefore incumbent upon Israel to welcome the covenant of the nations with the God of Israel."[31] The Noahide laws as elucidated in Judaism embody a paradox, a healthy ambiguity. From a particular historical narrative of encounter with the Divine comes an embrace of the world created by that Divine power, a world with differing histories, distinct narratives, and alternative cultures. God's graciousness and redemptive aspects are open to us all. The Noahide code builds a bridge of acceptance between Judaism and other traditions.

NOTES

1   See Babylonian Talmud, *Shabbat* 55a, which explains why Truth (*emet*) is the seal or signet of God.

2   *Midrash Rabbah: Genesis* [in Hebrew] (Jerusalem: Lewin-Epstein, 1959), 8.5 (my translation).

3   If these are the words of the angels, then the quoted verse is seen as their urging God to let Truth grow so that it will once again reach heaven. I find this explanation less convincing. For additional interpretations of this midrash. *See* Samuel Abraham Adler, ed., *Aspaklaria* [in Hebrew] (Jerusalem: Aspaklaria, 1994), 3:183–91. My thanks to Henoch Millen for pointing out this collection.

4   *Midrash Rabbah Bamidbar*, 13.

5   Babylonian Talmud, *Sanhedrin* 56a.

6   *Tosefta Sanhedrin* 81:3: "The righteous of the nations of the world have a share in the world to come."

7   See Jacob Katz, *Exclusiveness and Tolerance: Studies in Jewish-Gentile Relations in Medieval and Modern Times* (West Orange, N.J.: Behrman House, 1983), 25n1.

8   Jacob Katz uses this expression. See ibid., 35–36.

9   See, for instance, Jeremy Cohen, *The Friars and the Jews: The Evolution of Medieval Anti-Judaism* (Ithaca, N.Y.: Cornell University Press, 1982); and Hyam Macoby, ed. and trans., *Judaism on Trial: Jewish-Christian Disputations in the Middle Ages* (East Brunswick, N.J.: Associated University Press, 1982).

10   See Moses Maimonides, *Book of Judges, Mishneh Torah*, ed. S. Rubenstein (Jerusalem: Mossad Harav Kook, 1975), 398; *Sefer Halekutim, Mishneh Torah*, ed. S. Frankel (New York: Bnei Yosef, 1998), 364; and David Novak, *The Image of the Non-Jew in Judaism: An Historical and Constructive Study of the Noahide Laws*, Toronto Studies in Theology 14 (Lewiston, N.Y.: Edwin Mellen Press, 1983), especially 275–318. It is important to consider that both Spinoza and Moses Mendelssohn possessed corrupted texts of this work of Maimonides when they wrote. See Spinoza, *Tractatus Theologico-Politicus*, chap. 5, 47; and discussion in Katz, *Exclusiveness and Tolerance*, 69–179.

11   See note 6 above.

12   See the analyses in the works cited in note 10 above, as well as the reference in Katz, *Exclusiveness and Tolerance* (174), in which he alludes to the corruption in the Maimonides text used by both Spinoza and Mendelssohn. They had the text as I have translated it. A detailed examination of the textual issue is given by Eugene B. Korn, "Gentiles, the World to Come, and Judaism: The Odyssey of a Rabbinic Text," in *Modern Judaism* 14, no. 3 (1994): 265–87.

13   The controversy over this text—and its implications for halachic Judaism—per-

sists in some circles. For an explication of the differences between the views of Rabbi Abraham Isaac Kook and Rabbi Velvel Soloveitchik. *See* Korn, "Gentiles, the World to Come, and Judaism."

14 Quoted in Katz, *Exclusiveness and Tolerance*, 117.

15 Maimonides, *Book of Judges, Mishneh Torah*, 398.

16 E-mail discussion with Eugene B. Korn, October 14–15, 2007.

17 Katz, *Exclusiveness and Tolerance*, 193; Mary C. Boys, "The Covenant in Contemporary Ecclesial Documents," in *Two Faiths, One Covenant? Jewish and Christian Identity in the Presence of the Other*, ed. Eugene B. Korn and John T. Pawlikowski (Lanham, Md.: Rowman and Littlefield, 2005), 102.

18 I have not dealt here with the other category found in both biblical and rabbinic sources, that of *ger toshav*, or "resident alien." For further explication. *See* Novak, *The Image of the Non-Jew in Judaism*; and Korn, "Gentiles, the World to Come, and Judaism."

19 Katz, *Exclusiveness and Tolerance*, 168.

20 See Alan Levine, ed., *Early Modern Skepticism and the Origins of Toleration* (Lanham, Md.: Lexington Books, 1999).

21 Moshe Greenberg, *Studies in the Bible and Jewish Thought* (Philadelphia: Jewish Publication Society, 1995), 373.

22 Ibid., 386.

23 Ibid.

24 David Hartman, *A Heart of Many Rooms* (Woodstock, Vt.: Jewish Lights Publishing, 1999), 159.

25 Ibid., 161.

26 See Paul Mendes-Flohr and Jehuda Reinharz, eds., *The Jew in the Modern World: A Documentary History*, 2nd ed. (New York: Oxford University Press, 1995), 28–48, 123–36.

27 Mishnah, *Sanhedrin* 4:5 (my translation).

28 See Gershom Scholem, *The Messianic Idea in Judaism and Other Essays on Jewish Spirituality* (New York: Schocken Books, 1974), 282–303.

29 See Michael Wyschogrod, *Abraham's Promise: Judaism and Jewish-Christian Relations*, ed. R. Kendall Soulen (Grand Rapids, Mich.: Wm. B. Eerdmans, 2004), especially 179–82, 190–98.

30 Ibid., 185.

31 Ibid., 186.

10

Normative Islamic (Qur'anic) Teachings on Pluralism

Reflections on "The People of the Book"

RIFFAT HASSAN

On September 11, 2001, the United States arguably suffered the most serious foreign attack ever on its soil. American intelligence agencies identified the perpetrators as being of Muslim and Arab origin. The post–September 11 world is radically different from the world that existed before that fateful day. The sense of invulnerability and invincibility that characterized the consciousness of the world's lone superpower was suddenly, and irrevocably, lost. Understandably, many Americans wanted to lash out at those responsible for the dreadful terror. Most of the immediate perpetrators were dead and could not be punished. But still very much alive were others—such as Osama bin Laden—who were believed to have masterminded and financed the assault. Apprehending them seemed necessary to make a bleeding nation whole again and to restore confidence in the "manifest destiny" of the United States to lead and control the world.

In the aftermath of September 11, 2001, Islam and Muslims and the association of both with violence has been the focus of more attention than perhaps at any other point in modern history. Much of this attention— particularly in the case of mainstream American television coverage—has been negative, not only with regard to those who committed the criminal acts but also with regard to Islam, Muslims, and Arabs.

The September 11 assault on the United States has been condemned strongly by the global community including a large number of Muslims, ranging from leaders of Muslim countries to ordinary people. From the outset, however, the crisis was perceived and described in terms that polarized the world into two absolutely opposed camps. This worldview, which became dominant in the discourse of both the American administration and the U.S. media, was symbolized by expressions such as "us versus them," "either you are with us or you are against us," and "good versus evil." The dualism that permeated this discourse seemed, at times, to be cosmic in magnitude.

However one interprets the fateful events of September 11, 2001, one thing is clear. The world changed forever on that day. This change poses a serious challenge both for (non-Muslim) Westerners and for Muslims. Is it possible to "depolarize" the world and to build a bridge between "the West" and "the world of Islam" in the aftermath of 9/11? Reflection on this crucial question needs to recall the philosopher George Santayana's insight that those who do not remember the past and know their history are condemned to repeat it. In particular, we need to be aware of the West's long history of negative imaging and stereotyping of Muslims and Islam.

Edward Said has ably documented how Muslims, Arabs, and Islam have been misrepresented persistently by "Orientalists." Although Said may have succeeded in discrediting the term *Orientalist*, the aforesaid Orientalists have played a major part in shaping Western perceptions of Muslims, Arabs, and Islam. Their mind-set, exhibited by many media "experts" and non-Muslim academics such as Bernard Lewis (writing about "Muslim rage") and Samuel Huntington (writing about "the clash of civilizations"), is similar to that of the non-Muslim detractors of Islam in earlier times. In such an environment, bridge building between Muslims and non-Muslim Americans has become a most challenging task, one that is more vital today than ever before.

All too often two key shortcomings hinder interreligious dialogue: first, inadequate distinctions are made between the fundamental teachings of a religion and the cultural practices of its adherents; second, invidious comparisons are made between the highest ideals and best practices of one's own religion and the worst features of another religion. Given the persistent demonization of Islam in the United States and other parts of the world since September 11, it is evident to me that any serious effort to engage in authentic dialogue with Muslims must start with a review of normative Islamic—or Qur'anic—teachings on religious and ethical pluralism, rather than with perceptions of popular Muslim culture. Muslims regard the Qur'an as the highest source of authority. Therefore, I focus on identifying those major teachings of the Qur'an that are relevant in this context, particularly those passages referring to interaction among the *Ahl al-Kitab*, or "People of the Book": Jews, Christians, and Muslims.

The cardinal principle of Islam is belief in the absolute oneness of God, or *Tawhid*. In the opening chapter of the Qur'an, *Al-Fatiha*, God, is described as *Ar-Rahman* (the Most Merciful), *Ar-Rahim* (the Most Gracious), and *Rabb al-'alamin* (the Lord of all the peoples and universes). As noted by Fathi Osman, in the Qur'an God is related not to any particular place or people but to all creation.[1] The Qur'an affirms that God "cares for all creatures" (2:268). As numerous verses testify, its message is universal (25:1, 36:69–70, 38:87, 81:27–28). The Qur'an also affirms the universality of the prophet Muhammad's mission.[2]

Verses such as the following express the nonexclusive spirit of Islam, an often-repeated teaching of the Qur'an:

> Verily, those who have attained to faith (in this divine writ), as well as those who follow the Jewish faith, and the Christians, and the Sabians— all who believe in God and the Last Day and do righteous deeds—shall have their reward with their Sustainer; and no fear need they have, and neither shall they grieve. (2:62)

> Indeed, everyone who surrenders his whole being unto God, and is a doer of good withal, shall have his reward with his Sustainer; and all such need have no fear, and neither shall they grieve. (2:112)

> Be conscious of the Day on which you shall be brought back unto God, whereupon every human being shall be repaid in full for what he has earned, and none shall be wronged. (2:281)

Since God is the universal creator who sends guidance to all humanity, Muslims are commanded by the Qur'an to affirm (a) the divine message given to all the previous prophets and (b) the continuity of Islam with previous revelations and prophets. Muslims are also expressly forbidden to make a distinction among the prophets, as can be seen from the following verses:

> Say: "We believe in God, and in that which has been bestowed from on high upon us, and that which has been bestowed upon Abraham and Ishmael and Isaac and Jacob and their descendants, and that which has been vouchsafed to Moses and Jesus, and that which has been vouchsafed to all the [other] prophets by their Sustainer: we make no distinction between any of them. And it is unto Him that we surrender ourselves." (2:136)

> Step by step has He bestowed upon thee from on high this divine writ, setting forth the truth which confirms whatever there remains [of earlier revelations]: for it is He who has bestowed from on high the Torah and the Gospel aforetime as a guidance to mankind, and it is He who has bestowed (upon man) the standard by which to discern the true from the false. (3:13)

> Say: "We believe in God, and in that which has been bestowed from on high upon us, and that which has been bestowed upon Abraham and Ishmael and Isaac and Jacob and their descendants, and that which has been vouchsafed by their Sustainer unto Moses and Jesus and all the [other] prophets: we make no distinction between any of them. And unto Him do we surrender ourselves." (3:84)

> Behold, We have inspired thee [O Prophet] just as We inspired Noah and all the Prophets after him—as We inspired Abraham, and Ishmael. And Isaac, and Jacob, and their descendants including Jesus and Job, and Jonah, and Aaron, and Solomon; and as We vouchsafed unto David a book of divine wisdom; and [We inspired other] apostles whom We have mentioned to thee ere this, as well as apostles whom We have not mentioned to thee; and as God spoke His Word unto Moses: (We sent all these) apostles as heralds of glad tidings and as warners, so that men might have no excuse before God after (the coming of) these apostles: and God is indeed almighty, wise. (4:163)

> In matters of faith, He has ordained for you that which He enjoined upon Noah—and into which We gave thee [O Muhammad] insight through revelation—as well as that which We had enjoined upon Abraham, and

Moses, and Jesus: steadfastly uphold the (true) faith, and do not break up your unity therein. (42:13)

One major reason why the prophet Abraham is so important in the Islamic tradition is that he symbolizes Qur'anic teachings regarding the unity of all believers. Not only is he the prophet most often mentioned in the Qur'an after Muhammad, but he is also regarded in a significant way as the first *muslim*—a term signifying total submission to God. The Qur'an states that "Abraham was neither a 'Jew' nor a 'Christian,' but was one who surrendered himself unto God; and he was not of those who ascribe divinity to aught beside Him" (3:67). The Qur'an regards Abraham as a model monotheist who was *haneef* (true in faith). Referring to him as *khaleel Allah* (a friend of God), the Qur'an asks rhetorically, "And who could be better in faith than he who surrenders his whole being unto God and is a doer of good withal, and follows the creed of Abraham and turns away from all that is false—seeing that God exalted Abraham with His love?" (4:125).

According to the Qur'an, Abraham's spirit enabled Muslims (and other believers in God) to become witnesses for humankind: "And strive hard in God's cause with all the striving that is due to Him: it is He who has elected you [to carry His message], and has laid no hardship on you in [anything that pertains to] religion, [and made you follow] the creed of your forefather Abraham. It is He who has named you—in bygone times as well as in this [divine writ]—'those who have surrendered themselves to God,' so that the Apostle might bear witness to truth before you, and that you might bear witness to it before all mankind" (22:78).

Among the God-given rights strongly affirmed by the Qur'an, the following are particularly pertinent in the context of religious and ethical pluralism:

The Right to Life: Upholding the sanctity and absolute value of human life, the Qur'an says: "Do not take any human being's life [the life] which God has declared to be sacred—otherwise than in (the pursuit of) justice: this has He enjoined upon you so that you might use your reason" (6:151). Emphasizing that the life of each individual is comparable to that of an entire community, the Qur'an also states: "We ordain[ed] unto the children of Israel that if anyone slays a human being—unless it be [in punishment] for murder or for spreading corruption on earth—it shall be as though he had slain all mankind; whereas if anyone saves a life, it shall be as though he had saved the lives of all mankind" (5:32).

The Right to Dignity: The Qur'an categorically and emphatically proclaims, "We have conferred dignity on the children of Adam" (17:70). Therefore, the humanity of all persons, regardless of other differentiating factors including religious belief, must be respected by Muslims.

The Right to Free Belief in Religion: The well-known Qur'anic proclamation that "there shall be no coercion in matters of faith" guarantees freedom of religion and worship (2:256). According to fundamental Islamic teaching, non-Muslims living in Muslim territories should have the freedom to follow their own faith traditions without fear or harassment. Numerous Qur'anic passages clearly state that the responsibility of the prophet Muhammad is to communicate the message of God but not to compel anyone to believe. For instance: "And say: 'The truth [has now come] from your Sustainer: let, then, him who wills, believe in it, and let him who wills, reject it'" (18:29). The Qur'an also makes clear that God will judge human beings not on the basis of what they profess but on the basis of their belief and righteous conduct (2:62, 5:69).

The Qur'an regards diversity of peoples and religious and ethical perspectives as a part of God's design. In a remarkable passage in which reference is made to the unity and diversity of humankind, the Qur'an states: "O men! Behold, We have created you all out of a male and a female, and have made you into nations and tribes, so that you might come to know one another. Verily, the noblest of you in the sight of God is the one who is most deeply conscious of Him. Behold, God is all-knowing, all-aware" (49:13). This verse makes clear that one of the basic purposes of diversity is to encourage dialogue among different peoples and also that a person's ultimate worth is determined not by what group he or she belongs to but by his or her degree of God-consciousness.

Additional Qur'anic verses attest that a plurality of religions and ethical viewpoints is sanctioned by God:

> Every community faces a direction of its own, of which He (God) is the focal point. Vie, therefore, with one another in doing good works. Wherever you may be, God will gather you unto Himself: for verily, God has the power to will anything. (2:148)

> Unto every one of you have We appointed a (different) law and way of life. And if God had so willed, He could surely have made you all one single community: but (He willed it otherwise) in order to test you by means of

what He has vouchsafed unto you. Vie, then, with one another in doing good works! Unto God you all must return; and then He will make you truly understand all that on which you were wont to differ. (5:48)

Having lived in the West for the greater part of my life, I am all too painfully aware that many people in the West—including many Christians and Jews who, like Muslims, are "People of the Book"—see Islam as a religion spread by the sword and Muslims as religious fanatics who are zealously committed to waging "holy war" against non-Muslims or even against nonconforming Muslims. While it is beyond the scope of this essay to examine the historical roots of these perceptions, I stress that my Muslim identity means not turning away in hatred or anger from those who regard Muslims as "adversaries" but engaging in dialogue with them in a spirit of amity and goodwill, as prescribed by the Qur'an in the following verse: "Do not argue with the followers of earlier revelation otherwise than in a most kindly manner—unless it be such as are bent on evildoing—and say: 'We believe in that which has been bestowed from on high upon us, as well as that which has been bestowed upon you, for our God and your God is one and the same, and it is unto Him that we [all] surrender ourselves'" (29:46).

The ethical imperative central to Qur'anic teaching and the normative Islamic worldview is to enjoin the good—*al-ma'ruf*—and forbid the evil—*al-munkar*. Within the parameters of this categorical imperative, Islam is open to accepting and cooperating with any religious or ethical perspective.

CONTRIBUTORS' QUESTIONS FOR RIFFAT HASSAN

1. All three Western monotheisms are based on a revealed "book" or scripture (Tanakh, New Testament, Qur'an). None of these religions depends on its scripture alone; interpretive traditions are normative as well. Is it really possible to go back directly to the foundational scripture (in your case, the Qur'an) and yet remain true to the religious tradition as it has been shaped over history and come down to us? Is not any attempt to go back directly to the founding document (of any of our traditions) in fact a proposal for a radical reform that introduces a break with a religion as we have received it? Can such a "return" succeed, as you seem to imply, in closing the gap between the founding

teachings and the "cultural practices" evident in the Islamic world over the centuries?

2. You have outlined Qur'anic views that embrace pluralism; can you identify values shared by the three Abrahamic religions that could form a basis for needed trialogue, particularly in contexts that include the Holocaust and twenty-first-century violence and counterviolence that implicate all three of the major monotheistic traditions? What are the main issues of difference that such trialogue needs to engage?

RESPONSE BY RIFFAT HASSAN

Jews, Christians, and Muslims do not understand the meaning of "revelation" in identical ways. While Jews and Christians take their respective scriptures to be "divinely inspired," the human authorship of these texts is not denied. The vast majority of Muslims, however, do not regard the Qur'an as a "divinely inspired" text that was written by one or more human authors. They staunchly believe that the Qur'an is the Word of God "revealed" by the archangel Gabriel to the prophet Muhammad, who transmitted it, without change or error, to others. This process of revelation and transmission took place over a period of almost twenty-three years. As written by officially designated scribes, the Qur'an was completed during the lifetime of Prophet Muhammad, who is believed to have recited the Qur'an in its entirety in the last Ramadan of his life.

I have noted that the Qur'an is the highest authority in Islam. The text is distinct from, and has primacy over, what may be called "the Islamic tradition." Over many generations, however, Muslims have interpreted the Qur'an through the lens of the cultural milieus in which "the Islamic tradition" developed. As the central point of reference in Islamic theology and religious thought, the Qur'an has played pivotal roles at critical times in Muslim history. For instance, in the nineteenth and twentieth centuries, when much of the Muslim world was under colonial rule, the rallying cry of the Muslim modernist reformers and would-be liberators was "Back to the Qur'an, forward with jihad." This admonition implied that to identify Islam's core ethical principles and values and to get Muslim history back on track, Muslims should return to the foundation of their faith: the Qur'an. Having done so, they had to exert their mental capabilities (jihad) to figure out how best to implement those principles and values in the current context.

Should the modernist movement that advocated a return to the Qur'an be seen as calling for radical reform entailing a break with traditional religion? This question can be answered both positively and negatively. The modernist movement was radical in that it did not regard tradition as sacrosanct and challenged the claim of the conservative *ulema* (scholars) regarding the "finality" of the popular schools of Muslim law. Muhammad Iqbal (1877–1938), arguably the most outstanding Muslim thinker since Jalal al-Din Rumi (1207–1273), believed it necessary "to tear off from Islam the hard crust which has immobilized an essentially dynamic outlook on life, and to rediscover the original verities of freedom, equality, and solidarity with a view to rebuild our moral, social, and political ideals out of their original simplicity and universality."[3] In another sense, however, the modernist movement was not radical. It did not aspire to break with the Islamic religious tradition but wanted a return to foundations that would free the tradition from fossilization and stagnation and make it live vibrantly again.

Elsewhere in my writings, I have discussed the discrepancy between normative Qur'anic teachings and the way women are treated in most Muslim cultures. As a feminist theologian and activist, I have found that the best hope for the empowerment of women in Muslim societies and communities lies in demonstrating in a compelling way that negative cultural ideas and attitudes toward women are not warranted by a correct reading of the Qur'anic text, a text that is highly affirming of women's rights and dignity. While patriarchy has colored most interpretations of women-related Qur'anic texts, I affirm that the Qur'an itself represents the justice and mercy of God and is free of cultural biases. I believe that as more and more Muslim women and men become aware of the non-patriarchal and compassion- and justice-centered teachings of the Qur'an, the gap between God's intentions and cultural practices will diminish.

In response to the second question posed to me, I list key ideas, beliefs, and values shared by the Abrahamic faiths, followed by a listing of differences among the three traditions. First, here are elements that can advance the needed trialogue among Jews, Christians, and Muslims:

1. The three traditions share belief in the One God, who created all that exists. Since all human beings are created by One God, they are equal in terms of their creation.

2. According to Genesis 1, Adam was created in the image of God, and according to the Qur'an, God conferred dignity on all "children of Adam." These texts imply that, owing to its special status in God's creation, humanity has special responsibilities, namely, to be God's steward on earth.

3. The figure of Abraham is central to the three monotheistic faiths and is a powerful symbol of unity among Jews, Christians, and Muslims.

4. The prophets mentioned in the Hebrew Bible are recognized as such not only by Jews but also by Christians and Muslims. They are a connecting link among the three traditions.

5. Common to the three Abrahamic faiths is an ethical framework in which primary emphasis is placed on justice and compassion. Working collaboratively for the welfare of disadvantaged or marginalized people—something stressed by all three Abrahamic faiths—would make the interaction among Jews, Christians, and Muslims a solid basis for peace building.

6. Common to the three Abrahamic faiths is the imperative to be instruments of peace in the world. (The Qur'anic text, for example, claims that justice is a precondition for peace and, therefore, no genuine peace building can take place without a concurrent effort to create a just environment.)

With regard to the main issues of difference that trialogue among Jews, Christians, and Muslims needs to engage, I wish to note that since the late 1970s I have been intensively and extensively engaged in interreligious dialogue among the three Abrahamic religions. While this dialogue/trialogue has contributed to my personal growth as a Muslim woman, theologian, scholar, teacher, and activist, I have not seen it making a visible difference "on the ground" in terms of relationships between Muslims and non-Muslims (Christians and Jews). Salient reasons for this outcome are that Muslims feel that in general Jews and Christians (a) lack adequate knowledge of Islam, (b) do not regard Islam as being on a par with Christianity and Judaism, and (c) expect that interreligious dialogue should be carried out on their terms (mostly Christian), which may be alien or even hostile to Muslims' experience and understanding of Islam.

Development of a sound methodology for interreligious dialogue among Muslims, Jews, and Christians is crucial. In my view, the following ideas should be central to this methodology:

1. Trialogue participants should have sound knowledge of the normative teachings of the three faiths.

2. Authentic dialogue cannot exist without mutual respect. Respect for Islam entails that its basic terms are understood and referred to correctly. It also entails that the meaning given to terms of central significance in Islam should be recognizable and acceptable to Muslims (*jihad*, for example, which is generally and often misleadingly translated as "holy war," in fact refers to moral, intellectual, and spiritual struggle for the development of the self and the community).

3. In the modern period, numerous Muslim thinkers and activists sought to reform aspects of the Islamic tradition. These reformers were instrumental in liberating the Muslim world from Western imperialism and colonialism by the mid-twentieth century. However, colonialism was followed by neocolonialism in a number of Muslim countries, and new reform initiatives were undertaken by progressive Muslims in areas such as women's rights, literacy programs, poverty eradication, and economic development. Interreligious trialogue would be enhanced if these initiatives were better recognized and supported by Western countries, especially the United States. Unfortunately, these steps have been largely ignored while attention has focused on extremist views.

4. Social transformation can come only from within; it cannot be imposed from without by force. Strengthening the moderates in Muslim societies seems to have become the agenda of many governments in today's world.

5. A course of action that would be effective in enhancing interreligious dialogue would be to provide leadership training for select groups of Muslims and non-Muslims. These groups could be educated in particular regarding the normative teachings of Islam and the ways in which these teachings are being violated by a number of cultural practices.

Currently, a widespread feeling among Muslims is that Islam is misunderstood and unfairly maligned. A new methodology for interreligious dialogue, one that embraces the points mentioned above, can encourage Muslims, Christians, and Jews to address difficult problems collaboratively and constructively.

NOTES

1   Fathi Osman, *Concepts of the Qur'an: A Topical Reading*, 2nd ed. (Los Angeles: Multimedia Vera International Publications, 1999), 23.
2   For instance. *See* Qur'an 34:28.
3   Muhammad Iqbal, *The Reconstruction of Religious Thought in Islam* (Lahore, Pakistan: Kitab Bhavan, 1962), 156.

11

Reflexivity and *Tawallî* between Jews, Christians, and Muslims

BÜLENT ŞENAY

The twenty-first century is beset by seemingly intractable problems which point to the fact that we are suffering a deep spiritual crisis. Despite positive developments in many spheres of life, scientific breakthroughs among them, humanity still lacks the wisdom to keep our differences and disagreements within safe and appropriate boundaries. Because so many of us see the earth as a resource to consume rather than as something holy, we not only risk environmental catastrophe—*halaak* (utter destruction) or *shoah* (catastrophic destruction)—we have also lost our sense of the sacred inviolability of the individual human being. The darkest epiphanies of our century—the Holocaust, Rwanda, Bosnia, and Nagorno-Karabakh, among others—reveal that our ability to harm and mutilate one another has kept pace with our development, our "progress." Threatened by self-destruction, we need a spiritual revolution that can take us beyond those theological disagreements and interreligious conflicts which continue to inflame violence.

Religion ought to cultivate wisdom regarding the inviolability of the human being. Although religious traditions provide much of the spiritual groundwork that could enable human beings to overcome the phenomenon of exclusivity, intolerance and religiously motivated terrorism abound. Of course, if seen in isolation from the whole of their traditions, individual scriptural passages in the Hebrew Bible, the New Testament, and the Qur'an can easily be utilized to sanction violence and cruelty. The scriptures have been and are still being used in this way, thus serving to set in motion some of the darkest episodes of our recent history. Our response to this phenomenon should be self-criticism and, especially, *reflexive listening.*

From Moses through Jesus to Muhammad (peace be upon them all), we have a spiritual heritage that remains relevant and important because—and this point may shock many who think they are "religious"—the insights and messages of the founders of our traditions reflect relatively little interest in formal doctrine or theology. These spiritual giants taught that what matters is not solely *what* one believes but *how* one believes. The founders did, of course, teach us rituals to help keep us close to their message, but they mainly emphasized the ethical significance of what they taught. Morality must be at the heart of spiritual life. The only way we could genuinely encounter God, Allah, or any aspect of divine reality is to live a compassionate life, a life with *rahmah* (compassion or mercy) and *wadd* (love).

Although these teachers lived and had to survive in often violent societies, Moses, Jesus, and Muhammad all preached the importance of empathy and compassion; they taught that people must abandon their egotism and the violence that can so easily follow from self-centeredness. Despite the fact that aspects of teachings purported to them have often been used to legitimize "cleansing" massacres or crusades to "purify" the world and the "sacred order" of things, such readings of holy texts distort their essential messages: *kindness* in Jewish thought, *love* in the message of Jesus, and *afw* (forgiveness) in the Qur'an and Sunnah (the whole of lawful practices followed in Islam). Thus Muslims say "peace be upon them" every time they hear the names of these teachers. Moses, Jesus, and Muhammad all preached benevolence that was not to be confined to one's own people but should be extended to the entire world.

The golden rule of this spiritual anthropology was—and remains—"Do not do unto others what you would not have done to yourself." Without departing from our own traditions, we can learn from others how to enhance our particular pursuit of the ethical life. This insight helps explain why Islam was originally called *tazakkah*, a word related to *zakaat*, or "purity." Its meaning combines traits of purification, generosity, and compassion, indicating that anyone who enters into Islam should develop these characteristics. Working to do so is the ultimate jihad, or striving in God's cause.

The key question is how we deal with our differences, particularly, but not only, the differences found in the Abrahamic traditions of Judaism, Christianity, and Islam. Any dialogue/trialogue is an attempt to straddle borders of difference. If we generally agree that it is better to venture beyond the thresholds of our own *intellectual* borders, then we might acknowledge that we also need to venture beyond the thresholds of our *spiritual* borders. In dialogical or trialogical encounter, we need to cross these thresholds. Surely, the experience of crossing thresholds—especially when we are not quite certain at what point we have crossed—is the experience of discovery, surprise, and even risk. Inhabiting such borders may be termed an "in-between" condition. Crossing thresholds makes us vulnerable, as it makes the subject face the unfamiliar, the stranger, the "other." Spiritual and intellectual vulnerability characterizes all interreligious encounter—indeed, all encounters with the other. Dwelling on the borders is challenging and transformative, particularly with regard to facing the multiplicity of religious others in an age of globalization.

Alongside the multiplicity of religious otherness, the voices of tribalism, provincialism, and sectarianism resound; indeed, they often appear to be the dominant voices in religious discourse. However, I believe they are fighting what must be a losing battle. Though religious differences will certainly continue to exist, my strong belief is that humankind must move toward fellowship. Differences should not and need not lead to conflict. The sometimes unpleasant job of criticism must be carried out, yet with reflexivity (the practice of observing one's self as knower) and practical wisdom (*phronesis*, from Aristotle, or *al-hikmah al-amaliyyah*, from the medieval philosopher Abu Nasr al-Farabi) *conflict* can be avoided, and appreciation of diversity can be expanded.

Unfortunately, religions still legitimize ideologies that reinforce nationalist and cultural conflict. Elements within Islam, for example, function as a major source of anti-Western polemics. Fundamentalist Islam not only inspires violent understandings of jihad but also plays a central role in intra-Islamic conflicts in the Middle East and increasingly in Africa. Although most violence has ceased in Ireland, Irish Catholic nationalists remain at odds with Protestant Loyalists. Jewish religious fundamentalism poses a serious threat for peace in the Middle East and within Israel itself. (Sometimes, for example, the attitudes of Jewish fundamentalists toward

Jewish moderates seem to be more militant than their attitudes toward non-Jews are.) Conflict within and among the adherents of religions will remain a feature of the contemporary religious scene in the twenty-first century. No chance of Utopia here! Borders still exist. In order to keep two sides of the border together, what we need to do is listen to the other. Listening to the other requires reflexivity. Jesus had such reflexivity in mind when he told the Pharisees of his (and our) time: "Let the one who is sinless throw the first stone" (John 8:7).

In different stages of my life, I have been on a journey toward reflection and listening. I have visited Bethlehem and sat next to faithful Christians who, with their deepest love for Jesus, kissed the marble stone that traditionally marks his birthplace. I have stood at the Western Wall in Jerusalem where vibrations from the chanting of psalms rose into the sky, creating a spiritual atmosphere comparable with the Muslim pilgrimage of Hajj, where prayers uplift the spiritual traveler with love, devotion, and tears. I have sat next to a young Muslim who was quietly shedding tears of spiritual engagement with the Divine or the remembrance of Muhammad, the Prophet of Islam, during Friday prayer in the Masjid al-Aqsa in Jerusalem. During all these times, I could not help but consider what a strange fellowship this is: God seekers in every land lifting their voices in the most disparate ways imaginable to the God of all life.

Listening is at the core of my journey and its observations. Listening, I have found, is the first step toward straddling borders—or maintaining them respectfully. Listening is the beginning of reflexivity. Reflexivity, as I understand it, is the practice of observing and locating one's self as a knower within certain cultural and sociohistorical contexts, a process that entails awareness of the limits and relativities of those contexts. Reflexivity leads to self-awareness, scholarly accountability, and recognition of the range of human truths. Reflexivity requires objectivity in recognizing subjectivities across borders.

Reflexivity enhances awareness that religion includes three spheres of existence: (1) I and God (*nafs* [self] and Allah); (2); I and myself (I and my *nafs*); and (3) I and other selves (my *nafs* and other *nafses*). The third sphere concerns otherness. This third sphere, especially, should make us see that religion is not a theory. In particular, revealed religions such as Judaism, Christianity, and Islam propose principles and reflections—not theories— about how to live. Theories classify observations and seek to comprehend people in terms of the third-person plural. Theorizing about people and societies can create "otherizing," a mode of objectifying others. Theorizing about others may well create a "them" versus "us" situation. With regard to the "them" created by theorizing, Klaus Krippendorff argues as follows:

> All of "them" are labeled and assigned to particular classes on account of [those alleged] characteristics that all members of such classes are assumed to share. . . . In everyday languaging, third-person pronouns refer to those absent. Theorizing makes this absence a virtue that bestows on theorists the freedom to characterize others in ways radically different (and inferior) to themselves. . . . Theorizing [is] responsible for estranging others from ourselves. . . . If theorizing . . . continue[s] to dominate our understanding of other human beings, it [will] unwittingly [create a kind of] intellectual imperialism.[1]

Theorizing, in other words, has the potential to prevent us from engaging the other in authentic dialogue.

How must Muslims engage the religious other? My response begins with a word about tolerance. Tolerance can easily lead to arrogance. Tolerance means that there is the one who tolerates and the one who is tolerated, a relationship that keeps equality, let alone hospitality, to a minimum. Instead of tolerance, I propose coexistence based on recognition of the other-as-sacred. Adherents of "truth-claiming" religions need not drop their truth claims, although they should come to recognize, as a first step, a distinction between truth claims and what constitutes human responsibility toward the other. In my view, judging one another on the basis of absolute truth claims is not a genuinely religious act but rather a form of arrogance. Yes, each tradition may have its own definition of infidel, but such definitions easily lead to the creation of fixed borders. If they care about the good of humankind, adherents of different religions should come to recognize that it is ultimately in God's hands to judge who acts morally or immorally here on earth. The intrinsic religious value of other traditions can be acknowledged through making a clear distinction between God-as-sole-judge and human beings as finite moral agents.

As an example of what I mean, consider that the Qur'anic concept of *Ahl al-Kitab* (People of the Book) acknowledges the intrinsic value of the Judeo-Christian tradition, an idea different from mere tolerance. Qur'anic verses—such as those that advise "no compulsion in religion," that God is the Most Loving (*al-Wadood*), and that "it may be that Allah will grant love [and friendship (*tawallî*)] between you and those whom ye (now) hold as enemies" (Qur'an 60:7)—provide clear guidance with regard to how Muslims should relate to the religious other.[2] The Qur'anic vision of how to encounter the other can be termed "the ethics of *tawallî*."

Some verses in the Qur'an scarcely encourage amicable relations among the three Abrahamic communities. Examples include:

> O ye who believe! Take not the Jews and the Christians for your friends and protectors: They are but friends and protectors to each other. And he amongst you that turns to them (for friendship) is of them. Verily Allah guideth not a people unjust. (5:51)

> Never will the Jews or the Christians be satisfied with thee unless thou follow their form of religion. Say: "The Guidance of Allah, that is the (only) Guidance." Wert thou to follow their desires after the knowledge which hath reached thee, then wouldst thou find neither Protector nor helper against Allah. (2:120)

Those familiar with the *usool*, or methodology, of Islamic exegesis will know that these rulings are not absolute but conditional in that the message implies "Do not take them as friends (or rulers) if and when they cooperate against Muslims."

However, many Muslims read these verses in the context of colonialism, evangelization, and Orientalism. Such interpreters take these contexts to be the contemporary manifestation of a centuries-long anti-Islamic bias often encouraged by Jews and Christians. Verses such as those cited above are then read in radical/fundamentalist ways rooted in Muslim distrust and suspicion of everything Western. Given such common perceptions, many Muslims may be unable or unwilling to distinguish between the objective and profound Western Islamologists and those who are biased, hostile, and superficial. This inability, of course. Seeps into public perceptions as well. With such perceptions as background, youths poorly educated in Islam may consider these verses to be legitimate grounds for violence at a time when other conditions feed a sense of siege in a particular geographic location. Such circumstances can make it difficult for Muslims to comprehend that there is no single verse in the Qur'an that categorically excludes or casts blame on the People of the Book. In other words, the Qur'an is not essentialist regarding the religious other, a point that is crucial for our understanding of Islam. All the verses in the Qur'an that criticize Jews or Christians—mostly Jews—do so by blaming "those among them" who engage in unethical, hostile, or arrogant behavior.

The Qur'an speaks negatively not about religions but about certain kinds of religious individuals. It recognizes the plurality of religious communities. Verses that criticize the religious conduct of non-Muslims do not negate religious pluralism and should not be used to do so. In any case, far more numerous are Qur'anic passages that emphasize mutual recognition and insist on dialogue between Muslims and the People of the Book. Without necessarily denying the authenticity and universality of the truth claims of the message of the Qur'an as Sacred Text, we must also recognize that there are texts in that scripture that need to be understood in their historical context and in parallel with co-texts, that is, with other similar verses. Then we will easily realize that the ethics of *tawallî* is at the core of the Qur'anic message.

The Qur'anic term *jidal* (dialogue) is also helpful for understanding this ethic. Believers are invited to enter *al-jidal al-ahsan* (the fairest debate): "Invite (all) to the Way of thy Lord with wisdom and beautiful preaching; and argue with them in ways that are best and most gracious: for thy Lord knoweth best, who have strayed from His Path, and who receive guidance" (Qur'an 16:125). Unless we understand the texts in their rightful context, our century will continue facing a serious threat to world peace. As for the Islamic world, it is not difficult to realize that the fundamental clash is located *within* the Muslim community rather than between Muslims and non-Muslims.

Muslim societies must rediscover an "ethics of disagreement" already established in Islamic tradition. This ethics of disagreement is also needed for relationships between Muslims and non-Muslims. An ethics of disagreement is at the core of *al-jidal al-ahsan*. *Al-jidal al-ahsan* is the sole path to authentic trialogue. The first rule of *al-jidal al-ahsan* is self-criticism. As I suggested above, genuine religion requires reflecting on the "ethical I" rather than on "them." Typically, "them" is an essentialist category. True religion should not offer fixed categories encompassing the religious other. The kind of religious philosophy I believe to be authentic is one that relates otherness to goodness. If a particular person is good, that individual is good whether or not he or she is classified as an "infidel" in historical or cultural terms. Calling on the existing heritage of the wisdom traditions represented by the Abrahamic religions, we need to develop an unconditional ethical relationship with the other that does not allow us to dominate him or her, that does not deny the other's differences from me, and that does not remove these differences in the name of a conceptual unity in which he or she is objectified by me. Without establishing such an ethical philosophy, there will be no recognition of the other in his or her genuine otherness. We need an ethics that does not attempt to assimilate the other into an object determined by my categories of thought.

As Seyyed Hossein Nasr wisely observes, no basis exists in history for Islam to be "disturbed theologically" by the coexistence of other religions:

The existence of other traditions is taken for granted, and in fact Islam is based on the conception of the universality of revelation. The Quran among all sacred scripture is the one that speaks the most universal language and Muslims believe in the existence of a large number of prophets. . . . Although generally only the Abrahamic tradition has been considered, the principle of the universality of revelation applies to all nations. . . . The spiritual anthropology depicted in the Quran makes of prophecy a necessary element of the human condition. . . . Islam also considers itself to be the reassertion of the original religion, of the doctrine of Unity. . . . Muslims have always had an innate feeling [and belief] of possessing in their purest form the doctrines that all religions have come to proclaim before.[3]

Today, however, many Muslims seem to have forgotten the call of *rahmah* (compassion, care) and *wadd* (love) that the Qur'an and the Sunnah have taught for centuries.

Alwi Shihab, an Indonesian authority on Islamic law, sums up both the challenge and the promise presented to all Abrahamic traditions by the Qur'an:

The challenge is for all of them to live by the moral and spiritual dictates of the Torah, the Gospel and the Qur'an. The promise is that if they do so, both the sky and earth would freely bestow on them their blessings; "were they to abide by the Torah, the Gospel and that which was sent down to them from their Lord, they would have provisions from above them and from beneath their feet" (5:66).

Can Jews, Christians and Muslims hear the voice of God to each in their own language? This is indeed the real challenge of the hour.[4]

Such a challenge brings us to a major crossroads between theology and ethics. Trialogue should first and foremost concern itself with ethical positions rather than with theological differences, though the latter surely can be juxtaposed with ethics at certain points. Authentic trialogue will not sweep uncomfortable scriptural texts and historical disasters under the carpet in order to maintain scholarly "civility." Those committed to trialogue should study difficult texts, ask searching questions, and analyze past failings. However, after all this we should also remember that trialogue cannot be a purely intellectual affair; it should also be a genuine spiritual process. So much suffering engulfs the world; theologies will not be of much help in relieving it. *Tawalli* is the way forward. People who have neither time nor any yearning for *salat-namaz* (Muslim prayer) could, at a minimum, recall Muhammad's insistence that religion and sincerity are synonymous, that no one gains access to the world to come unless he or she is a believer, and that no one can truly become a believer until all love one another.

CONTRIBUTORS' QUESTIONS FOR BÜLENT ŞENAY

1. You claim that judging one another on the basis of one's own absolute truth claims is not "religious" in and of itself. "Adherents of different religions," you contend, "should come to recognize that it is ultimately in God's hands to judge who acts morally or immorally here on earth." Do these statements mean that we should put aside the question of truth in the course of trialogue and that only ethical tasks remain significant? Are truth claims not intrinsic to religious convictions?

2. You plea for the adherents of different religions to concentrate on ethics rather than on theological differences. In so doing you appear to presuppose the existence of some common ethical ground underlying all three Abrahamic traditions, a ground that can serve as a criterion to judge religious behaviors. Can we so clearly distinguish ethics from theology? Can we separate the moral from the spiritual dimension of faith? Might it be the case that the origin of the tensions among the monotheistic religions resides in the fact that we do not sufficiently accept and appreciate theological differences? Further, if it is the case that "all the verses in the Qur'an that criticize Jews or Christians . . . do so by blaming 'those among them' who engage in unethical, hostile,

or arrogant behavior," why does the text not simply criticize anyone who is unethical or arrogant, rather than a Jew or Christian who may behave in this way? How might your response to these questions be affected by the fact that we live in a post-Holocaust world whose political context contains twenty-first-century violence and counterviolence implicating all three of the major monotheistic traditions?

RESPONSE BY BÜLENT ŞENAY

Yes, indeed, truth claims are intrinsic to religious convictions. However, when a believer enters into dialogue with others, what happens is the unfolding of a communication between two human beings. Human beings are limited in their understandings. Understanding is nothing but "standing under" something we want to grasp. A Muslim believes and claims that Islam is the ultimate truth, yet the very same Islam tells him or her to leave judgment of the ultimate truth in the hands of God when the "Day" comes. In the words of contemporary religious thinker Frithjof Schuon, "Truth is situated beyond forms, whereas Revelation, or the Tradition which derives from it, belongs to the formal order . . . but to speak of form is to speak of diversity, and so of pluralism."[5] The very diversity of human life on the face of the earth requires an ethical worldview based on the "common good."

The Islamic vision of the earthly life is based not on theologically absolute claims but on the idea of *ma'roof* (common good). The word *ma'roof* itself comes from the root word *'urf*, which means something that is commonly known and recognized by people. The word *'urf* is associated with the word *Ma'ruf* (what is right, common good) in the Qur'anic text. With the concept of *al-ma'roof*, Islamic teachings provide a profound ground for basic human rights (loosely translated as *hoqooq al-'ibaad* [the rights of God's servants]). It is because of the *hoqooq al-'ibaad* that competing with regard to truth claims is not the purpose of religion, and judging one another on the basis of one's own absolute truth claims is not "religious" in and of itself. In Qur'anic and Islamic outlooks, that which is religious is identified with faith-based action—and especially with regard for others. *Amal al-saaleh* (moral deeds) are crucial. Islam judges the actions (whether they are good, decent, moral, etc.) in this earthly world, and Allah judges intentions and faith in the hereafter. If Allah so wishes, of course, he also can judge his servants in this world. Ethics begins with others. Instead of focusing on theologically absolute claims, the Qur'an enjoins believers to live a moral life (*amal al-saaleh*). *Ma'roof* proposes a framework for morality/good deeds, yet cannot itself impose values on or rules for a diverse society.

The "common good" is not the result of a theological truth claim, but emerges instead from moral claims that bring about such a life based on dialogue/trialogue. Such dialogue/trialogue requires guidance. Guidance, in turn, needs to be based on principles. These principles are "establishing justice" (*qist*), "eliminating prejudice" (*zann*), and "alleviating hardship" (*yusr*). The laws of the Qur'an and the Sunnah promote dialogue and cooperation (*taarof*) as well as mutual support within the family and the society at large. All these are indications of an ethical vision beyond theological formulations.

Arguably the most controversial and volatile concept in the Qur'an is jihad (holy war). Frightening to many non-Muslims, both inspiring and confusing to many Muslims themselves, it is primarily an ethical, judicial, and spiritual term all at once. With regard to jihad, Muslims frequently accuse Islam's critics of quoting Qur'anic verses out of context; Islam is thus unfairly portrayed as a violent religion. The problem is that today it is often Muslims who quote verses from the Qur'an out of context or fail to take into account that there are other verses that explain and qualify the verses they quote. A fundamentalist/literalist Muslim reading of the Qur'an and the Hadith is as harmful to humanity as a Christian Zionist reading of the Bible or a Jewish Zionist reading of the Tanakh.

In addition to the Qur'anic verses that refer to each community's being given a separate "way" (*shir'ah, minhaaj*), the following quotations offer clear proof that religious diversity is part of the Divine Will. God's servants (Muslim or non-Muslim) are allowed to follow their own paths until God "tells them the truth." The Qur'an (*Surah al-Hajj*) 22:40 proclaims that permission to engage in fighting is given to "those who have been expelled from their homes in defiance of right (for no cause) except that they say, 'our Lord is Allah.' Did not Allah check one set of people by means of another, there would surely have been pulled down monasteries, churches, synagogues, and mosques, in which the name of Allah is commemorated in abundant measure. Allah will certainly aid those who aid his (cause); for verily Allah is full of Strength, Exalted in Might, (able to enforce His Will)." This verse demands the protection of religious freedom and diversity. In other words, the purpose of legalizing jihad is to struggle against injustice (*zulm*). One does not even need to mention the verses that clearly forbid murder, for example, Qur'an 17:33. Unfortunately, many popular writers misquote the Qur'an or deliberately distort various verses. Most widely quoted verses are the few that refer to the "battles" between the pagan Arabs and the new Muslim community. And in those verses the word used for "battle" is *moqaatala/qaatal*, not *jihad*. Jihad has spiritual connotations that qualify its sense of just or holy war, taking into account the validity of religious diversity identified in the Qur'anic verse quoted above (22:40).

Many Qur'anic verses warn Muslims, believers, and all of humanity against arrogance. But the question at hand at the time of revelation was the sharp opposition and offensive actions from particularly Jewish and, later, Christian foes. The particularity of the revealed verses needs to be understood in the context of how to deal with those who attacked the new believers (Muslims) at the time. Beside this framework, the divine presence exists through the love (*al-wadd*) and compassion (*ar-rahmah*) of Allah (Qur'an 50:16, 11:90, 85:14). The ultimate ethical grounds for relationship with others are based on the teachings of the Prophet in the Qur'an and Hadith: for example, "You will not go to Paradise unless you have the faith, you will not have faith unless you love each other" (*Sahih Muslim*, Book 1, Hadith 96). This passage enjoins Muslims not to engage in arguing or enforcing theological absolute claims but rather to live together by creating a public space based on the common good, that is, *al-ma'roof*. Thus we are in the presence of an ethical (*akhlaaq*) rather than a theological claim.

In response to the second question posed to me by the contributors to this volume, yes, we can distinguish but not necessarily separate ethics from theology. And let us recall that theology, in the Christian sense of that word, does not exist in Islam. What is loosely called "Islamic theology" is the study of *Kalaam*, which means the study of the Word rather than *Theos*, the deity. This distinction marks the difference between ethics and theology. Truth claims are important, and they may be diverse in their formulations; we shall leave their adjudication to God's judgment, and we shall focus on eliminating injustice, oppression, and terror. Yes, distinguishing ethics from theology presupposes the existence of some common ethical ground underlying all three traditions, a ground that serves as a criterion for judging religious or nonreligious conduct. In my view, what is "moral" is not separate from that which is "spiritual." "Spiritual" does not necessarily refer to theological understanding. We are engaged in morality. The Qur'anic text does criticize anyone who is unethical or arrogant (*mostakber*). The verses that criticize Jews and Christians for certain actions and dogmas do so insofar as these two religious communities were the immediate and often hostile neighbors of early Muslims. There were no Buddhists or Hindus in Mecca or Medina. The particularity of the Qur'anic revelation refers to the reality during the immediate period of revelation.

From the Qur'anic text—and context—we learn that *zulm* (injustice) has to be eliminated. Certainly, the Holocaust is considered to be a *zulm* (oppression, persecution, tyranny). This is why it is believed by Muslims throughout the world today that Jews are to be the first people to understand the suffering of the Palestinians under Israeli occupation, let alone the fact that many Jews survived in history thanks to the Islamic practice of a form of protection that was not merely tolerance. Palestinians should stop suicide bombings and rocket firings. The occupation and the daily humiliation of the Palestinians must stop too. The inhuman conditions of the refugee camps should be tackled seriously. All of these matters are related to morality rather than to theology. However, if any faith community develops a theology that allows power to be exercised without morality, then we are in serious danger. Morality is therefore both crucial and central in the Qur'anic vision. Commitment to *al-maʿroof*, to the common good, prepares the necessary ground for dialogue/trialogue.

We do live in a post-Holocaust world whose political context contains twenty-first-century violence (including state terrorism) and counter-violence implicating all three of the major monotheistic traditions. The roots of violence can be found in the lack of an ethics of disagreement. Therefore scholars have the responsibility to work on such an ethics and hermeneutics of disagreement both *within* and *between* faith traditions. The Qur'anic concept of *al-maʿroof* can provide a starting point for such an ethics and hermeneutics and for movement forward in dialogue/trialogue.

NOTES

1 Klaus Krippendorff, "Ecological Narratives: Reclaiming the Voice of Theorized Others," in *The Art of the Feud: Reconceptualizing International Relations*, ed. Jose V. Ciprut (Westport, Conn.: Praeger, 2000), 8, 9, 12.

2 With the exception of some Qur'anic material in quotations from other scholars, all of this chapter's translations from the Qur'an can be found online in the database of the Center for Muslim-Jewish Engagement, University of Southern California, http://www.cmje.org/religious-texts/quran. This online version of the

Qur'an contains English translations by Abdullah Yusuf Ali, Marmaduke Pick-thall, and M. H. Shakir. I mainly have used the translations by Yusuf Ali.

3   Seyyed Hossein Nasr, *Sufi Essays* (Albany: State University of New York Press, 1972), 131–32.

4   Alwi Shihab, "The Qur'an Recognizes Plurality," January 2, 2006. Available online at http://www.upf.org/component/content/article/178/2076.

5   *The Essential Frithjof Schuon*, ed. Seyyed Hossein Nasr (Bloomington, Ind.: World Wisdom, 2005), 149.

12

Encountering the Other

Enemy or Stranger?

HUBERT G. LOCKE

Unless one takes a longer view of history and considers the Andalusian period in medieval Spain when Muslims, Christians, and Jews lived side by side and, "despite their intractable differences and enduring hostilities, nourished a complex culture of tolerance," the exchange of ideas and opinions between adherents of the three religious traditions is a comparatively recent occurrence.[1] It is even more recent with respect to conversations of Jews and Christians with Muslims than those between Jews and Christians. Some lessons from the latter experience, therefore, might be relevant.

If there is anything Christians and Jews have learned from decades of dialogue, it is the danger of failing to speak with candor to one another. In the United States, a benign tradition of polite, interfaith conversations, bolstered by annual Brotherhood Week exercises and Passover Seders in church social halls, left both communities, some sixty years ago, unprepared for the earnest encounter demanded by the confirmation, in 1945, that millions of Jews had been murdered in the heart of Christian Europe. Leaders in the two faith communities have struggled ever since to overcome this tragic chapter in their shared history.

As Christians and Jews turn to their Muslim colleagues in the hope that a serious, threefold conversation can be initiated, this earlier experience between two of the three participants in the discussion should be remembered. It is even more imperative to do so when the discussion is burdened by contemporaneous events that risk distorting both perspective and judgment.

We cannot proceed, for example, as though we are oblivious to the significant tensions between the Islamic community and the Judeo-Christian West. Furthermore, the temptation to resort to inaccurate categorical assertions needs to be resisted: modern Islam is no more monolithic than its Jewish or Christian counterparts, while the "Judeo-Christian West" may depict a fading cultural heritage far more than it does a contemporary political reality. Nevertheless, Islam, Judaism, and Christianity confront and engage one another across a geographical and cultural divide that events of the past several decades have only served to heighten. Placing these events and their participants in an appropriate analytic framework and perspective is one of the several, foundational tasks we face.

Ultimately, the challenge of trialogue for all three religious traditions may lie less in discussions of religious differences than in how each faith confronts the modern era. The tensions between Judaism, Christianity, and Islam may have to do, in other words, far more with the perceived ways in which each tradition addresses the realities of the twenty-first century than with divergences in religious dogma and practices. Three externalities, in this regard, are of particular significance.

The Abrahamic Faiths and the Theocratic Impulse

The modern era presents all three religious traditions with possibilities, circumstances, and challenges that, while not unique, are unprecedented in their scope and significance. Of the myriad possibilities, none is greater or more alluring than the impulse to use the mechanisms and instruments of the state to advance religious ideals and convictions.

We know the theocratic impulse to be among the oldest and most enduring of human allurements. A conviction of "the supremacy and transcendency of God over the world" leads easily to the notion that a nation's laws ought to be fashioned and the lives of its people ordered in accordance with the divine will.[2] This theocratic urge appears to have a renewed appeal in the modern era. The prospect of enlisting the machinery of the state in the effort to establish divine rule over societies that are viewed as morally corrupt and unjust seems to be compelling to many believers.

Modernity confronts these theocratic sentiments with stark realities that are features of the current world landscape. Technology makes changing ideas and opinions, the diversity of habits and tastes in dress and music, and the messages of literature and film almost instantaneously available around the globe and accessible to millions. Urbanization, with the individual freedoms it provides under the cloak of personal anonymity, makes efforts to enforce a uniform lifestyle of any sort problematic. Globalization creates new economic possibilities and pressures in societies that change expectations and patterns of behavior in both developed and developing nations.

Religions may respond to these realities in several ways. They may choose to rail against some of the outcomes of modernity, particularly those that seem to challenge or threaten religious principles and beliefs. They may reject the outward features of modernity as completely as possible and choose to live instead in a premodern existence devoid of technological and other devices. Or they may actively oppose modern trends and developments as inimical to religious belief. The last of these responses is most apt to turn to the authority of the state for assistance in curbing what are viewed as religiously impermissible ideas or behavior.

Whenever a religion pursues such a course, the effort will be flawed— not because it cannot be attempted, but because it is achievable only by some degree of force or coercion. Coercion where religious belief and practices are concerned is rejected by voices of moderation and enlightenment in all three religious traditions and throughout the modern religious world.[3] The essential idea of religious commitment is contradicted, in principle, wherever theocratic beliefs seek to hold sway over modern societies and, in practice, whenever religious groups seek, with government assistance or support, to require specific religious practices or behavior as public observances. In the United States, for example, some Christian groups have been slow to learn this lesson with respect to issues such as prayer in public schools and various antigambling proposals.

The ultimate failing of the theocratic impulse, however, lies in the fact that it allows no place for the Other. If there is but one way to believe and behave, then those who do not conform are a threat to the order and stability of the theocratic society. At best, they must be dealt with as second-class citizens who are not entitled to the full rights, privileges, and protections of the state; at worst, and far more frequently, they are subject to various degrees of punishment that the state imposes in the name of whatever theocratic rule it upholds.

Asserting the importance—indeed, the necessity—of maintaining a distinction and a distance between religious authority and the power of the state admittedly flies in the face of deep-seated tradition and experience, especially in the Christian and Muslim worlds and, to a lesser extent, in Judaism as well. All three faiths have, at points in their history up to and including the present time, sought to impose religious rule by utilizing the power of the state. At times, such policy has been considered not simply a matter of tradition but a tenet intrinsic to the religious faith itself.

In such cases, a second, unavoidable problem is encountered—one that is also amply documented in the course of religious history in all three religious traditions. The theocratic impulse requires not only the imposition of a generally religious view of conduct and behavior on a society but also and inevitably the imposition of a particular creed or dogma, derived from the teachings of a specific group or sect within the larger religious community; the state is then called upon to uphold and enforce this doctrine. The fact that there are dissenters to this particular understanding and other interpretations that compete for recognition and acceptance as authentic beliefs is the source of much of the religiously rooted conflict and violence that plagues many societies in our time.

Theocratic worldviews, therefore, are essentially incompatible with the realities of modernity. The theocratic outlook may have great relevance and meaning as a personal moral compass; as an external guide for social order and political decision making, it can only result in conflict and societal chaos.

The Abrahamic Faiths and the Fundamentalist Instinct

All religions are judged not only on their professed ideals but also on the behavior and practices of their adherents. In a fair and balanced appraisal, one sets aside the bizarre and the episodic; one cannot, however, dismiss what appear as major trends or patterns. These factors in the religious calculus make the fundamentalist phenomenon problematic in the traditions of Judaism, Christianity, and Islam. Because fundamentalism displays many characteristics of the aberrant in religious life, it is tempting to treat it as a marginal and untutored sidebar to the main story that is religion in human experience. Current features and expressions of fundamentalism, however, make the marginal appear, in some settings, as mainstream and therefore as matters of major consequence in the modern world.

To an alarming degree, fundamentalism seems to be an ingrained, instinctual, or inherent characteristic of religion. As Martin E. Marty and R. Scott Appleby, important scholars of fundamentalism, have said: "Religious fundamentalism has appeared as a tendency, a habit of mind, found within religious communities . . . which manifests itself as a strategy, or set of strategies, by which beleaguered believers attempt to preserve their distinctive identity as a people or group. . . . [For fundamentalists] a selective retrieval of doctrines, beliefs, and practices from a sacred past . . . serves as a bulwark against the encroachment of outsiders who threaten to draw the believers into a syncretistic, areligious, or irreligious cultural milieu."[4]

This understanding of fundamentalism as an instinct or "habit of mind" focuses attention on one of fundamentalism's most troubling characteristics. It highlights the fact that the core beliefs of fundamentalists are not, per se, the problem. Textual scholars may dispute their analyses of various sacred writings, and historians may quarrel with their interpretations of sundry religious eras and events; no one, however, would deny fundamentalists the right to their own understanding of religious faith and its practice.

Fundamentalism, however, does not return the favor. Fundamentalism has, in all three traditions, an immense capacity for intolerance that sets it apart from other expressions of belief and religious behavior. Virtually by definition, the fundamentalist worldview in every religious tradition understands itself to be the correct or valid expression of that tradition, with either the implicit or explicit understanding that all other beliefs and practices are incorrect or false.

This essential intolerance of religious beliefs and practices that it does not uphold or sanction makes fundamentalism especially problematic in the modern era. Intolerance as an outlook or behavior is a disruptive element in any society in any period; in an era when the migration of people in huge numbers—and their ideas and customs—between different societies and cultures produces an immense and increasing diversity of religious beliefs and practices in the world's nation-states, intolerance is a volatile and dangerous ingredient in any society. When the rejection of the Other is a violent one, religious intolerance becomes anathema to civilized peoples and cultures.

The perceived threat that outsiders present to a worldview that fundamentalists deem sacred inclines them to see the Other as the Enemy. While the task is best left to etymologists and ethnographers, a nonspecialist finds it interesting to speculate whether the word that designates a stranger in Arabic (*gharib*) and Hebrew (*ger*) came, under fundamentalist influences in both traditions, to take on far more negative connotations that paved the way for contemporary pejorative usages (e.g., *goy* in Hebrew and Yiddish). Christianity has a counterpart in its use of the term *heathen*, although etymologically it is more difficult to trace. In any case, a return to an understanding of the Other as the Stranger would be a welcomed development because the latter tends to have a uniformly positive meaning in all three traditions, eliciting corresponding senses of obligation on the part of believers in Judaism, Christianity, and Islam.

Mainstream religious traditions rightly reject the secular tendency to discuss religion as though its core beliefs and its fundamentalist outcroppings were all of a single piece. At the same time, what fundamentalism has set itself against is a reality that mainstream religion cannot ignore. If fundamentalism is best understood as a "religiously inspired reaction to aspects of the global processes of modernization and secularization," then it should be apparent to all except the most obtuse that these processes are not likely to abate in the future.[5] Fundamentalism's reaction, in some settings, takes on a violent form that threatens the stability and security of entire societies. How each religious tradition will address the fundamentalist instinct in its midst becomes one of the great challenges of the modern era.

The Abrahamic Faiths and the Majoritarian Conviction

Religions have a regrettable record of supporting the ideas of religious freedom and tolerance in societies and periods in which they find themselves among the minority faiths and of becoming notably intolerant of other faiths when they become the dominant religious tradition. Unfortunately, the impression is thereby conveyed that religious tolerance is a virtue only when it is a necessity and that the status of the majority exempts a religious faith from forbearance and open-mindedness.

It might be argued that in societies where the overwhelming majority of the populace adheres to a particular religious faith, that faith should enjoy a certain primacy and that even a theocratic system of government— possibly one modeled on fundamentalist beliefs—should be both permissible and workable. The most basic of democratic principles, in fact, would seem to support the idea that, in such circumstances, the theocratic ideal is as valid and as entitled to be honored as any other political vision.

Modernity, however, once again makes this proposition difficult to advance and sustain. Since World War II, many communities that were bicultural or virtually homogeneous have become multicultural in character. For instance, one of the largest Hindu temples in the world has been built in Atlanta, Georgia—a city once a symbol of a bifurcated black and white urban community that today is also home to a mosque that serves five thousand Muslim worshippers. Germany and the Scandinavian countries—monochromatic and monocultural societies well into the second half of the twentieth century—have become home to an astonishing diversity of people and customs. Clearly, today's monolithic societies are likely to become tomorrow's multicultural communities.

At their best, the institutions and processes of religion can advance these developments positively—uniting and amalgamating diverse groups of people into collaborative, tranquil communities. At worse, religion will be a tool that serves to delay this eventuality by serving both as a rationale and as a force that produce and perpetuate societal turmoil.

The majority in the populace will determine in which direction the society will move, but that reality can be highly problematic. Social scientists have focused attention increasingly on the majority not only as the distributor of power, position, and privilege but also as the source of conflict in a society.

> It is the majority . . . which sets the cultural pattern and sustains it, which is in fact responsible for whatever pattern or configuration there is in a culture. It is the majority which confers upon folkways, mores, customs, and laws the status of norms and gives them coercive power. It is the majority which guarantees the stability of a society. It is the majority which requires conformity to custom and which penalizes deviation—except in ways in which the majority sanctions and approves. It is the majority which is the custodian of the mores and which defends them against innovation. And it is the inertia of majorities, finally, which retards the processes of social change.[6]

In religious terms, this configuration places the moral onus on the majority in any social situation precisely because the majority is the center of power and authority. The majority is challenged—indeed, obligated, in this schema—to make the interests of the minority a principal consideration.

In this sense, each of the three religious traditions will perform a crucial role in the way in which societies respond to modernity in the twenty-first century. To speak of the realities that modernity presents is not to imply that religion must accept them uncritically; it is only to posit that they are givens and not likely to be altered by religious dissent or resistance. It is also to suggest that religion will have its principal impact when it informs and inspires those who make up the majority to act in ways that are consonant with the highest and best in every religious tradition.

Religious faiths and their traditions can set forth models of human behavior that overcome the depersonalizing features of modern societies and invest life in the twenty-first century with spiritual meaning. Religions are at their best when they set forth values and ideals that cause individuals to reach beyond their ordinary selves and strive for decent and noble purposes in life. Down through history, religion has failed whenever it has attempted to transform entire communities. No human institution, in fact, is capable of producing such transformation. As Reinhold Niebuhr so acutely discerned, the achievements that are possible for individuals "are more difficult, if not impossible, for human societies and social groups."[7]

We return, then, to the vision and the experience of medieval Spain and the remarkable era of religious tolerance that also spawned an extraordinarily rich period of artistic, literary, and scientific enlightenment, all under the aegis of a Muslim culture that "defined [its] version of Islam as one that loved its dialogues with other traditions."[8] Would not such an achievement by the three faiths—each cultivating a climate of religious goodwill wherever it constitutes the majority—be well worth their mutual striving in our time?

CONTRIBUTORS' QUESTIONS FOR HUBERT G. LOCKE

1. You state that "religion will have its principal impact when it informs and inspires those who make up the majority to act in ways that are consonant with the highest and best in every religious tradition." While this hope is, of course, an ideal, it also raises the question as to what constitutes the *highest and best* in a religious tradition, and who is authorized to make that claim. It also raises the question of the status of those who disagree, or find a different "highest and best," such as, for example, those who insist that the "highest and best" is a messianic call to purification. To what extent is your hope for a religion that fulfills its

"highest and best" in a certain way different from any other monolithic or even fundamentalist claims about what a religion should "really" be about?

2. Your essay emphasizes two key points: (a) fundamentalists do not allow others the same tolerance that they themselves are allowed, and (b) the majority is the "custodian of mores," a custodian, moreover, whose inertia retards processes of much-needed social change. In a sense your essay calls for the diversity and recognition of pluralism embodied in the coexistence of faiths in Muslim Spain. Will you suggest concrete ways in which the majorities of each of the traditions might overcome their inertia and enter into fruitful conversation with one another, particularly in light of the Holocaust and its aftermath and in a historical context that contains twenty-first-century violence and counterviolence often implicating all three of the major monotheistic traditions? Will you suggest ways in which the majority can speak, as you suggest, with a candor that addresses key issues that call for joint reflection?

RESPONSE BY HUBERT G. LOCKE

Both trenchant questions speak to an implicit theme of my essay: while "the highest and best" in every religious tradition is admittedly a value judgment, those who adhere, as believers or followers, to such ideals are presumed to constitute the majority sentiment in each tradition. But majority sentiment often fails to consider religious diversity and pluralism among its highest and best religious ideals. That result produces conflicts between religious traditions, and those tensions threaten social order and stability throughout the world.

Each of the three religious traditions under consideration fosters a personal piety that embraces the ideals of compassion and generosity toward strangers, benevolence toward the poor, and a dutiful regard for the order of family and community. These values are taught as part of the core of one's religious obligation; a likely consensus exists that these values are essential features of a religious tradition's highest and best ideals.

This consensus implies a corresponding rejection, in principle at least, of greed, violence, and anarchy as authentic religious values or ideals. These hostile inclinations are invalidated as authoritative religious ideals, in one respect, by the minority of adherents who hold them. Assuming the majority sentiment in each religious tradition embraces ideals of compassion, benevolence, and social order, a crucial need is for the majority to discern that those key ideals imply, indeed entail, the key importance of religious pluralism and diversity. They do so because the ideals of compassion, benevolence, and social order cannot be realized apart from respect for the Other, which requires openness to difference. This openness, of course, is not indiscriminate. To the contrary, respect for the Other and openness to difference also require resistance against those who pervert the religion's highest values and their implications for religious pluralism and diversity.

It is imperative to promulgate diversity and pluralism in religion as authentic values, rather than regard diversity and pluralism as secular impediments or cultural hindrances to genuine religious belief. Here, contemporary experience is challenging centuries of religious teaching in all three religious traditions. For decades now, at least in the Western world, increased numbers of people find themselves having to adjust—in where they live, in the workplace, in their choice of friends, even within their families—to those who do not share their religious beliefs or traditions. Increasingly, such circumstances are coming to be perceived by religious adherents everywhere as a reality of life in modern times—not as a breakdown in the social order or as a regrettable collapse of religious hegemony.

In point of fact, this new reality should be the occasion for discussions that need to take place intensively *within* each religious tradition; perhaps, in fact, they ought to precede those that occur *between* the three religious faiths. Only as each majority within Christianity, Islam, and Judaism is moved to engage those in its own midst who resist the ideas of religious diversity and pluralism as authentic values can the ground be prepared for fruitful collaboration between the three traditions on these important issues.

In one sense, then, the contemporary interreligious conversation takes place in the wrong quarters. Enlightened (or perhaps more modestly, eager) representatives from the three traditions seek active ways in which the search for understanding and peaceful accord can be advanced. They do so by engaging in tripartite discussions; such endeavors are not undertaken easily, but they are easier than having to confront those who ostensibly share the same tradition but who disavow the values that motivate and inspire the quest for religious accord.

The task, therefore, is that of elevating the ideas of religious diversity and pluralism to ideals that carry the same import as those of compassion and benevolence and of making the former as binding as the latter. It can be argued that the nature of the world society in which we find ourselves demands no less. If we learn anything from the technological age in which we find ourselves, it is how enormously constricted both time and space have become on this planet. It no longer takes extended periods for ideas to reach and have an impact on the various communities and cultures around the globe. The distances that once served as effective barriers between peoples and traditions are breeched in seconds by the marvels of modern communication.

In such a world community, we can ill afford those sentiments—political, cultural, or religious—that give rise to hostility or conflict between nations and people. The Holocaust is one—arguably the worst, to date—of the unfortunately repeated modern examples of what can happen when we do not aggressively work to overcome false ideologies in our midst. It is only when we take seriously the imperative of religious respect and accord among all religious faiths that we have any hope of a world society that can enjoy some modicum of peace.

NOTES

1   Maria Rosa Menocal, *The Ornament of the World: How Muslims, Jews, and Christians Created a Culture of Tolerance in Medieval Spain* (Boston: Little, Brown, 2002), 11.

2   C. P. Tiele, professor of the history of religions at the University of Leiden (1877–1901), gave the Gifford Lectures in 1896–98 "on the elements of the science of religion" in which he posited a "theocratic type" as one of two "directions of development" that religions have moved in over time. See John Baille, *The Interpretation of Religion* (New York: Abingdon Press, 1928), 394–95.

3   See Barry Hankins, "Religious Coercion in a Postmodern Age," *Journal of Church and State* 39, no. 1 (1997): 5–35. The editorial opens with the following statement: "In America and much of the West, we have lived for some time in an era that has prided itself on its tolerance in matters of religion. Not only have most major Western governments ceased official policies of religious coercion, but also the modern academy and every major faith group have come around to positions of expressed tolerance, if not full-fledged religious liberty" (5). The classic religious statement on coercion is that of the Qur'an: "Let there be no compulsion in religion: Truth stands out clear from Error: whoever rejects evil and believes in Allah hath grasped the most trustworthy hand-hold, that never breaks. And Allah heareth and knoweth all things" (2:256). This translation, by Abdullah Yusuf Ali, can be found in the Qur'an online database, Center for Muslim-Jewish Engagement, University of Southern California, http://www.cmje.org/religious-texts/quran/verses/002-qmt.php.

4   Martin E. Marty and R. Scott Appleby, foreword to *Islamic Fundamentalisms and the Gulf Crisis*, ed. James Piscatori (Chicago: American Academy of Arts and Sciences, 1991), xii.

5   Martin E. Marty and R. Scott Appleby, "Introduction: A Sacred Cosmos, Scandalous Code, Defiant Society," in *Fundamentalisms and Society: Reclaiming the Sciences, the Family, and Education*, ed. Martin E. Marty and R. Scott Appleby (Chicago: University of Chicago Press, 1993), 2.

6   Robert Bierstedt, "The Sociology of Majorities," *American Sociological Review* 13, no. 6 (1948): 709.

7   Reinhold Niebuhr, *Moral Man and Immoral Society* (New York: Charles Scribner's Sons, 1960), xi.

8   Menocal, *Ornament of the World*, 21.

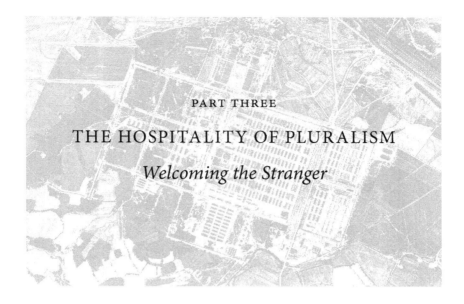

THE HOSPITALITY OF PLURALISM

Welcoming the Stranger

The legendary Irish musician Tommy Sands has shown for decades that seemingly fragile and powerless realities—for example, his guitar and voice singing songs that he recalls from the past or writes for the present and future—can be resilient sources of encouragement and strength, inspiring commitment to deepen understanding, cultivate respect, and heal discord. Two hallmarks of his music, which played important parts in the peace process that calmed the violent "troubles" long separating Protestants and Catholics in Northern Ireland, are persistence and inclusion.

"Carry on," says one of Sands's famous songs, "carry on, / You can hear the people singing, / Carry on, carry on, / Till peace will come again."[1] Traditional Irish music, and Sands's versions of it are no exception, is scarcely triumphal. It assumes no guarantees that what is right and good will prevail. Lamenting the wounding and loss of life, yearning for conditions that preserve and sustain the existence and good that people share, this music carries on by summoning resistance against the joy-robbing afflictions produced by disrespect for and exclusion of the other. Absent persistence that refuses to stop combating the causes of injustice and suffering, what Sands calls "the lonely years of sorrow" are likely to go on and on, leaving immense waste and no peace in their wake.[2]

Signs of Sands's persistence were visible during the summer of 2010, when he and his multitalented musical family accepted Leonard Grob's invitation to visit the Stephen S. Weinstein Holocaust Symposium, the eighth in a biennial series at Wroxton College in England. Sands and his family had recently returned to the United Kingdom after bringing their music and testimony to embattled Israelis and Palestinians, whose prospects for peaceful coexistence remain so fraught that even a Tommy Sands might have been deterred from trying to improve them. Far from being deterred, however, Sands and his family took their fragile instruments, their seemingly powerless music, and carried on by offering visions of alternatives that invited Israelis and Palestinians to join him in song and in creative politics too.

As Sands made clear to the Weinstein Holocaust Symposium in late June 2010, the alternatives he envisions emphasize inclusiveness, and his understanding of inclusiveness places a premium on hospitality, on welcoming the stranger, indeed on turning strangers into friends. "Let the circle be wide round the fireside," Sands sings, "and we'll soon make room for you / Let your heart have no fear / There are no strangers here / Just friends that you never knew."[3]

Are such sentiments more than feel-good wishful thinking? Perhaps not, and yet when Sands and his family sing this song, skepticism and cynicism can be laid to rest, if only momentarily. It is worth noting, too, that the contributors to *Encountering the Stranger* were once just that— strangers who came from religious traditions that have harbored and often intensified fear of one another. Some of us contributors—Jews and Christians—were strangers when we first met at the Wroxton symposia initially organized by Leonard Grob and Henry F. Knight in 1996. Friendship grew, and its circle expanded to include the Muslim contributors to this book—some of them strangers to one another as well as to their Jewish and Christian partners before they accepted the risky invitation to engage in trialogue and found friendship in that process. This small but expanding circle confirmed that Sands's vision—"There are no strangers here / Just friends that you never knew"—could be much more than sentimental, feel-good, wishful thinking.

As this book's trialogue unfolded, it became increasingly clear that the goal for our small circle and for the interreligious understanding needed so much in our twenty-first-century world is one and the same. In Sands's words, that goal is to "make room for you," to meet and treat one another well. Translated into the terms of interreligious relations, this goal means that Jews, Christians, and Muslims need to show hospitality to one another, and nothing is more fundamental to that hospitality than pluralism, which at its core entails that religious differences are more than "tolerated" or even "respected" but are welcomed. Even that way of putting the point, however, remains too abstract, for the key is that religiously different persons and communities need to welcome one another. For that to happen, people and communities often have to change internally as well as in relation to one another. Such work is easier said than done. It requires setting aside the exclusive and all-too-often violence-prone conviction that my way is right and yours is not; it entails embracing Sands's precarious but truthful insight that closing "our eyes to the other side" makes us "just half of what we could be."[4]

The chapters in Part Three of *Encountering the Stranger* are variations on Sands's themes of perseverance and inclusiveness, for they explore what is necessary to widen the circle of interreligious relationships so that they embody the hospitality of religious pluralism. As the chapters' diverse styles and contents make clear, no one-size-fits-all grasps what that hospitality of pluralism entails. For the three Abrahamic traditions, for the individuals and communities in which those traditions live, the hospitality of religious pluralism always must be attentive to needs, responsibilities, and opportunities that reflect the particularity and specificity of time and circumstance. Yet in those details, the shared, persistent, and inclusive goal of the hospitality of pluralism is to create and sustain welcoming conditions so that "there are no strangers here / Just friends that you never knew."

Sands suggests that the hospitality of pluralism involves sharing stories—"stories of old and new ones to be told / To carry away when you go."[5] Every Jew, Christian, and Muslim has a story, and the sharing of those stories is likely to confirm Sands's insight that "in the main, people are the same everywhere . . . in search of love, friendship, laughter, intrigue and a rightful place in the Family of Man."[6] In ways that resonate with Sands's version of the importance of the hospitality of pluralism, Henry Greenspan begins Part Three with stories and reflections that focus on his sister Carol, a troubled artist who sometimes called herself Ora, the Hebrew word for "light."

A psychologist, Greenspan has devoted his life to ongoing, in-depth interviews with a circle of Holocaust survivors, who once were strangers to him but have very often become his friends. This work has made him a keen listener, an essential element in the hospitality of pluralism, for he has to let the stories of others infuse his own consciousness so that he can begin to grasp what life has been for those persons. The difficulty of such work is intense and demanding. Greenspan's contribution to this book's trialogue takes an unconventional but highly important path by exploring how much is at stake when the need is to "let the circle be wide" but success in that regard eludes us.

Greenspan could not prevent his sister's demise, but his inquiry deepened his awareness of the importance of what he calls "the border between light and dark," the region of consciousness where we discern that truth is not found on one clear-cut side and untruth on another. "What I find most compelling," says Greenspan, is not "the moral drama of light *versus* dark, but the commingling of each with the other, a vision that I find most human and humane." If the hospitality of religious pluralism is to be realized, then that work requires making room for one another in the borderlands where differences are seen not as conflicts between "light and dark" but as instructive interactions that can replace crystal clarity with the more subtle and perhaps captivating rays of dawn or twilight.

The Christian thinker Britta Frede-Wenger also uses a story, the parable of the rings, to depict the hospitality of religious pluralism. This story pivots around a blurring of truth and identity. Is one ring more authentic than another? If so, which one fits that description and to whom does that ring belong? Or have circumstances unfolded in such a way that no one can answer those questions with certainty? Perhaps none of the rings can any longer be identified as the exclusively authentic one. Instead, the test of the rings' validity may depend on the actions of those to whom the rings have been entrusted.

Frede-Wenger draws not only on the parable of the rings but also on her German and Catholic traditions to assess how Christianity has dealt with religious differences. Her analysis leads to the conclusion that Christianity and indeed every religious tradition should practice the hospitality of pluralism, which is summed up in the conclusion of her main essay: "On the day of salvation, God will owe us not one but two answers: which religion is the true one, and why man has to suffer. And while we are awaiting answers, it is our common and supreme duty to work together for the end of the suffering that we ourselves have inflicted—and which we continue to inflict."

Sana Tayyen shares stories from her Muslim tradition to advance what she calls *litarafoo*, an inquiry process that involves not just questioning but deep interrogation of one's own religious identity. Thus, *litarafoo* can serve as "a source of bridge building whereby people of a given religion may come to understand and accurately perceive not only the other's religion but also their own." In particular, she recalls Salman al-Farisi, one of the prophet Muhammad's close companions.

Before his conversion to Islam, Salman knew religious non-Muslims who were righteous. After his conversion, Salman wondered what would happen to those persons when their earthly lives ended. Tayyen explains that Islam took into account Salman's consternation that these non-Muslims might receive eternal damnation. She emphasizes that the Qur'an corrected the error of that judgment as follows: "Those who believe (in the Qur'an) and those who follow the Jewish scriptures, and the Christians and the Sabians—any who believe in God and the Last Day, and work righteousness, shall have their reward with their Lord; on them shall be no fear, nor shall they grieve" (Qur'an 2:62).

This story illustrates how awareness of differences can prevent a religious tradition from becoming exclusive and rigid and lead it to make hospitable room for others. To paraphrase Tommy Sands, the challenge is for religious traditions to keep widening the circle so that the hearts of their adherents have no fear and we become more of what we can be by opening our eyes to the other side.

Rachel N. Baum, by telling the story of her interreligious marriage, deepens awareness of what it can and should mean to become more of what we can be by opening our eyes to the other side. She is Jewish; her husband is not. As a result of intermarriage, Baum continues to encounter a challenging question: Is she a "good" Jew? If she were a good Jew, some critics might say, she would not have married outside her religious tradition. Taking that step, the critics might add, threatens the future of her people, particularly because her husband chose not to convert.

Baum's narrative is bold and honest. It describes the struggles about identity that she continues to experience. Some of these struggles are familial; others reflect debates within the Jewish community. But Baum also underscores how her Jewish identity has been enriched and deepened in a marriage that allows her not just to see the other side but to embrace and be intimate with difference as it is embodied in her husband and in their family's life. Their home provides more than an image or a metaphor of the hospitality of pluralism. It makes room for the particularities of identity—in this case, Jewish and Christian—while at the same time showing how those particularities can be complementary and mutually supportive.

Intermarriage sometimes made Baum an outsider within her own Jewish community. Khaleel Mohammed's chapter begins with his experience as a Muslim in the United States, an identity that has sometimes made him not just an outsider but an "enemy" within his own country. That condition, he notes, existed before al-Qaeda's attacks on the World Trade Center and the Pentagon on September 11, 2001, but those events aggravated it. At the time of Mohammed's writing, neither the furor over the proposed Islamic community center in the vicinity of Ground Zero in New York City nor the threat of Qur'an burnings on American soil had erupted as they did during the summer and autumn of 2010. But American hostility toward Islam and Muslims has been in the news even more than Mohammed's chapter indicates. Hence his outlook is all the more important because it appeals so strongly to the importance of religious pluralism.

Mohammed's chapter does that work by pointing out that the Abrahamic traditions have emphasized theology too much and ethics too little. An emphasis on theology, he argues, tends to encourage exclusivism, but an emphasis on ethics has the potential to encourage inclusivism because the key moral ingredients of the three traditions are much more alike than they are different. Hospitality extended to the other, what Sands calls making "room for you," is at the heart of ethics in the Abrahamic faiths. Mohammed uses his chapter in particular to show how that teaching is and must be normative in Islam, a point he uses to criticize his tradition when it comes up short. The hospitality of pluralism is supported whenever the Abrahamic traditions are self-reflective in that way.

The Belgian theologian Didier Pollefeyt draws Part Three to a close with his reflections on Catholic approaches to religious diversity. As Pollefeyt traces the history of his own tradition, he raises a basic question: Do the three Abrahamic traditions all point toward the same "beyond," the same ultimate reality? Are they all paths—very different paths, to be sure—that reach the same destination at the end of the day? Pollefeyt's response emphasizes that "interreligious dialogue is possible, and it can be fruitful, but only so long as the participants agree that no one has direct and unmediated access to a reality 'beyond' and that this reality will finally remain unknown and mysterious for every person and religious system."

If Pollefeyt is correct, then the hospitality of religious pluralism entails a profound and humane humility that can help turn strangers into friends. Jews, Christians, and Muslims can and should care deeply about their traditions and about how to make them the best that they can be. They can even say that, for them, it would not really be thinkable to embrace another tradition as one's own. But at the same time, the hospitality of pluralism requires recognition that neither *my* way nor *your* way is *the* way.

A crucial message in Pollefeyt's chapter, indeed it is a unifying thread in every aspect of this book, is that all religious traditions—individually and even collectively—are incomplete, fallible, and in need of correction and revision as they encounter one another, probe themselves, and expand their horizons. To cite Tommy Sands once more, the Abrahamic traditions, each and all, need to see that if they close their eyes to the other side, they are just half of what they could be. But if these traditions open themselves in hospitality to one another, they will come closer to what shows itself to be right, good, and truly awesome—the "beyond," the divine, that each seeks and can find, at least in part, even while its fullness eludes our human grasp, as it must.

NOTES

1   For more detail on Tommy Sands. *See* his autobiography, *The Songman: A Journey in Irish Music* (Dublin: Lilliput Press, 2005). For Sands's commentary on the lyric quoted here. *See* 252–57.

2   See ibid., 256.

3   Although Sands indicates that he did not record "Let the Circle Be Wide" until 2009, he notes that he has sung this "song of welcome" repeatedly and around the world. See the comments by Sands that accompany his album *Let the Circle Be Wide* (West Chester, Pa.: Appleseed Recordings, 2009).

4   Quoted from Sands's "Let the Circle Be Wide."

5   Ibid.

6   See the comments by Sands that accompany his album *Let the Circle Be Wide*.

13

Ora

HENRY GREENSPAN

"The light," they say, "is near to the darkness."
—Job 17:12

Jerusalem, June 1971. I had not come to the Holy Land as a tourist. Several weeks earlier, I learned that my sister Carol was in an Israeli psychiatric hospital, diagnosed as schizophrenic. My parents told me that her doctors said that a visit from me might help her return to reality. We had always been close. I was then twenty-three; she was twenty-five.

Carol had come to Israel a year earlier, after she finished college, a bachelor of fine arts from Cornell. She had been a painter all her life, in love with colors. Most of her work was "abstract"; to me this meant that you couldn't find any definable stuff in it. It was never abstract to her, but the thing itself—colors forming, melding, and surprising one another as they burst in and over. "It is their relationship," she would explain to me. And she would show me a painting and ask me if I liked it. I'm a "stuff" kind of person. Although a writer, I find even poetry mostly inscrutable. Somehow, I managed—or she allowed me—to dodge the question.

Carol had come to Israel to find a new life. She was not a Zionist; her identity as a Jew—not impassioned—was typical of the suburban town outside New York City where we grew up. But she had found something in Israel—in the people, the colors, the not-suburban town—that drew her. She spoke of Israel more or less the way she spoke of Ralph Waldo Emerson, the nineteenth-century American writer about whom we playfully argued. "You have to feel it," she insisted. "Either you feel it or you don't." In the 1960s, that won the point as well as anything.

She felt it. During the first six months, she learned enough Hebrew to get through rudimentary conversation. She had had a few love affairs (we were never shy about sharing adventures). In Jerusalem she had rented a small apartment, which was also her art studio. She was painting continuously. She had changed her name to "Ora," which is Hebrew for "light," and, of course, the middle part of "Carol" read the Hebrew way, from right to left. When I look back at our letters from that period, letters that were long and philosophic, I remember it always felt silly to address as "Ora" the Carol I had known all my life. But she would not have accepted any other way.

There were no clear signs of madness in her letters, although they stopped coming during the weeks before I heard the news. When we talked once on the phone, there was a strain that I did not understand. I assumed it was one more thing that she "felt" and I didn't. So I was not prepared for the person I met when I arrived. Thin, vigilant, brittle, she accepted my hug but could not return it. When we went out to eat, she told me that there were things she could see but I wouldn't: what people said, a stranger's glance, the numbers on a bus or a bill or a restaurant's address. She was living with a kind of "mindfulness" to which some might aspire. She was awash in significance and meanings. But they all portended condemnation and doom. A prophet of God accepted this. Either you feel it or you don't.

Years later, Carol (she was "Carol" again) told me more about what had happened. During the weeks before her first psychotic break, she had started to paint compulsively, almost around the clock. She wanted to capture all the light that she saw. And, in Jerusalem, she saw it everywhere. And then painting became her enemy. She was seeing too much, and it was making her crazy. She couldn't stop painting, but she had to stop. It would be years before she felt strong enough to risk it again.

For me, before I knew any of this, what had happened was simpler. My sister was gone. She was crazy, and I knew it. But these were the days of R. D. Laing and "anti-psychiatry" and everyone has their reality and who knows what. I had never been with a psychotic person before, let alone one who was the closest person in my life. Maybe I was missing something. And I did not want to become another one of her persecutors (a situation, it was clear, she was anticipating). And I was there because I was supposed to help "bring her back to reality" (she was not the only one with delusions). So, with the person whom I already knew better and who knew me better than anyone in the world, I tried a kind of "interfaith dialogue." It was, in retrospect, both a very loving and a very silly thing for me to do.

One morning, about five days into the trip, I told her I couldn't meet her; there were some things I needed to buy. This was a lie. I simply couldn't take the strain of being with her. The numerology of everything, the threats of everywhere, and my own feelings of helplessness and anger toward Carol for being crazy were more than I could bear.

It was one of those Jerusalem days in which the sun is so bright that it is itself almost unbearable. The light of Jerusalem is famous. It is part of what brought Carol there and why, as Ora, she tried to become it and paint it until she couldn't anymore. It is not like the light of Florence, also famous, but much gentler. The light in Jerusalem, reflected everywhere in silica and sandstone, comes back hard to the eye. I cannot help but see something vicious in it. Or, like the mistral, perhaps something so unremitting it can drive you crazy. Or, like God, something so encompassing that it can command you to sacrifice your beloved Isaac or Ishmael just to see if you will do it. The Sun God tolerates no shade, no shadows, no idols, and no nonsense. The Sun God tolerates no other gods before it.

I needed to be by myself. Without planning it, I walked from the Jerusalem Young Men's Christian Association (YMCA)—a hostel well known to be the best deal in town—to the Mount of Olives. And, still without planning, I took a turn and found myself in Gethsemane.

Gethsemane in June is a riot of color. Had Jesus stayed around a few more weeks, he might have plea-bargained. Amid the lushness, the blooming, this was no place to meditate and die. It was a garden of a sort I had never seen, a passion of a different kind, and particularly in the city of sandstone that reflects rather than refracts. Washing out degrees and distinctions, that is why Jerusalem has much more light than color.

In Gethsemane, there were both—degrees and distinctions. And I remembered things Carol had said about color and imagined that I was beginning to understand. Not stuff, but colors themselves, and their relationships. Perhaps this was what I had come to find. Perhaps this was what I needed to crack the code to get my sister back. Perhaps some Force that she would understand had led me there.

Even the garden became too bright to linger in, and so I went into the church that was adjacent. I didn't know its name or significance at the time. Only later I learned it was the Church of All Nations, named in commemoration of the many countries that had contributed to its construction in the 1920s. It is also known as the Basilica of the Agony in commemoration of the Passion. Inside, there is a large rock on which it is said Jesus prayed the night before his crucifixion. The building itself is ecumenical in style: domes on all sides that could be taken for minarets, along with a Byzantine exterior. Earlier, there had been a Byzantine church on the site.

Coming in from the brightness of the garden, when I first entered the church I saw nothing—total darkness. I felt my way along a wall and to a bench. It took a long time for my eyes to adjust. And all I ever really saw was a diffuse light of purple blue that seemed to come from nowhere. Then I saw what appeared to be windows high up, which were the source. I later learned these were made of a translucent alabaster intended to reveal the interior only gradually. My own revelation, I imagined, was itself coming gradually. "You have to feel it." I convinced myself that maybe I did. I never noticed the rock or the mosaics depicting Judas's betrayal and Jesus' arrest.

When I saw Carol the next day, I was excited to tell her about the experience in Gethsemane. I thought this could be the start of a new bridge between us. But she was much too preoccupied with the voices and the numbers to hear anything I said. The rest of the trip was taken up mainly by my inventing reasons to limit our time together, looking for help from Carol's Israeli psychiatrists and not getting any, and counting down the days until I could leave. Call me Judas. Call me Ishmael.

Children of light; children of darkness. It is always in the light that the blessed live; and in the dark, the accursed. "For the Lord God is a sun and shield," says Psalm 84. It is said that the Dome of the Rock was once so bright that it was impossible to look directly at it. Saul was blinded by a brilliant light on the way to Damascus and could not see anything for three days, at which time, as Paul, he saw everything. "I am the light of the world. Whoever follows me will never walk in darkness, but will have the light of life," the Gospel of John (8:12) quotes Jesus. The Egyptian god H(or), in Greek Horus, is from the same root as *ora*, a source of light. So is Osiris, which was the Greek for Osar. But not only the sons of God radiate the sun of God. Golda Meir is said to have chosen that name because of its etymology. "Or" or "ir" with an "m" connotes "from becoming light" or "becoming awake" (i.e., enlightened). "Allah is the light of the heavens and the earth," says the Qur'an, "light upon light—Allah guides to His light whom He pleases" (24:35). "And God said, 'Let there be light,'" says Genesis (1:3). Thus ending (by creating) Day One.

The only part of the Yom Kippur liturgy that ever really moved me, besides the haunting Kol Nidre prayer with which the Day of Atonement begins, was *Neilah*, the closing service. Here we were told "the gates are closing": a last opportunity for repentance was at hand. The autumn light came into our synagogue at soft angles by that time of day. The border between light and dark always seemed more interesting—and, to me, more holy—than either one alone.

Too bad we don't hear more about the Children of Twilight or of Dusk.

Heavily medicated, Carol was brought back to the United States about a year after I saw her in Jerusalem. This time my parents went. They had arranged for her to be at a hospital outside Boston, where I lived at the time. Carol later told me that she thought I resented this, being put in the role of having to care for her again. She was not entirely wrong. And yet, it was wonderful to have dinner together every Sunday, and, over eight years, we shared our thoughts and reflections again. In our family, no one had a monopoly on madness. She and I had been the "groundlings," exchanging ironic asides while the others lost their heads. That was a large part of how we got through childhood, helping each hold on to as much reality as we could shelter.

People who live with schizophrenia (Carol never wanted to be called "a schizophrenic") very rarely recover. As with other chronic illnesses, many are able to contain and cope through support and medication. They themselves live in a twilight world in which the voices are never far away. When they hear them, they learn not to listen. Or they talk back. Or they talk with their friends or their brothers.

None of this should be sentimentalized. Living with schizophrenia also deserves a church of all nations and a basilica of agony.

At the end of August 2000, I got a call one Friday morning in Michigan. I had moved to Ann Arbor at the end of the 1970s. Carol and I saw each other a lot less, of course, and I was not good—I was, indeed, very bad—at keeping contact by phone. Still, the old closeness was there when we spoke or saw each other, even if there was that frightened, brittle part of her as well.

The voice said: "I am sorry to have to relay this. Your sister Carol has died."

She had been found on the floor of a bathroom early that morning. There was no sign of cause. She had been living for several years in a "halfway house" that she loved. She was close to many who also lived there, her illness brothers and sisters. For the past few years, she had started to paint again and had signed up for art classes that were to begin the next week. She had put together a portfolio that she was sending to galleries, and some of her work was for sale in Boston restaurants. Again, it was about colors mixing and melding.

The autopsy showed nothing. But the toxicology report, which came back a few weeks later, showed an unusually high level of the drug Clozaril, which she had been taking and which, it's now known, can cause sudden cardiac death. Was it an impulsive overdose? An accident? The result of an interaction with one or more of the several other drugs she was taking? There were many bottles full of pills in her room, some prescriptions just filled. If she had wanted to kill herself, she had a lot of options.

We will never know. There is a general belief that suicides are always clear in retrospect—there was some sign, some indication. That is probably not true. But whatever it means, even looking back, no one close to Carol could find any such hint. If anything, she seemed to be looking forward in her life. But one should never underestimate the power of impulse and of many years in the company of loneliness and shadows.

My wife and I "made arrangements." My parents had both been gone for several years. My older sister and Carol had been estranged even before Carol had gone to Israel. I had an uncle in New Hampshire who knew a Jewish funeral home in Boston. That was what we arranged, the rest to be decided when we arrived.

I went there to "view the body." Her face was cold, of course, and she did not look peaceful. Her mouth, stitched closed, could not break into one of the ironic asides that I still expected from her. I could not help saying what she would have anticipated me to say under the circumstances. "Carol, we have a problem. You're dead. And I'm not sure what to do." After a couple of beats—she had perfect comedic timing—I heard her saying in my head: "Well, geez, Hank. We should probably have a funeral."

Because it was Labor Day weekend, we had some extra time to think things through. Carol's religiosity had included a little bit of everything since she had lived in Boston. Like many others in that city, she was a Jewish-Christian-Buddhist-polyspiritual kind of person. In general, she went wherever she felt warmth, which had become more important than light.

The funeral home told us about a new Jewish cemetery well out in the Boston suburbs, not far from Emerson's old haunts. And, indeed, the Jewish cemetery was immediately adjacent to an archetypal New England cemetery, which had, among its interred, Revolutionary War veterans and the full nineteenth-century panoply from Whigs and Democrats to Victorians (with a Civil War obelisk marking the divide) as well as those who had died more recently.

Because the Jewish cemetery section was so new, one could pretty much pick the spot. And so my wife and I strolled around it in the waning September afternoon, talking about the advantages and disadvantages of the "view" Carol would have (keeping in mind her horizontal plane) from this plot versus that one. "View" is important. Almost universally, we imagine it is for them rather than for us. It is a way of persisting in our care.

We settled on a plot midway between sun and shadow. Facing East, wonderfully tall elms and oaks shaded it until about noon. Then the sunlight crept in slowly, dappled, careful, as the afternoon progressed. Even later in the day, there was enough give in the branches that the light was constantly modulating, so that a change in the breeze could easily transform it.

Saul/Paul would not have been blinded or enlightened here. Amid the unpredictable shade and shadows, Abraham might have given things a second thought, and Jesus might have sustained the possibility that he really was forsaken after all.

It was a good place for lingering reflection and communion. And for the sanctity of beloved uncertainties and good-byes.

CONTRIBUTORS' QUESTIONS FOR HENRY GREENSPAN

1. Your essay is filled with powerful symbolism and rich metaphor, but in the context of dialogue, its message appears dark and hopeless. Here and there are flashes of light and possibility, but, in the final analysis, you seem to say, in the words of Ecclesiastes, that all is "empty and fruitless." Is this what you wish us to conclude regarding Jewish,

Christian, Muslim dialogue/trialogue? Or (as one alternative among others) might your emphasis on twilight, shadows, dusk—your celebration of the ambiguity of vision that triumphs over blinding clarity—be intended to serve as an evocation of *uncertainty* as a fundamental truth of human existence, leading us to value authentic dialogue/trialogue all the more?

2. Your essay appears to force the reader to grapple with the question, "What does it mean to be religious?" If I am religious, does that mean I am so blind that I cannot tolerate difference? Do I walk the path of blinding light and crush all tints and shades? Am I engulfed in religious pride—that is, am I a "mighty" Muslim, Jew, or Christian? Or am I a listener? Can I learn new insights from interreligious dialogue—and change? Was it your intent to raise such questions? Particularly in light of the Holocaust and its reverberations and in a historical context that contains twenty-first-century violence and counterviolence implicating all three Abrahamic traditions—none of which is going away— what would be your best-case scenario about what it might mean to be religious?

RESPONSE BY HENRY GREENSPAN

In several respects, I take the questions asked to be different facets of a single question, and so I will respond in an integrated way.

My reflection, "Ora," is not a position paper. It is a short personal memoir, a story. It retells the time I went to Jerusalem to visit my sister Carol, who had been diagnosed as schizophrenic. She was, indeed, psychotic, and her madness centered on a series of religious delusions—all fearful—which tortured her. Carol was the closest person in my life at that time. I tried in every way I could to find a bridge, a dialogue, with her. And yet, I could not—at least not during the time I was in Jerusalem. If there is anything "hopeless" in the piece, it is in the description of that week.

Afterward, the story retells how much there was between us that was anything but hopeless. During the years Carol lived in Boston, we saw each other every week. As I wrote: "It was wonderful to have dinner together every Sunday, and, over eight years, we shared our thoughts and reflections again. In our family, no one had a monopoly on madness. She and I had been the 'groundlings,' exchanging ironic asides while the others lost their heads. That was a large part of how we got through childhood, helping each hold on to as much reality as we could shelter." Although Carol continued to struggle with her illness, our weekly dinners were occasions of joy and of peace.

On another level, "Ora" is a meditation about a particular kind of religiosity. In taking the Hebrew name "Ora," Carol was identifying with the light that she also tried to contain in her painting. But this was a light that consumed her. She was not alone. In psychiatry, there is discussion of "Jerusalem syndrome," in which people quite typically become preoccupied with "purity" and the color white (which includes all other colors).[1] I was myself struck by the light of Jerusalem, which I experienced as "hard," "unremitting," "intolerant." As metaphor, I made reference to "sun gods" more generally—and the images of being "blinded by the light," "immersed in the light," a "child of the light." The association of all-consuming light with holiness seemed to me to be common to the three Abrahamic faiths and to other traditions (which speak of "enlightenment") as well.

There is no doubt that this version of religiosity is the counterplayer in my story. It stands in contrast not simply to tolerance but to an authentic *love* for shade, twilight, the intermingling of light and dark. At the end of the piece, set against the dappled light that played across Carol's grave, I invoke the peace of "lingering communion and reflection" and an uncertainty that I call "beloved."

It is, therefore, no secret what I find most compelling. Not the moral drama of light *versus* dark, but the commingling of each with the other, a vision that I find most human and humane. I associate it with the philosopher William James's celebration of the "margin," the "ever-not-quite," the otherness that always escapes domination by any single perspective (theological or political).[2] I think also of the Holocaust survivor Primo Levi, who praised "impurity" in contrast with the obsession with purity that he identified with fascism: "In order for the wheel to turn, for life to be lived, impurities are needed, and the impurities of impurities in the soil, too, as is known, if it is to be fertile. Dissension, diversity, the grain of salt and mustard are needed: Fascism does not want them, forbids them, and that's why you're not a Fascist; it wants everybody to be the same, and you are not. But immaculate virtue does not exist either, or if it exists it is detestable."[3]

Personally, then, I am what James called a "radical empiricist": Someone who believes that the world really is as complex and diverse as we typically experience it—"blooming" and "buzzing," as James famously put it.[4] Given those convictions, which do not lend themselves to any kind of monism (including monotheism), I have been surprised that "Ora" has been embraced by my friends whom I consider most "religious." This is not simply because they identify with my love for my sister (although it is partly that). As I have understood them, it is rather because the piece *affirms* diversity and uncertainty. And those who are most centered in their faiths seem to find that affirmation most compelling. They can be who and what they are. And meet the other as who *they* are. And what is celebrated and interesting is the *space between* them: the space that allows for surprise and learning something new. That is why uncertainty, for these friends, is also "beloved."

To say it differently, I learned that the opposite of faith is not doubt. It is an insistence on stasis—a universe in which nothing lives, nothing dies, nothing is new, and nothing is old. I understand that such a vision of eternity, of pure being, is compelling to some. In my own being, the best I can do, if they are willing, is to join such people in conversation—this conversation, for example, about that sort of vision.

Therefore, I cannot answer the question of "what it might mean to be religious." I can only say that I, personally, do not consider myself "religious." And so, for that very reason, I have been moved by the fact that this "space between" is also beloved by many who are. In my own view of things, I do not know our purpose or our destiny. But what I do know, and embrace, is conversation about such questions. That conversation is palpable. It requires no special faith; only passionate interest. And so I have found such conversations to be, for me, the essential ground, *whatever* may be our destiny. To say it differently, such conversations—probing, challenging, but always a struggle mutually engaged—have brought me as close to ecstasy as anything I have known. That experience is the result of sharedness across difference, that tension honestly engaged, and the cocreation of space that permits and even encourages such sharing and engagement.

It is unnecessary to say what this suggests about interfaith dialogue or trialogue. For me, such encounters, indeed, can be everything. And from those who have more "faith" than I do, I have come to understand that faith—at least at its best—is precisely what permits encounters with otherness that are joyous and embracing rather than fearful and violent. But the joy can be lived, and the revelations can come, even for those like me who live within a faith of a different kind.

For me, that is enough. For me, that is much more than enough.

NOTES

1   See, for example, Yair Bar-El, Rimon Durst, Gregory Katz, Josef Zislin, Ziva Strauss, and Haim Y. Knobler, "Jerusalem Syndrome," *British Journal of Psychiatry* 176 (2000): 86–90.

2   See William James, *The Principles of Psychology*, 2 vols. (New York: Henry Holt, 1890); and James, "On a Certain Blindness in Human Beings," in *Talks to Teachers on Psychology: And to Students on Some of Life's Ideals* (New York: Henry Holt, 1899), 229–64.

3   Primo Levi, "Zinc," in *The Periodic Table*, trans. Raymond Rosenthal (New York: Schocken, 1984), 34.

4   See William James, *Essays in Radical Empiricism and a Pluralistic Universe*, ed. Ralph Barton Perry (New York: Dutton, 1971). The phrase "blooming, buzzing confusion" appeared originally in James's *Principles of Psychology* (1:488). I have argued that the image goes back to James's memories of the Amazon jungle, where he spent memorable weeks as part of the Thayer Expedition in 1865. Like Carol, James himself was formally trained as a painter. See Henry Greenspan, "William James's Eyes," *Psychohistory Review* 8 (1979): 26–46.

14

Bearers of the Rings

Reflections on Christian Spirituality and the Theology of Religions

BRITTA FREDE-WENGER

The situation could hardly be more complex: a Jew who raises a Christian orphan girl is challenged by a Muslim sultan to respond to the question, "Which religion is the true one?" To make matters even more complicated, the scene takes place in Jerusalem. How will the Jewish man respond?

In a time like ours, which is characterized by ongoing violent conflicts at least partly associated with religion, we might not be optimistic that fruitful discourse will ensue. And yet, the situation does not escalate; the dialogue between Nathan, the Jew, and Saladin, the Muslim sultan, does not consist of mere polemics.

The encounter I have described exists in literature, but probably the dialogue never took place in fact—at least not during the Third Crusade (1189–1192), the context in which important literary accounts place it. One version of the dialogue is found in Giovanni Boccaccio's fourteenth-century allegorical work *Decameron*. In the eighteenth century, Gotthold Ephraim Lessing took up Boccaccio's tale and wrote his own version: a drama titled *Nathan the Wise* (*Nathan der Weise*), one of the most prominent works of the German Enlightenment. How might these literary versions of interreligious dialogue relate to challenges that Jews, Christians, and Muslims face in the twenty-first century?

In both works, Nathan answers Saladin's question with a story that is often called the parable of the rings. In this chapter, I use this parable as a basis for reflection—specifically from a Roman Catholic perspective—on Christian spirituality and a branch of Christian theology known as "theology of religions." Lessing's drama not only sketches a theology of religions but also depicts a successful interreligious dialogue. Thus it invites us to reflect on how theological models may influence the spirit of dialogue.[1]

My analysis begins by presenting three models of Christian theology of religions: exclusivism, inclusivism, and religious pluralism. I then introduce insights from the contemporary German theologian Jürgen Werbick and comment on the parable of the rings. Finally, building on both Werbick and the parable, I suggest that what Christians may be able to bring to interreligious dialogue—indeed, what they have to bring—is modesty in response to the face of the other, a modesty that grows out of the eschatological dimension of Christian hope.

Models of Christian Theology of Religions

Historically, Christian theology divided humankind into two groups: those on the path to salvation, that is, those who were baptized Christians, and those who were damned, that is, nearly everybody else. The Church believed that Christ is the definitive and all-encompassing revelation of God, and it specified the content and meaning of this revelation in articles of faith. The Church took its authority in these matters to mean that no salvation was possible outside the Church (*extra ecclesiam nulla salus*), and both membership in the Church and salvation itself depended upon confessed belief in these articles of faith.

In line with this thinking, some missionizing groups felt driven to bring the Gospel to non-Christians. Interpreting Matthew 28:19 in the light of their ecclesiological position, they considered this work to be their duty: "Go therefore and make disciples of all nations, baptizing them in the name of the Father and of the Son and of the Holy Spirit and teaching them to obey everything that I have commanded you." But what about people who had heard the Gospel of Christ and still refused to become Christians—in other words, Jews and Muslims? Christian logic entailed that an open refusal of Christ, the son of God, was damnable. Imagery from the Gospel of John (8:44) was used to demonize the Jews, who were collectively vilified as "Christ killers." God's covenant with Israel was broken, the Church maintained, and Christianity was now the "true Israel." That claim meant that Islam would be branded a deplorable heresy and its adherents infidels.

For much of its history, Christianity has practiced exclusivism, which is a dualistic approach based on the concept of an in-group and an out-group. To reach salvation you had to be "in." While Christian theologians could find hopeful words for those non-Christians who had not yet been reached by the word of Christianity, it had very little but contempt and spite for those who *chose* not to be baptized (sometimes refusing even under pressure).[2] Violence against "unbelievers" has been a long and devastating chapter of Christian history.

With the Second Vatican Council's "Declaration on the Relation of the Church to Non-Christian Religions" (*Nostra Aetate*) in 1965, a paradigmatic shift took place. This shift grew out of changes in Christian ecclesiology and anthropology, on the one hand, and perceptions regarding the historicity of human life and religious traditions, on the other. If God is the creator of all men and women, everyone is to be looked at as born in the image of God. Thus the concrete historical reality of human life—not only humankind's abstract nature—found a place in theological reflection.

From these insights, two lines of thought were drawn by the council. One was that certain questions unite all people and that all religions offer answers to them. For example, what is man? What is the meaning of life? Where do I come from and where do I go? The other was that diverse people may perceive God in various ways. As the second part of the declaration states, "From ancient times down to the present, there is found among various peoples a certain perception of that hidden power which hovers over the course of things and over the events of human history."[3]

Consequently, speaking of non-Christian religions, the council stated: "The Catholic Church rejects nothing that is true and holy in these religions. She regards with sincere reverence those ways of conduct and of life, those precepts and teachings which, though differing in many aspects from the ones she holds and sets forth, nonetheless often reflect a ray of that Truth which enlightens all men."[4] Considering Muslims and Jews in particular, the council spoke "with esteem" of Muslims who believe in the Creator, honor Abraham and Mary, and revere Jesus as a prophet. The ties to Judaism were found to be even closer: "The Church, therefore, cannot forget that she received the revelation of the Old Testament through the people with whom God in His inexpressible mercy concluded the Ancient Covenant. Nor can she forget that she draws sustenance from the root of that well-cultivated olive tree onto which have been grafted the wild shoots, the Gentiles."[5] Vatican II did much to mute talk of heresy and condemnation of other monotheisms.

However, the fundamental article of faith, the universal role of Christianity in the history of salvation, was left untouched by *Nostra Aetate*. That fact is reflected in the name—inclusivism—by which some key doctrines in the declaration are known in the theology of religions. Even though "rays of truth" may be found in other religions, the full truth and salvation are still found in and through Christ alone. Other religions are seen and valued in terms of their closeness to or distance from Christianity. Inclusivism, the second conceptual model, remains decidedly hierarchical.

While *Nostra Aetate* left little room for continued disrespect of other religions, it also measured them by Christian standards rather than by their intrinsic value. Nevertheless, although the document contains and applies a very specific Christian perspective, *Nostra Aetate* has enhanced the possibility of true dialogue between Catholicism and other religions. In particular, it has revolutionized Jewish-Christian understandings. Dilemmas remain, however, because *Nostra Aetate* replaces the "hard" dualism between those who are "in" and "out" of salvation with a "softer" dualism—but dualism nonetheless—between precepts and teachings that are (perhaps) "partly true" and "fully true." Hence a key question must be asked: Does inclusivism ultimately overcome the exclusive character of dualistic thought patterns?

Religious pluralism, the third model, offers a totally different approach insofar as it is non-dualistic. The philosopher of religion John Hick has advanced this outlook by distinguishing between the "Real" and *perception* of the "Real." According to Hick, while these perceptions and their transformations into plural religions may differ according to underlying cultural backgrounds, the ultimate reality behind these religious "dialects" remains the same. Consequently, he proclaims that "the world religions" may all transform human existence in valid ways that do not privilege one over another: "In distinguishing between the Real itself and the Real as it is thought and experienced by men, I attempt to analyze the pluralistic hypothesis that the world religions include different experiences, concepts, and, consequently, reactions to the Real as a result of the main aspects of human life and that in each of the world religions there can be found a transformation of human existence from a concentration on the self to a concentration on the Real."[6]

While inclusivism as put forth by *Nostra Aetate* depicts a hierarchy of religions with Christianity on top, pluralism attributes equal value to the different religions. While inclusivism distinguishes between "the truth," one that can only fully be found in Christianity, and "rays of truth" in other religions, pluralism abandons altogether the idea that absolute truth resides in any one religion.

At first glance, pluralism seems to be highly attractive, for it seems to allow religions to meet on an equal footing. The Catholic Church, however. *Sees* the problem of relativism lurking in religious pluralism. The Church, it seems, cannot accept a position that compromises the eminence of Christianity, which the relativizing implications of religious pluralism entail.[7]

The Question of Truth in Lessing's Parable of the Rings

In response to the Catholic position regarding religious pluralism and its relativistic implications, the contemporary German theologian Jürgen Werbick helpfully argues in two directions. While he criticizes the Holy See's line of argument against pluralistic theories, he also argues against pluralism's notion of abandoning the question of truth:

> If truth was pluralistic in the end, the different claims to truth and religious paths could remain indifferent to each other. We would each follow our own path and would have to concede that all the others are probably on the right path, too. If we really take each other seriously, however, we must be ready to get into the others' truth claims in a way that they can challenge us to discursively explain or even to correct our own beliefs. Your claim to truth must not leave me indifferent. It asks to be negotiated with everything that I hold to be true. A radical pluralism tends toward an ideology of leaving-each-other-alone and possibly sends the signal that one wants to be left alone, too.[8]

If I take both myself and the other seriously, it is irresponsible—indeed, impossible—to neglect the question of truth.

With Werbick's position providing an important context, consider again Saladin and Nathan and, in particular, a provocative claim that Lessing attributes to the former: "Of these three / Religions only one can be the true one."[9] Nathan does not address Saladin's claim directly; he changes the genre of the discourse to follow. Where Saladin (and we) expect a theory—or at least arguments to prove a point—Nathan offers a parable. This move is significant: a fruitful response to the implied question may not lie in timeless abstractions; it can only be discovered in a story.

The parable of the rings is a mini-drama in itself: "In days of yore, there dwelt in east a man" who had been given a precious ring "from a valued hand" (141). This ring had the power to let its bearer find favor in the eyes of both God and men, if—and here is a noteworthy qualification—the owner was confident about the truth it represented. The ring was to be handed down through the generations to the most beloved son of a father. The father in this tale had three sons and dearly loved each of them; he thus promised the ring to them all. As death approached, he was at a loss as to what to do, so he ordered an artist to make two perfect copies of the ring. After the father died, all three sons claimed ownership of the true ring. Nathan concludes: "Comes question, strife, complaint—all to no end; / For the true ring could no more be distinguished / Than now can—the true faith" (143).

The dilemma is perfect. All of the sons had trusted their father—and none of them had a reason for trusting their father less than the other two did. Not surprisingly, the sons call on a judge to decide the matter. At first, the judge refers to the internal criterion of the ring's truth: all three sons possess the ring and trust that theirs is the true one. However, none of them has found favor in the eyes of the others. So the true ring must be lost. The parable, however, does not conclude in this manner. At this point, the wisdom of the judge reveals itself in a distinctive turn. He urges the sons not to look back for proof or explanation but to leave the question open and turn to the future: "If each of you / Has had a ring presented by his father, / Let each believe his own the real ring" (146). He continues:

Let each endeavour
To vie with both his brothers in displaying
The virtue of his ring; assist its might
With gentleness, benevolence, forbearance,
With inward resignation to the godhead,
And if the virtues of the ring continue

To show themselves among your children's children,
After a thousand thousand years, appear
Before this judgment-seat—a greater one
Than I shall sit upon it, and decide.
So spake the modest judge. (146)

A Critical/Self-Critical Reappraisal of Inclusivism

It would go beyond the scope of this essay to discuss thoroughly the parable of the rings.[10] Instead, I want to highlight some aspects of the parable in light of my reflections on a theology of religions.

1. *"Comes question, strife, complaint—all to no end; / For the true ring could no more be distinguished / Than now can—the true faith"* (143). The parable does not fully propose religious pluralism. While the plurality of religions is not to be doubted, the question of "truth" does not disappear. The true ring was neither lost, nor was it melted into three rings. However, the parable does not propose an exclusivist vision either. The father's impulse to make copies of the ring grew from love of all his sons. He saw all of them as worthy of the ring and wanted none of them to be excluded from its salvific power.

2. *"In days of yore, there dwelt in east a man / Who from a valued hand received a ring / Of endless worth"* (141). When reflecting upon the ring's nature, we inevitably look back and ask, where does it come from? The loving father himself was a descendant of a man who had been given the ring "from a valued hand." This "valued hand" is the parable's only allusion to God. The search for truth, therefore, goes hand in hand with a reflection on the nature of this loving grace, the gift of a power that gives because it cares. A call for reflection of this kind may well assist us as we search for truth in interreligious dialogue.

3. *"After a thousand thousand years, appear / Before this judgment-seat—a greater one / Than I shall sit upon it, and decide"* (146). The central role of the life, death, and resurrection of Jesus Christ has often led Christians to neglect the eschatological dimension of their faith. However, our truth as Christians is a reasoned hope that anticipates the good that may come but has not yet arrived. We don't "have" but "await." This eschatological dimension not only allows us to respect others in dialogue, but it opens up a space in which we are asked to be ready to let ourselves be challenged by their eschatological hopes. In the German language, followers of

other religions are called *Andersgläubige*: they are different, but they are also believers. For Werbick, the possibility of interreligious dialogue rests on each person's readiness to participate in discourse recognizing that the full arrival of the truth lies *ahead*. This discourse *reaches* out to a common religious truth that lies *ahead*. It is not available here and now. However, this truth is starting to become apparent because the path leading toward it can be seen and walked. Meanwhile, if claims about this truth happen in anticipation, as they should, then they have to allow alternative ways of claiming religious truth. Such awareness can produce helpful questioning, correction, and enrichment all around.[11]

Thus Werbick proposes an inclusivist vision for a Christian theology of religions. But his inclusivism is eschatologically intensified. Because the giving love that Christians experience in the story of Jesus Christ desires the salvation of all humankind, nobody will be excluded from salvation. However, this inclusivism is eschatologically open; it waits for God's revelation of the truth of the hope upon which I stake my life. And it trusts God to make my life true where I might fail.

4. *"So spake the modest judge"* (146). This line does far more than conclude Lessing's parable of the rings. In my view, it offers us the key virtue for successful dialogue among Christians, Jews, and Muslims today: modesty. If this "modesty" has found its reflection in the judge's advice, it calls for two things: passion and patience. We are enjoined to be passionate and confident about our own faith. We are called to live passionately and lead a life that gains the respect of others. At the same time, we are called to be patient and leave it to God to reveal Himself. And might this patience not even lead us to a readiness to hear God's voice in the life of others, too?

Werbick calls for a critical/self-critical inclusivism. In his eyes, Christian inclusivism today must remain critical, that is, we must continuously ask ourselves to what degree we judge others solely by our own standards. We have to be on guard against all forms of usurpation. Moreover, we have to be self-critical; we must allow ourselves to be challenged by others. This demand is as old as Christianity: "Always be ready to make your defense to anyone who demands from you an accounting for the hope that is in you; yet do it with gentleness and reverence" (1 Peter 3:15–16).

POSTSCRIPT

Like the biblical Job (or should I say the Job of the Qur'an?), Nathan lost his wife and seven sons. His wisdom and readiness to await God's revelation, therefore, prompts us to reflect on the question of theodicy. On the day of salvation, God will owe us not one but two answers: which religion is the true one, and why man has to suffer. And while we are awaiting answers, it is our common and supreme duty to work together for the end of the suffering that we ourselves have inflicted—and which we continue to inflict.

CONTRIBUTORS' QUESTIONS FOR BRITTA FREDE-WENGER

1. You explain that the "giving love that Christians experience in the story of Jesus Christ" is a love that "wants the salvation of all humankind." Yet if Christian love is rooted in the belief of Jesus' salvific work—if the portal to the salvation of all humankind is based on a specific form of "eschatological intensification"—how does such love become truly universal? If it is *the Christ* who wants the salvation of *all*, is a Christian eschatology truly open? Does not belief in the divinity of Jesus play a privileged role in the eschatological drama? In a post-Holocaust world, is your notion of a self-critical inclusivism—one that responds with "patience and modesty" to the other—enough of a shield against supersessionist tendencies?

2. Church theology is institutional, formulated by thinkers who gave potency to faith-based constructs that may or may not have been sanctioned by Jesus. Thus you speak of Jürgen Werbick, who proposes an inclusivist vision of Christian theology that is eschatologically intensified. Given the reality of the Holocaust and its aftermath, as well as the world of Islam, to what extent do movements within contemporary Roman Catholicism encourage a reexamination of Christian creedal formulations in ways that might change the course of inter/intrafaith relationships?

RESPONSE BY BRITTA FREDE-WENGER

The opportunity to respond to the questions posed by my fellow contributors allows me to explain further an aspect of my essay that is prone to misunderstanding. On the one hand, I propose that God's saving grace includes all humankind regardless of their religion; on the other hand, I do not give up the Christian idea that Christ will play a role in the eschatological drama. Does this outlook offer a truly open and self-critical inclusivism? Does it provide an adequate shield against supersessionism?

My response begins with a story. In the nineteenth century, the brothers Grimm published a collection of fairy tales. Among them is the story "The Hare and the Hedgehog." In this fairy tale, a hedgehog challenges a hare to race. The hare, however, does not stand a chance of winning because the hedgehog's wife has hidden at the end of the furrow. Whenever the hare arrives at the end of the furrow, the hedgehog's wife steps forth and greets the hare with the sentence: "I am here already!" One might be reminded of this tale when Christians talk about eschatology. While Christians claim that followers of other religions will reach salvation, too, they might do so with an aura that claims, "We are there already." Such reasoning is rightly perceived as supersessionist. Christians are challenged to rethink their eschatology in a way that avoids supersessionism *without* disconnecting their eschatological hope from the story of Jesus.

My essay includes Lessing's parable of the rings because it illustrates the existential dimension of religious commitment. Taken together, the eschatological orientation of Christian hope and the existential dimension of religious commitment may not constitute a shield against supersessionism, but at least they put forward a "Stop!" sign. Such a sign does not guarantee that no one will cross a certain line. However, it reminds us Christians that violating the sign's imperative is likely to harm others and also ourselves.

One of the basic problems of Christological teaching is the question of Jesus' divine and human nature. My essay uses a carefully chosen phrase when I refer to "giving love that Christians experience in the story of Jesus Christ." A baffling experience marked the beginning of what was to become Christianity: the early Christians simply could not talk about the God of Israel without talking about Jesus at the same time. Why? Because the caring love of God for humankind—a love that revealed itself at creation, during the exodus from Egypt, and onward in the history of the people of Israel—had revealed itself once again. As Jesus' disciples proceeded to understand his fate, God's caring love could be understood as having gained a new quality. In the words and deeds—in the life, death, and resurrection of Jesus—the early Christians felt touched by the divine. Many years later, the Council of Chalcedon (451 CE) described the human and divine in Jesus as being neither melted together nor separable. So while God's passionate love for humankind and God's promise to save humankind were revealed to Moses, to Abraham, to Noah—if not to Adam and Eve—this same love and promise, Christian thinking affirms, will be present in the eschatological drama. For Christians, this love and promise are inseparably tied to the story of Jesus Christ, but that particularity does not contradict the inclusivism of this outlook. My own reflections remain within the inclusivist framework.

I can clarify these claims by referring to the Jewish philosopher Emil L. Fackenheim, whose definition of faith is indebted to the Christian existentialism of Søren Kierkegaard. "Faith," says Fackenheim, "may be defined as the positive answer, given by way of personal commitment, to existential questions of ultimate significance, which reason can still raise, but no longer answer."[12] An existential leap lies at the core of religious commitment. For Fackenheim, theology follows upon this existential decision. In Fackenheim's words, "Theology is the explication of the faith into which a leap has been made."[13]

With Fackenheim's views in mind, consider once more the parable of the rings and my reflections on a theology of religions. In the parable, the judge before whom the three brothers present their case does not presume to decide which ring is the authentic one. So he encourages each brother to trust that his ring is the authentic one: "If each of you / Has had a ring presented by his father, / Let each believe his own the real ring."[14] As the parable suggests, confidence about this matter, or, by analogy, confidence in one's own religious commitment, allows the bearer of the ring, or, by analogy, the committed religious believer, to find favor and respect in the eyes of other men and women as well as in the eyes of God.

With respect to the followers of different religions, the judge's words contain two important implications. The first is that the multiplicity of rings, each with an inner beauty and power of its own, should be a constant reminder about the existential dimension of religious commitment and theological reflection. Thus my reflections in this volume (along with those of other contributors) are shaped by the perspective of faith. Furthermore, while for Kierkegaard the alternative to faith is despair, Fackenheim, writing from a post-Holocaust perspective, says, "I would now categorically reject all theological attempts to set up alternatives of faith and despair: there is both despair within faith and serene confidence without it."[15] The sons in Lessing's parable do not have "serene confidence," which, Fackenheim suggests, faith does not provide. Instead, their faith entails the risk of commitment, which includes acknowledging and respecting the commitments of others. This acknowledgment and respect go beyond mere tolerance; they involve a critical/self-critical challenge that calls for openness to hear the voice of the divine through and in the other.

The second implication is that the closing words of the "modest judge" allude to eschatological events: "After a thousand thousand years, appear / Before this judgment-seat—a greater one / Than I shall sit upon it, and decide."[16] My response to the contributors' questions began with the story of the hare and the hedgehog, and I want to return to it now. Lessing's parable ends with the three sons (representing three religions) standing *side by side* facing the ultimate judge. None is a (speciously) triumphal "hedgehog" appearing *next to* the judge and saying to the others, "I am here already!"

The right mixture of passion, patience, and modesty can help us see and heed the "Stop!" signs that need to be observed if interreligious dialogue is to be at its best and provide, in particular, adequate safeguards against supersessionist tendencies. At least to some extent, such "Stop!" signs have been recently observed, and I point out one instance as a partial reply to the contributors' asking me whether there are movements within Roman Catholicism that reexamine Catholic doctrine and contribute to a change in the course of inter/intrafaith relationships. One recent event that ignited inter/intrafaith turmoil was the renewed authorization in 2008 of the Tridentine Mass, whose Good Friday liturgy includes a problematic prayer for the Jews. The fact that this 2008 event led to intense, if unresolved, discussion not only outside but also within the Roman Catholic Church should be seen and valued as a sign that the enormous twentieth-century changes in Roman Catholic teachings have not been reversed. At the same time, vigilance continues to be needed to ensure that the "Stop!" signs crucial for advances in interreligious dialogue and intrareligious integrity are maintained and heeded.

NOTES

1   On this point, note Tiemo Rainer Peters's argument that theology after Auschwitz "has to keep in mind that theological statements can have and have had political effects." Tiemo Rainer Peters, "Thesen zu einer Christologie nach Auschwitz" [Theses on a Christology after Auschwitz], in *Christologie nach Auschwitz* [Christology after Auschwitz], ed. Jürgen Manemann and Johann Baptist Metz (Münster: Lit Publishing House, 2001), 3 (my translation).

2   Bertram Stubenrauch, "Die Theologie und die Religionen" [Theology and the Religions], in *Fundamentaltheologie* [Fundamental Theology], ed. Klaus Müller (Regensburg: Verlag Friedrich Pustet, 1998), 340–67.

3   Second Vatican Council, *Nostra Aetate*, "Declaration on the Relation of the Church to Non-Christian Religions," October 28, 1965, pt. 2. Available online at http://www.vatican.va/archive/hist_councils/ii_vatican_council/documents/vat-ii_decl_19651028_nostra-aetate_en.html.

4   Ibid., pt. 2.

5   Ibid., pt. 4. Note the use of the present tense for the verb "draws."

6   John Hick, "Gotteserkenntnis in der Vielfalt der Religionen" [The Knowledge of God in the Plurality of Religions], in *Horizontüberschreitung: Die Pluralistische Theologie der Religionen* [Moving beyond Horizons: The Pluralistic Theology of Religions], ed. Reinhold Bernhardt (Gütersloh: Gütersloher Verlagshaus, 1991), 62 (my translation).

7   The declaration *Dominus Iesus*, on the unicity and salvific universality of Jesus Christ and the Church (August 2000), caused ongoing irritation in the inner-Christian ecumenical movement. However, the declaration was directed primarily against the theory of religious pluralism. For a critique of the document. *See* Jürgen Werbick, "Theologie der Religionen und kirchliches Selbstverständnis aus der Sicht der katholischen Theologie" [The Theology of Religions and the Self-Image of the Church as Viewed from the Perspective of Catholic Theology], *Zeitschrift für Theologie und Kirche* [Journal for Theology and Church] 103 (2006): 77–94.

8   Ibid., 82 (my translation).

9   Gotthold Ephraim Lessing, *Nathan the Wise*, trans. William Taylor of Norwich (Champaign, Ill.: Standard Publications, 2007), 138. For subsequent quotations from this text as cited in my main essay, page numbers are given in parentheses and refer to this edition.

10 Karl Josef Kuschel, *Vom Streit zum Wettstreit der Religionen: Lessing und die Herausforderung des Islam* [From Argument to Challenge: Lessing and the Challenge of Islam] (Düsseldorf: Patmos, 1998).

11 Werbick, "Theologie der Religionen," 84.

12 Emil L. Fackenheim, *Quest for Past and Future: Essays in Jewish Theology* (Boston: Beacon Press, 1970), 104.

13 Ibid., 99.

14 Lessing, *Nathan the Wise*, 146.

15 Fackenheim, *Quest for Past and Future*, 9.

16 Lessing, *Nathan the Wise*, 146.

15

Litarafoo: The Dialogical Method

SANA TAYYEN

So-called newsworthy information concerning "others" and their societies around the world often reveals a lack of dialogical interaction. We often encounter cultural and religious differences without understanding the contexts of these differences and our relation to them. We settle for the media's snapshots that depict little of the richness and complexity of the other's lived experience. The often threatening nature of the images or snippets of information conveyed through media outlets can produce unjustifiably negative perceptions. Without constructive dialogue and respectful understanding, enmity toward and demonization of the other frequently follow.

Religious communities are particularly prone to accept and promote such biased perceptions. To contribute to Jewish-Christian-Muslim trialogue that can help counter the propensities of religions to depict the religious other in biased ways, I introduce the dialogical method found within Islamic scripture and tradition. The Qur'an and Sunnah (the prophetic tradition of Muhammad) support and encourage a dialogical relationship among multireligious communities, a relationship that is dialectical in nature. This dialectic becomes a source of bridge building whereby people of a given religion may come to understand and accurately perceive not only the other's religion but also their own. I call this process *litarafoo*.

Litarafoo *in the Qur'an*

To understand Islam, one must realize the position that the Qur'an plays within Islamic theology and hermeneutics, especially when contemporary issues are being addressed by religious scholars and sheikhs. As Imam al-Tahawi (ca. 843–935) maintained in the ninth century: "The Qur'an is the Word of God that emanated from Him without modality in its expression. He sent it down to His messenger as a revelation. The believers accept it as such literally. They are certain it is, in reality, the Word of God, the Sublime and Exalted. Further unlike human speech, it is eternal and uncreated."[1] This theological statement, accepted by Islamic scholars and sheikhs throughout much of Islamic history, plays an essential role in Qur'anic exegesis; at all times, Muslim scholars must be cognizant of the context it creates.[2] As the eternal and uncreated word of God, the Qur'an shall not be subject to static interpretation, nor shall it be overwritten by human whim and desire. Therefore, *Ulum al-Qur'an*, or "sciences of the Qur'an," has been created by Muslim scholars to give present-day meaning to that which is eternal and uncreated.

Recognizing both the norm expressed by al-Tahawi and the global socioreligious situation in which encounters with religious differences are unavoidable, a growing number of contemporary Muslim scholars, within and outside the predominantly Muslim regions of the world, interpret the Qur'an in ways that emphasize the importance of interreligious dialogue and authentic communication. These interpretations allow for the possibility of respectful and hospitable coexistence among members of many religious traditions. It is no longer the case, as it was in the old city of Damascus, that people can be separated into neighborhoods inhabited, respectively, by Jews, Christians, or Muslims. Although these homogeneous neighborhoods may have created "comfort zones," they can no longer exist without the forces of "otherness" encroaching upon them. These social challenges encourage the development of Qur'anic exegetical interpretations that have not been accepted until recently. The recognition of these interpretations is a reflection of the spirit of our times.

Particularly in the first decade of the twenty-first century, Muslim scholars have enhanced understanding of the following verse from the Qur'an: "O mankind! We created you from a single (pair) of a male and a female, and made you into nations and tribes, that you may know each other (not that you may despise each other). Verily the most honored of you in the sight of God is (he who is) the most righteous of you."[3] Recent interpretations emphasize that this verse promotes the value within Islam of multireligious coexistence. "That you may know each other" epitomizes the dialogical position that the Qur'an understands as the way to honor human diversity. The term *litarafoo* denotes this dialogical process, which is, I believe, an inherent ingredient of Islamic tradition.

As suggested by the Qur'anic verse quoted above, *litarafoo* acknowledges that diversity comes from the Creator.[4] Only within such diversity does *litarafoo* even begin to make sense. As the Qur'anic commentator Abdullah Yusuf Ali suggests, this verse is addressed to humankind, as opposed to the Muslim brotherhood/sisterhood, which is usually addressed with the phrase "Oh you who believe!"[5]

Litarafoo—"that you may know each other"—entails a deep and deepening relationship between others. This relationship requires a respectful exchange of ideas and hospitable behavior; it seeks expanded awareness of each other's identity and does so in ways that advance peaceful coexistence. To know someone is to know what defines him or her from the inside and out. It is to probe further than the typical "multicultural exchange" currently in fashion within diverse communities and nation-states. It is to encounter the other with the questions: "Who am I?" "What is it that defines me?" "Who are you?" "What is it that defines you as I search to define myself in relationship to and with you?"

Litarafoo, the process of building such relationships, depends on dialogical encounter. In that encounter between self and other, a new dialectic unfolds as probing questions and open inquiry add insight and depth in mutual comprehension of religious traditions and their differences. Profound encounters with the other further define the self. As a Muslim, I am unaware of certain aspects of my religion until I encounter the other. In the words of Anselm K. Min, it is precisely "the 'other' [who] pushes one into one's own interiority and challenges one's existing self-identity."[6] Hence my Islamic identity expands its horizons in relation to my religious other. By virtue of *litarafoo*, my Muslim self becomes further and even better defined by the Jewish or Christian other. Yet *litarafoo* is the means to an even greater end. *Litarafoo* aims for people to attain the human attribute that God finds most significant. According to the Qur'an, this attribute is righteousness as God-consciousness, *At-Taqwa*.

Study of the Qur'an also emphasizes *asbab al-nuzul,* or the occasions and circumstances surrounding revelation. It is well accepted in the tradition that the Qur'an was revealed piecemeal to the prophet Muhammad over a period of twenty-three years. Muslims believe that the Qur'an's verses were revealed to the Prophet by God through the archangel Gabriel. Often the Prophet received the revelations in the company of his companions and within the context of the uncertainties and challenges posed by events taking place at the time. The specific circumstances within which revelations occur have been studied by Muslim scholars and jurists and categorized as *asbab al-nuzul*. This area of study offers enormous insight into the mental energy and focus of the nascent Muslim community during the Prophet's life.

One event found in the *asbab al-nuzul* highlights Salman al-Farisi, or Salman the Persian, a prominent Muslim companion of the Prophet, and in particular Salman's relationship with non-Muslims. Before becoming a Muslim, Salman encountered numerous religious men who were not Muslim; he lived and worshipped with them in the course of seeking God. At one point, Salman shared with the Prophet his deep concerns about the soteriological status of non-Muslims. "They are in hell," the Prophet told Salman. At the time, the Prophet's reply could not have been otherwise, for the Prophet was strictly limited to basing his responses to such questions upon Qur'anic revelation as it had thus far unfolded. The Qur'anic verse that would become the accurate and normative response of Islam with regard to Salman's inquiry had not yet been revealed.

Salman's previous interactions produced profound encounters with numerous religious non-Muslims who were righteous and sincere worshippers. He formed bonds of admiration with them. Thus it is not surprising that Salman found the Prophet's initial response difficult to accept, so much so, the *asbab* indicates, that the earth became darkened for him. But immediately after the Prophet gave his initial and limited answer, the following verse was revealed as a correction: "Those who believe (in the Qur'an) and those who follow the Jewish scriptures, and the Christians and the Sabians—any who believe in God and the Last Day, and work righteousness, shall have their reward with their Lord; on them shall be no fear, nor shall they grieve" (Qur'an 2:62). Upon hearing this word, Salman said, "It was as if a mountain had been lifted off of me."[7]

Salman's dialogical encounters with non-Muslims and his internal struggle to understand the religious other set in motion a dialectical movement within himself, with the Prophet, and with God. Salman responded with great sincerity to the righteous human soul, Muslim or not. An encounter with a respected religious other prompted the asking of salient questions; responses to these questions eventually came to define Islamic teachings toward the self and other.

Litarafoo *in the Prophetic Tradition*

The current need for constructive interreligious dialogue is unprecedented. Like the other Abrahamic faith traditions, Islam contains valuable resources that can help meet this need. To advance my argument further, consider some additional ways in which the life and teaching of Prophet Muhammad support multireligious coexistence and authentic interreligious communication in the twenty-first century. As an example, I cite the Prophet's reception of a delegation from Najran during the late Medina (Madinah) period of the life of the Prophet.[8] After the return of the Muslims to Mecca (Makkah), Prophet Muhammad and his companions received many delegations seeking conversion to Islam or a pact with the Prophet in order to receive protection for their people. One particular delegation consisted of sixty Christian men who had arrived from Najran, a Christian community in southern Arabia. Upon their arrival in Medina, the delegates were received in the mosque by the Prophet and were given space to say their prayers. They spent several nights as the Prophet's guests. During that time a number of issues were discussed, including theological perspectives about the nature of Jesus and the Christian belief regarding his divinity versus the Muslim belief in Jesus' prophethood and his role as a messenger of God.[9] The Muslims and Christians reached no consensus on these matters. The Christian delegation returned home after making a favorable treaty with the Prophet according to which, in return for the payment of taxes, they were to have the full protection of the Islamic state for themselves and their churches.[10]

The encounter between the Christians from Najran and the Prophet took place in a respectful manner. Far from being dismissed by the Prophet, the Christian theological position was respected. Neither Christians nor Muslims were required, let alone forced, to compromise their theological positions for the sake of coexistence. They stated their positions, paid attention to their differences, and respected those differences and each other.

The encounter between the Najran delegation and the Prophet calls to mind Diana Eck's emphasis on the importance of interreligious dialogue both within the academic arena and beyond. Especially in an essay titled "Dialogue and Method," Eck emphasizes that religious communities exist not in isolation but in interrelation with one another; they must be understood in that dynamic relationship.[11] She calls this reality "georeligious," noting, for example, that mosques exist in the American Bible Belt and churches can be found in Muslim Pakistan. As she depicts this "georeligious" reality, Eck urges that we must distance ourselves from any method that colonizes or objectifies the other, leading us to dismiss or ignore the other's voice (132–35). For Eck, getting to know the other, whether for the sake of academic research or for interreligious communication, requires dialogue that pays careful attention to the other's voice. Dialogue is the discipline of thought that enables us to gain clarity about our own situatedness (140). Further, Eck writes, the mutuality and critical awareness that shape the give-and-take of dialogue are the very investigative tools that enable us to become more sharply aware of our own consciousness, ethics, and voice (142). Prophet Muhammad and the Christians from Najran exchanged theological beliefs grounded in their respective scriptures; this exchange reflected the attention to "voice" that is a critical aspect of Eck's methodology. Each group listened to the other; their listening assisted them in grappling with both similarities and differences in their worldviews. Their dialogue helped each party define better their positions on the subjects under discussion.

In their encounter with the Christians from Najran, the Muslims made known the teachings of Islam. Prophet Muhammad was believed to be the messenger of God. As such, it was his duty to relay the Islamic message: "Let there be no compulsion in religion: truth stands out clear from Error: whoever rejects Evil and believes in Allah hath grasped the most trustworthy handhold that never breaks."[12] The Christians' disagreement with Islamic teachings about Jesus, including the rejection of his divinity, was not interpreted by the Muslims as hatred of Islam; nor, it seems, were the Christians threatened by the Muslim position.

All parties to dialogue come with an agenda, big or small; interlocutors stating those agendas up front create stronger bridges to genuine communication, ones not based on false premises. A vital and distinctive element of *litarafoo* can be characterized as follows: to know the other is to also know his or her agenda. In the seventh-century Muslim-Christian encounter involving the delegation from Najran, both sides had an agenda. Mutual knowledge about these matters made Muslims and Christians better able to communicate their intentions and to be truthful to one another.

The Hadith (the collective body of traditional accounts of Muhammad's sayings and actions) reports that when a Jewish funeral procession passed before the Prophet, he stood in respect for the deceased. Asked by his companions why he stood, Muhammad replied, "Is it not a living being (soul)?"[13] The Qur'an and the prophetic tradition state that every human being is a soul created by God. The Prophet of Islam recognized this aspect of humanity in all people, regardless of their ethnicity or religion.

As a Muslim, I take the Qur'an and the tradition of the Prophet to be the basis for my interaction with all of humanity. Every human being—Jew, Christian, Muslim, Hindu, Buddhist, or other—is a soul deserving respect and the right to be accurately understood in the context of his or her tradition. The practice of *litarafoo* gives humanity the ability to transcend ignorance of and disrespect for the other. The Qur'an supports the intimate relationship of dialogue between every human soul; it supports mutual understanding among religious communities, an understanding that allows each of us to better comprehend our position within our own religious traditions.

CONTRIBUTORS' QUESTIONS FOR SANA TAYYEN

1. You argue that *litarafoo* was enacted at the meeting of the Prophet with a Christian delegation. You go on to say that the parties "stated their positions, paid attention to their differences, and respected those differences and each other." Further, you aver that "each group listened to the other . . . their dialogue helped each party define better their positions on the subjects under discussion." Thus you seem to indicate that more transpired at this time than can be termed "tolerance" of one another's positions. Does *litarafoo* allow for *fundamental* rethinking of one's *core* beliefs? In interreligious dialogue/trialogue inspired by *litarafoo*, how far can one go in subjecting one's own tradition to critique? For example, what might happen in such interreligious dialogue/trialogue when an interlocutor of a different faith tradition has a radically different perception of moral values with regard to issues such as euthanasia or abortion rights or the use of violence? In a post-Holocaust world whose historical context contains twenty-first-century violence implicating all three of the major monotheistic traditions, how might such *litarafoo*-inspired dialogue/trialogue bear fruit?

2. How does abrogation of earlier Qur'anic verses by later ones affect Muslims who wish to use *litarafoo* as a basis for dialogue? For example, some verses in the Qur'an inveigh against Jews and Christians; others, which you cite, honor the diversity of humankind. Further, some Muslim sects deny any authenticity to Muslim traditions other than their own. How is intra-Muslim dialogue, inspired by *litarafoo*, being used as a dialogical tool to engage theological "strangers" *within* Islam? How might it be so used? How might intra-Muslim ecumenism assist interfaith dialogue/trialogue?

RESPONSE BY SANA TAYYEN

The sincere practice of *litarafoo* in interreligious encounters draws "people of understanding," as the Qur'an calls them, into profound reflection and rethinking.[14] The act of "getting to know the other" causes the new to emerge from the old. For a society to grow in this way, it must allow itself to be sufficiently permeable for exchanges of ideas to take place. Such moments of exchange can helpfully open identities and traditions to challenges from the other.

Particularly challenging for Muslims is the Islamic tradition's insistence that emerging or evolving ideas are acceptable only if they are consistent with the Qur'an and Sunnah, the two most authoritative guides for Muslim communities. Hence as new ideas confront and permeate Muslim communities, Islamic scholars can adapt or modify the ideas to fit within the boundaries established by the Qur'an and Sunnah, or they will have to reject them insofar as the new ideas are not consistent with the authority of these sources. *Litarafoo* does not necessarily undo one's core beliefs, but it does challenge a community to avoid stagnancy and to allow for intellectual, spiritual, and practical growth as that community encounters communities of the other.

In interreligious circumstances where interlocutors from different traditions get to know one another, the question remains, how far can and should the mutual challenges go? No one-size-fits-all response is possible; the answer lies in the hands of individuals and communities. But *litarafoo* always stresses the importance of respectful consideration of the views of the other, including those views that challenge us most. On issues such as abortion, euthanasia, and twenty-first-century violence, Muslim scholars and practitioners should consider new approaches and perspectives, testing them to see whether they contain insights about the "good" that might properly expand Muslim horizons. However, if embracing the new approaches and perspectives would be inconsistent with the Qur'an and Sunnah, then such embracing would constitute an unacceptable loss of Islamic identity.

In response to the second question posed to me, the abrogation of verses in the Qur'an as agreed upon by traditional Muslim scholars does not affect the verse on which *litarafoo* is based. The meaning of *litarafoo* and its implications for multireligious coexistence and dialogue rely on traditional interpretation that has more recently been directly applied in the context of interreligious dialogue by major Muslim scholars both in the Islamic world and in the West.

As my analysis above emphasizes, the study of the science of the Qur'an—known as *asbab al-nuzul*, or the circumstances surrounding revelation—is vital to traditional Islamic exegetical interpretation, and a simple reflection upon what is abrogated in the Qur'an is not sufficient to gain full scholarly understanding of Islamic thought and practice. To understand the Qur'an without considering these contextual events brings foreign meanings and ideas into the Qur'an, thus creating an un-Islamic perspective that is not supported by the main body of Islamic sources and scholarship. The necessary consistency with the essence of Islamic identity is lost. Hence exegetical interpretation of the Qur'an has traditionally studied the contextuality of verses before any application to modern times is undertaken.

The Muslim *umma*, or community, neither is nor should be monolithic. Within the unifying principles of Islam, Muslim diversity is a fact—historically and presently—and a blessing. Hence although *litarafoo* is found within the Qur'an and Sunnah, it also is something to be discussed and applied by contemporary Muslims. The ways of *litarafoo* are applicable for all Muslims and indeed for people of all religions.

Importantly, *litarafoo* shows that not all exegetical interpretations are accurate, correct, or consistent with the entirety of Islamic authoritative sources. Scholars, imams, and sheiks are not infallible. *Litarafoo* encourages Muslim scholars and practitioners to use their critical thinking skills in the service of exegetical interpretations that are truly consistent with the essence of Islam and the global, interreligious situation in which Islam now exists.

As for the claim that "some verses in the Qur'an inveigh against Jews and Christians"—a view that a traditional Muslim perspective will find odd—it is important to remember that very often Muslim leaders have allowed for diverse interactions among Jews, Christians, and Muslims. History is full of important exchanges of ideas among adherents of the Abrahamic traditions; this can be seen in the writings of philosophers, theologians, and scientists and in the arts as well. Islamic civilization has greatly contributed to the growth and development of these endeavors. By no means did this interaction begin or end with Muslims alone. For example, Islamic philosophy, or *al-falsafah*, was born as a result of the meditation of traditional Islamic thinkers on the philosophical ideas of the Hellenic and Hellenistic worlds and to some extent the philosophical heritage of India and pre-Islamic Persia.[15] Further, according to Seyyed Hossein Nasr, Islamic philosophy is a philosophy born of the synthesis of Abrahamic monotheism and Greek philosophy, giving rise to a type of philosophical thought that has had great influence in both the Jewish and Christian worlds.[16]

According to G. W. Bowersock, a look into the Near Eastern world from late antiquity to well into the Islamic period demonstrates to the modern world that the investigation of mosaics as historical documents can inform us about the religion and society of the region.[17] In his book *Mosaics as History*, Bowersock provides instructive glimpses of interreligious encounters from the past. Giving detailed attention to historical mosaics, he argues that as Muslims gained control of the Near East, they encountered people with different languages, cultures, collective memories, and religions. Surviving from both sacred and secular buildings, mosaics from the sixth to eighth centuries reveal key elements of religious interaction during those times.[18]

Apparently, it was not unusual for Muslims to pray inside Christian churches, nor was it rare for Muslims to build churches for Christian communities with which they hoped to establish diplomatic or filial bonds. Significantly, Bowersock's work details historical events that are illustrated in Muslim sources and thus taught within the traditional Islamic framework. Included in these events is the second caliph of Islam, Umar ibn al-Khattab, who is said to have prayed on the steps of the Church of the Resurrection in Jerusalem as well as in the church at the tomb of the Virgin Mary at Gethsemane. An Umayyad governor of Iraq built a Christian church at Kufa in honor of his mother, who was Christian. Further, Bowersock notes that al-Mansur, the second Abbasid caliph, contributed to the construction of a church in Damascus.[19] Historical examples of this kind contrast with allegations that verses from the Qur'an "inveigh against Jews and Christians."

In any case, the spirit of respect and cooperation found in those ancient examples should take precedence over claims of opposite conduct. *Litarafoo* among Muslims should shape the Muslim world by reviving the traditional Islamic spirit toward the religious other. Once so alive and engaging, that spirit enabled Islamic civilization to be a major contributing force toward the advancement of humanity for nearly a thousand years. That spirit can do the same in the next millennium and beyond.

NOTES

1   Al-Tahawi, *The Creed of Imam al-Tahawi*, trans. Hamza Yusuf (Hayward, Calif.: Zaytuna Institute, 2007), 54.

2   At one point in Islamic theological history, the argument regarding whether the Qur'an is the uncreated or created word of God was hotly debated among Muslim philosophers. The idea of the Qur'an's being the created word of God was rejected by the majority of Sunni theologians and jurists and by other Islamic scholars.

3   *The Meaning of the Holy Qur'an*, trans. Abdullah Yusuf Ali (Beltsville, Md.: Amana Publications, 1991), 49:13. In this chapter, citations from the Qur'an refer to this translation.

4   For two reasons, I use "the Creator" here instead of "God." First, I wish to signify the status of all humanity as God's creation. All three Abrahamic religions recognize and worship the Creator as the One who has created all of humanity. Second, "the Creator" identifies one of the central defining characteristics of what religious men and women mean when they say "God."

5   See comments in *Meaning of the Holy Qur'an*, 1342, 49:13.

6   Anselm K. Min, "Towards a Dialectic of Truth: Contemporary Reflections on Hegel's Conception of Truth," in *Truth: Interdisciplinary Dialogues in a Pluralist Age*, ed. Christine Helmer and Kristin De Troyer (Leuven, Belgium: Peeters, 2003), 161.

7   Jalal al-Deen al-Suyuti, *Asbab al-Nuzul* [The Contexts and Occasions of the Revelation of the Qur'an] (Damascus: Dar Qutaiba, 1987), 8 (my translation).

8   The life of Prophet Muhammad is divided into the Mecca and the Medina periods. The Mecca era is often characterized by hardship and oppression, while the Medina era is characterized by lesser hardship and greater prosperity.

9   Sources for this event come from Martin Lings, *Muhammad: His Life Based on the Earliest Sources* (Rochester, Vt.: Inner Traditions International, 1983), 324. See also Safi-ur-Rahman al-Mubarakpuri, *Ar-Raheeq al-Makhtum* [The Sealed Nectar] (Medina, Saudi Arabia: Maktaba Dar-us-Salam, 1995), 450–51.

10   Muslim dominance, it should be noted, put the Najran community into *dhimmi*, or secondary, status. Contemporary interpretations and standards would see this

status as neither liberating nor egalitarian. However, the point is not to criticize events that took place well over fourteen hundred years ago but to gain an internal appreciation of the meaning of these occurrences. It is vital to understand such events in their cultural, sociopolitical, and theological contexts.

11 Diana Eck, "Dialogue and Method: Reconstructing the Study of Religion," in *A Magic Still Dwells: Comparative Religion in the Postmodern Age*, ed. Kimberley C. Patton and Benjamin C. Ray (Berkeley: University of California Press, 2000), 131–50. Further citations to this volume are indicated in parentheses.

12 *Meaning of the Holy Qur'an*, 2:256.

13 *Sahih Bukhari*, Chapter 23, Hadith 399, trans. M. Muhsin Khan. Available online at http://www.searchtruth.com/book_display.php?book=23&translator=1&start=64&number=392.

14 "He granteth wisdom to whom He pleaseth; and he to whom wisdom is granted receiveth indeed a benefit overflowing; but none will grasp the Message but men of understanding" (Qur'an 2:269).

15 Seyyed Hossein Nasr, *Islam: Religion, History, and Civilization* (San Francisco: HarperCollins, 2003), 163.

16 Ibid., 164.

17 G. W. Bowersock, *Mosaics as History: The Near East from Late Antiquity to Islam* (Cambridge, Mass.: Harvard University Press, 2006), 113.

18 Ibid., 111.

19 Ibid., 109.

16

Loving the Stranger

Intimacy between Jews and Non-Jews

RACHEL N. BAUM

I am a Jew. There is no branch of Judaism that would deny this, despite my maternal grandmother's marriage to a non-Jew, despite my having celebrated Christmas throughout my childhood, despite my occasional affection for bacon, lettuce, and tomato sandwiches. I am a Jew, because my mother is a Jew, and her mother before her, and her mother before that.[1]

Am I a good Jew? I admit that I bristle at the question. Yet the question "Is person X a good Jew, Christian, Muslim, etc.?" lies at the heart of much conversation within and among religious communities. Many debates within religious communities can be understood as disagreements over what it means to be a good member of the community. What is *essential* to the community, what must one have or be in order to identify with that community?

The branches of Judaism define its essence differently. Halacha (the body of Jewish religious jurisprudence) is central to Orthodoxy; Jewish ethics is of fundamental importance to Reform Judaism. Yet the determination of what makes a "good Jew" is not limited to religious Judaism, but extends to secular Jewish culture as well. And here, despite the differences between the religious and the secular, there is a surprising amount of agreement on the challenges facing the Jewish community.

From this vantage point, I am seen as a "good Jew" because I am a professor of Jewish Studies, and specifically a Holocaust scholar; because I volunteer my time within the Milwaukee Jewish community; because I belong to a synagogue; because I belong to the Jewish Community Center; because I give to the Jewish Federation annual fund; because my children attend Sunday school and Hebrew School; because I celebrate the Jewish holidays.

I am a bad Jew because my husband is not Jewish.

I experience these two sides to my Jewish identity in irreducible tension. The "badness" that my husband is not Jewish is not mitigated by my positive Jewish actions, but rather adheres to our family, like a scarlet I: *Intermarried.*

Intermarriage is the bogeyman of the Jewish community, the event that is most feared. Given that institutional antisemitism has been largely eradicated in the United States, intermarriage is experienced as the most serious threat to the survival of the American Jewish community. When the 1990 Jewish Population Survey reported that more than half of American Jews were "marrying out," the community responded by promoting programs to encourage "continuity," asking potential donors to consider whether their grandchildren would identify as Jews.[2]

That the non-Jew is seen as a threat to Jewish survival is, I would argue, significant to any interfaith conversation between Jews and non-Jews. While there are religious objections to intermarriage, what is so striking is the relative agreement among all the denominations of Judaism that intermarriage is a problem and that the best relationship for a Jew is with another Jew. Thus even Jews who do not observe halacha participate in the cultural condemnation of intimate relationships between Jews and non-Jews.

This outlook is significant, because it suggests a resistance to the non-Jewish other that exists *despite* the religious tradition of openness that several contributors to this volume note. Intermarriage is often siphoned out of interfaith conversations, as if a Jewish community's perspective on intermarriage has no bearing on how it thinks about non-Jews. This essay addresses that blind spot.

While some people claim that the traditional Jewish attitude toward intermarriage is racist, that contention is unnuanced and cannot stand scrutiny. The Jewish concern with intermarriage is not about "blood"; marriage between a Jew and a convert to Judaism is acceptable. Even for the Orthodox, a marriage between a Jew and a person converted halachically to Judaism would not be considered an intermarriage. At the same time, it is disingenuous to suggest that the Jewish fear of intermarriage has nothing to do with how the community sees non-Jews. It is of great significance that much of the Jewish world remains in fear of its children being too intimate with non-Jews, lest they marry. If we are to look for ways that the faith communities can open themselves, one to the other, then we must move away from the patterns of thought that create fear of the other—and fear of intermarriage.

Two positions dominate the debate about intermarriage: first, the tide of intermarriage must be stanched in order to save the Jewish community; second, intermarriage is a fact of modern life, and those who are intermarried should be welcomed into the community to encourage their chances of identifying as Jews. These two perspectives are often subject to debate as if resistance or acceptance provides the only options vis-à-vis intermarriage.

I want to add a different perspective: The Jewish community needs to think creatively about intermarriage *so that the community can thrive*—not simply so that it will thrive with the addition of intermarried families, but so that it will thrive by upholding a dynamic understanding of its own identity. The American Jewish community is in danger of ossifying Jewish identity, and nowhere is this clearer than in the debate about intermarriage.

The Jewish community's conversation about intermarriage is based on a number of assumptions about the individual, the nature of community, and the experience of marriage itself. These presuppositions are assumed, but not spoken; they underlie how the community thinks about itself in relationship to non-Jews, particularly the existence of non-Jews within the Jewish community. For Jews to think differently about the non-Jewish other will require a new understanding of identity, of what it means to *be* Jewish, and of the nature of communal belonging and human connection.

For much of the mainstream Jewish community, Jews who "marry out" are seen as essentially different from in-married Jews, *regardless of their Jewish behavior*. To be intermarried is to be ontologically different, Jewishly speaking. While halachically Jewish, the intermarried Jew is seen by most mainstream American Jewish organizations as somehow less Jewish, less part of the community, even if he or she expresses a desire to be included in that community.

The notion that to be intermarried is to be *by definition* a "bad Jew" is at the heart of the Conservative movement's decision not to allow the intermarried to work in its schools or camps as teachers, rabbis, cantors, educators, or executive directors. The 1991 statement by the United Synagogue Commission / Department of Education informs members of the Conservative movement "that our schools are not permitted to employ individuals as educators in either administrative or teaching positions who are intermarried. While as a movement we are ready to reach out to the non-Jew who has married a Jew, we have never been prepared to accept intermarriage as desirable. We should not permit anyone who has intermarried to hold educational positions and thus serve as negative models for our children."[3]

Highlighting this point, Joel Roth and Daniel Gordis note that intermarried Jews should not serve as elected officials in synagogues because "they are more than passive members of a halakhically improper marriage—they made an active decision to enter into that relationship, a relationship which we consider of paramount danger to the Jewish community. That they should understand the fact that their marriage must affect their status in the Jewish community is not unfair or unethical; it is obligatory and desirable."[4]

Thus at the heart of the Conservative responsa (the body of rabbinic responses to questions of law) is the idea that intermarriage is a choice by which a Jew has decided to hurt the Jewish community, and therefore he or she must accept the consequences. There is, to be sure, a halachic prohibition against intermarriage, but the Conservative position goes beyond halacha. Nowhere does it state that Conservative Jews who violate other aspects of halacha, who are not *shomer Shabbat* (those who observe the Sabbath laws) or do not observe kashrut (Jewish dietary laws), place themselves on the outskirts of the community, or should be prevented from contact with the children of the community.

Nor are intermarried Jews simply told to keep their relationships private or to promote in-marriage when teaching children. There is something intrinsically wrong (one might say "bad") about the intermarried that suggests that young people must be protected from any contact in which they might experience the person as *not bad*. Nor is any distinction made between intermarried couples who have a Jewish home and those who do not, or between intermarried couples who are raising their children as Jews and those who are not. At the heart of the Conservative movement's decision is a belief about the very state of being intermarried, outside of any particular religious choices a couple might make.

While dissenting from the Conservative movement's views about intermarriage, I find validity in the claim that intermarriage makes the Jew ontologically different. Our very being *is* altered through deep connection with others who are different from us. The possibility—at times even the desirability—of such alteration is the very basis of dialogue: we are not the same people after the dialogue as we were before. Dialogue changes us, reshuffles our identity. Precisely this reshuffling is what the Jewish community fears.

One of the strategies to dissuade couples from intermarrying is to point out the challenges of living with difference. Dennis Prager and Joseph Telushkin go so far as to suggest that people with different religions cannot truly share the same values. In *The Nine Questions People Ask about Judaism*, one question asked is, "Why shouldn't I intermarry—doesn't Judaism believe in universal brotherhood?" The authors answer bluntly: "Our answer depends entirely on the values you share with us and your prospective mate. Do you care if the Jewish people and its distinctive values survive? If you do, then sharing common concerns and values, it is relatively easy for us to communicate on the issue of intermarriage. We have only one question: Does the person you are considering marrying also hold these commitments and values? If the answer is yes, marry that person. Judaism welcomes converts."[5]

Of course, whether the non-Jewish spouse converts or fails to convert says little about the survival of the Jewish people. Whether the non-Jew is supportive of Judaism in the home matters, and how the couple raises their children matters, but Prager and Telushkin cannot imagine that a non-Jew might be supportive of Judaism and his or her Jewish partner without wanting to convert.

Prager and Telushkin go on to mock the reader's claims of love: "Unless you subscribe to such romantic notions as 'love conquers all' or that you can only love one person, it should be obvious to you that the more values and concerns which you share with your husband or wife, the greater the likelihood of a happy and successful marriage."[6] The authors cannot envision that anyone not blinded by love could see themselves having more values and concerns in common with a non-Jew than with a fellow Jew.

The Prager-Telushkin approach to intermarriage reflects an impoverished view not only of relationships between Jews and non-Jews but of love itself. They regard love as a matching of similarities, a finding of oneself in the other. For Prager and Telushkin, a successful marriage is built on identifying as many correspondences as possible—politics, musical tastes, values, commitments—and religion trumps because it includes them all.

For most people in long-term relationships, however, the experience is not only one of overwhelming sameness but also of difference. Similarities make companionship possible and enjoyable—appreciating the same leisure activities, sharing the same values and commitments, agreeing about how to spend one's money. But significantly, marriage, gay or straight, also involves the experience of difference and the utter alterity of another person. The *interplay* between sameness and difference makes marriage rich. The key dimensions of this interplay include the experience of the complete otherness of someone who you had started to think was your own self and, sometimes, the relief of similarity when the other seems so alien.

Love risks vulnerability. One can be misunderstood or unappreciated by another or even lose oneself to the other or to the "us" of the partnership. Such risks, which are intrinsic to relationship, are akin to those facing the Jewish community in relationship with non-Jews. Each marriage between a Jew and a non-Jew is a microcosm of something greater: Jews and non-Jews facing each other.

Prager and Telushkin suggest that sameness can mitigate this fear, can make a relationship safe and secure, one without risk. It may be safest to fall in love with someone from your own community—not only for the Jewish community but also for other religious and ethnic communities. But as philosopher Annette Baier reminds us:

> It is not very "safe" to love another. If safety is what one values most,
> the womb or the grave is the best place for one, and, between the two,
> one will want the best approximations one can get to these places where
> one is sheltered from or beyond hurt. One will opt for places where one
> cannot respond emotionally to the emotions and other states of mind of
> others, cannot be pleased by their pleasure, disappointed at their lack of
> pleasure, hurt by their indifference, angry at their failure to be angered
> by insults, saddened by their choice to withdraw rather than forgivably
> harm, and so on. There is no safe love.[7]

Baier's words remind us that the risk of love is the risk of responding emotionally to others, the risk of being *affected* by them. In the debate about intermarriage, these relationships have been reduced to the discourse of "assimilation," where the Jewish partner is simply overrun by what is generally figured to be his or her Christian companion.

This fear of intermarriage creates a culture of anxiety that revolves around Jewish emotional engagement with non-Jews. Jewish parents are told that if their children socialize predominantly with non-Jews, they risk having them fall in love with non-Jews and marrying them. Despite Judaism's traditional welcoming of the stranger, the community fears the stranger *among* us, the stranger who is no longer strange.

Cultural critic bell hooks explains that fear often supports the status quo. While she is not writing specifically about the Jewish community, her words speak to the issue at hand: "Fear is the primary force upholding structures of domination. It promotes the desire for separation, the desire not to be known. When we are taught that safety lies always with sameness, then difference, of any kind, will appear as a threat. When we choose to love we choose to move against fear—against alienation and separation. The choice to love is a choice to connect—to find ourselves in the other."[8]

At the same time, I cannot ignore the reality of the risks to the Jewish community. If all intimate relationships bear the risk of losing oneself to the other, then certainly the more fragile half of the partnership, here the Jewish partner, risks more. But Judaism has already taken that risk, has already decided that the benefits of being part of non-Jewish culture outweigh the danger to a traditional Jewish life. Judaism has already changed through the encounter with modernity, through the encounter with non-Jews. To suggest "yes, that, but no more" is disingenuous. Judaism is either a pure system, untouched by the non-Jewish world, or it must face the complexity of "finding itself in the other."

To find oneself in the other is not to give one's self away. It is the language of fear and domination that must always see the other as a threat to oneself. Engaging with the other can return me to my self, made anew.

I see this movement in Jane Lazarre's memoir, *Beyond the Whiteness of Whiteness: Memoir of a White Mother of Black Sons*. Lazarre, a Jewish woman, has been married for more than three decades to her African American husband, raising two sons with him. Her thoughtful memoir traces the ways in which raising Black sons as a white woman called her to new levels of growth and consciousness. Lazarre is painfully aware that had she not fallen in love with her husband, her privilege as a white woman would have protected her from the experiences of racism that she now sees. She writes, "The fortunate accident of loving a Black man and becoming a mother of Black children has enabled me to see the world more truth-fully."[9]

Lazarre's text focuses on the interracial nature of her relationship, the fact of her being a white woman raising Black sons. The reader has no idea if she donates money to her local federation or belongs to a synagogue. But her Judaism is woven through the text and is clearly an essential part of her identity. She is first-generation, her father a Russian Jew from the ghetto who later became an American communist. Her sense of Jewish identity is part of what fueled her sense that she could relate to her sons' experiences of being outside—and her realization that it was not that simple.

Lazarre's experiences model how the love of someone who is differ-ent can enrich the Jewish community. She understands something now, through her loving relationships with people who are different from her, that she could not have understood before. Her sons are Jewish, and while they may not identify with the Jewish community in uncomplicated ways, they carry their Judaism with them. Should they marry Jewish women, their marriage would be an "in-marriage," although still not of the stereo-typical sort.

Is it possible that those of us who marry non-Jews have the opportunity to learn something new as well—not necessarily about racism, as Lazarre learned from marrying her husband, but of difference and connection? Is it possible that marrying a non-Jew might help us understand Judaism better. *See* something against a new background, which we couldn't see in the sea of sameness? Is it possible that we, above others, embody most profoundly Judaism's injunction to love the stranger?

Perhaps I am a good Jew after all.

Yet having been in a relationship with a non-Jew for more than two decades, I am no Pollyanna about the challenges. My in-laws are German, I am a Jewish Holocaust scholar, and I have experienced firsthand many of the challenges of intercultural dialogue. Earlier in my relationship, I wished that things could be different, that I would have fallen in love with a Jew, or that my partner would at least convert. Now, with the distance of age, and two children later, I am able to see the fruits of difference, the particular gifts my husband brings to our family, and the ways that the challenges have shaped me. I am the Jew that I am because of my love of a non-Jew. This realization has been hard-won, and writing it down feels too simple, too linear. So I will say it again: I came to know myself by knowing someone other.

This is, when all is said and done, my central point: that the Jewish community must rise to the challenge of modernity in all its complexity. The pluralistic world in which we live is not going away, nor do we want it to, and we must learn how to move within it gracefully. Not with fear. Not with hatred. Not by giving ourselves away. But with love and a willingness to engage fully with those whose differences challenge us.

CONTRIBUTORS' QUESTIONS FOR RACHEL N. BAUM

1. You ask whether marrying a non-Jew might help a Jew understand Judaism better. Regarding your marriage to a non-Jew, you go on to say that engaging with the other can return you to yourself, "made anew"; you add that you came to know yourself by knowing someone other. How, concretely, has your marriage to "the stranger" helped you develop a sense of Jewish identity in ways that might not have happened otherwise? How, concretely, has it helped you know yourself better? How much of such increased knowledge might be the result of the particular "other" to whom you are married?

2. Implicit within normative Judaism's fear of intermarriage is a concern that the non-Jewish partner will not share the values common to Jews or support the Jewish partner's attempts to live by these values. You speak of benefits that lasting encounters with the stranger might bring to Judaism. You also say that you are the Jew that you are because of such an engagement, an engagement that has been "hard-won." Can you elaborate how these fruits have been hard-won? Reflecting in particular on the fact that yours is a post-Holocaust marriage situated in a world where relationships between Jews and Muslims and between Christians and Muslims are widespread and increasingly dangerous, please address some of the challenges of engaging the stranger in the ways you have chosen. In the face of such challenges, can you proffer a generalization about the survival of a Judaism that embraces intermarriage in a post-Holocaust world?

RESPONSE BY RACHEL N. BAUM

Let me begin with two snapshots from my post-Holocaust, interfaith marriage:

One Christmas, my sister-in-law put together a photo album for my husband and me. We had recently had our first child, and she wanted us to have a family history that we could someday pass on to him. It was a labor of love, as she had looked through many family photos before making her selections and color-copying them, writing captions in a silver pen underneath. Half the book was blank, with the idea that I could put my family photos in it, thereby giving our child a complete sense of his genealogy.

On one of the pages there was a picture of an uncle in his military uniform, a swastika on his armband. Underneath, in the silver pen, was the simple caption: *Hubert, the youngest son, during WWII. He was stationed in Russia and lost a leg in battle.*

My sister-in-law did not understand why my husband and I were upset about her inclusion of this photograph or why the presence of a swastika in a family album might complicate the circumstances under which we would give the book to our son. To this day, neither my husband's sisters nor his parents understand why that swastika upset us so much. This gap of understanding exists not because they feel a connection to the symbol but because they feel none. In fact, my mother-in-law told me, "It's just a symbol, like the American flag."

II

When my father died, my family sat shivah for him. This is a weeklong period of mourning in which people come to the house to express their condolences and to help make up a minyan, the group of ten Jews needed to say the Kaddish, the mourner's prayer. One night, we had only nine Jews. Nobody else was counting heads, of course—the house was full of people—but I counted Nine Jews.

I was upset in ways that do not entirely make sense. I am not a halachic Jew. I eat bacon, I drive on the Sabbath. *And yet.* At the time, it felt like a sign. We weren't two Jews shy of a minyan; we were missing one. My husband. My father. Loss surrounded me.

My husband didn't understand—was actually angry, my grief-stricken, soft-spoken husband. How, he wanted to know, could a Jew off the street be counted and he, who my father considered as a son, not count?

My father would have agreed with my husband. A secular Jew, he wouldn't have cared at all about whether there were ten Jews. He knew who his tribe was, and it included my husband.

Yet my father was buried in the traditional fashion, in a Jewish cemetery. In death, he was claimed by a people and buried as his father and grandfather before him. This continuity is not without meaning, and it sometimes upsets me that unless my husband converts, I will not be buried near my parents. It pains me that should I die first, my husband will not count in the minyan, will not be recognized as part of the community that will say Kaddish for me. My children will, but not my husband. My family divided.

I begin with these snapshots because they capture moments when my husband and I were acutely aware of our differences—not differences in values but in identity. Each of us stood on a divide of history and peoplehood that shaped our identity before we were born.

Between us was a gap that could be traversed but not erased.

And so I say that my current embrace of my interfaith marriage has been hard-won. Like others, I have given in at times to the idea that I could be protected from difference, that sameness would insulate me from conflict. If I had married a Jew, there wouldn't be swastikas in the family album, wouldn't be Nazis in the family tree (I was outraged when my father-in-law told me, about a decade into my marriage, that a great-uncle, to whom I had written a lovely card upon our marriage, remained loyal to the Nazism of his youth). There wouldn't be any doubt about the Jewishness of my family or about our participation in Jewish ritual.

In other words, if I had married a Jew, it would have been easier. I probably would have felt more secure in my Jewish identity earlier on, because it wouldn't have been challenged. This is, after all, the Jewish model: Your identity as a Jew gives you a particular vision of the world and a set of responsibilities. Everything starts from the identification of yourself as a Jew.

Yet because I fell in love with my husband before I fell in love with Judaism, I could not begin from my identity as a Jew. Instead, I began from the knowing I had gained through my experience with another person and shaped a Jewish identity that would support and nurture that knowing. On the most basic level, we joined a Reform synagogue because no other movement would fully accept us. Our celebrations run closer to the spirit of the holiday rather than the letter of the law. More complexly, my sense of myself as a Jew, of what it means to live a holy life, always already includes non-Jews. My reality reflects a simple truth: who we are is shaped through our encounters with other people. While we are born into some identities, we give those identities meaning through the experiences that mark us.

Judaism by definition must exclude non-Jews to some extent, yet my love of a non-Jew forces me to investigate those boundaries and to see Judaism through my husband's eyes. The places where my husband sees things differently than I do—such as with the Kaddish minyan—force me to clarify my beliefs. Were my husband Jewish, I might not have had to think about whether it matters where you are buried and whether I believe in an afterlife where my husband and I can be together.

More to the point, I might not have to ask myself if I believe in a God who would bring two people from different faiths together, in love. That I do believe in such a God shapes my worldview and my perspective on interfaith work. It also significantly divides me from my own tradition, which cannot conceive of its God blessing a marriage between a Jew and a non-Jew.

In the wedding vows I spoke to my husband, I noted his generosity of spirit. It is one of the things I most admire—his ability to give freely, without keeping score as I too often do. It is this generosity of spirit that has created our Jewish home. My husband never sees things in terms of whose tradition is "winning," because if he did, clearly it would be mine. He has followed me into the land of the Israelites as surely as Ruth followed Naomi.

So, yes, my feelings about intermarriage have everything to do with the particular "other" I married—but isn't that precisely the point? I didn't marry an abstract Non-Jew; I married a particular man who has taught me, through his example, about generosity. The idea that we can best serve God, or even our community, with people who are like us is a limited view and ignores the extent to which we are drawn to people who have qualities that we may not have. These qualities sometimes come directly from the other person's tradition and his or her different experiences.

To believe that a Jewish home can only be nurtured by two Jews is to create a zero-sum game where one side must always take something at the expense of the other. Ultimately, I think this is an impoverished view of the world and of God.

Is my embrace of intermarriage dangerous? Indeed it is, in a number of ways. It is dangerous to Judaism precisely because identity is challenged.

Including non-Jews in the Jewish family changes how Jews think about themselves and their community. There is a danger that Judaism will be unrecognizable after such changes, that the center will not hold.

It is dangerous to me personally. I feel more emotionally rent through this experience than I imagine I would have felt had I married a Jew. At family gatherings with my in-laws, I am aware of being the only Jew, aware of standing alone when the conversation turns to religion.

Yet focusing on the danger of embracing something new sometimes blinds us to the dangers of not changing. Identity can be a narcotic that lulls us into a comfortable sense of belonging. It can encourage us to raise our walls and resist connection with others.

The Jewish community has spent a very long time talking about the dangers of engaging with those who are different from us. It is time to talk about the dangers of not engaging.

If not now, when?

NOTES

1 I begin the essay this way, intentionally echoing the final words of *Wall Street Journal* reporter Daniel Pearl, who was murdered by terrorists in Pakistan in 2002. Pearl saw himself as a cultural Jew, and he was married to Mariane Pearl, a non-Jewish Buddhist. It is with bitter irony that I note that Daniel Pearl's bravery has been rightly lauded by the American Jewish community, which has claimed him as a Jewish hero. Yet had he lived, he would have simply been an intermarried Jew, considered on the outskirts of the community, and his cultural Judaism would have placed him among the "unaffiliated."

2 By the 2000 National Jewish Population Survey (NJPS), United Jewish Communities (UJC), which oversaw the NJPS, would retract the 52 percent statistic, placing the true figure at 43 percent, but it hardly mattered, as a decade of programs dedicated to continuity were already in place. See Nacha Cattan, "New Population Survey Retracts Intermarriage Figure," *Jewish Daily Forward*, September 12, 2003, http://www.forward.com/articles/8112.

3 Quoted in Rabbi Jerome M. Epstein, "Issues regarding Employment of an Intermarried Jew by a Synagogue or Solomon Schechter Day School," approved by the Committee on Jewish Law and Standards of the Rabbinical Assembly on September 17, 1997. Available online at http://www.rabbinicalassembly.org/sites/default/files/public/halakhah/teshuvot/19912000/epstein_employment.pdf?phpMyAdmin=GoIs7ZE%2CH7O%2Ct%2CZ1sDHpI8UAVD6.

4 Quoted in ibid.

5 Dennis Prager and Joseph Telushkin, *The Nine Questions People Ask about Judaism* (New York: Touchstone, 1986), 146.

6   Ibid., 147.

7   Annette Baier, *Moral Prejudices: Essays on Ethics* (Cambridge, Mass.: Harvard University Press, 1995), 47.

8   bell hooks, *All about Love: New Visions* (New York: William Morrow, 2000), 93.

9   Jane Lazarre, *Beyond the Whiteness of Whiteness: Memoir of a White Mother of Black Sons* (Durham, N.C.: Duke University Press, 1997), 69.

17

When Certainty Becomes Immaterial

KHALEEL MOHAMMED

North America, and in particular the United States, has never allowed me to forget who I am. Long before the 9/11 attacks on the World Trade Center and the Pentagon in 2001, I was made to know that I was the outsider. As a Muslim living on a continent where religion plays a larger part in discourse than most people like to admit, I could only note with impotent sadness that press coverage on Islam was overwhelmingly negative.[1] The 9/11 attacks drastically intensified that negativity. Like my coreligionists, I am no longer just the outsider: I have become the enemy within. Mass media coverage about my religion overwhelmingly portrays it as murderous and intolerant, pitted against the advanced enlightenment of the other two Abrahamic faiths.

Against this pervasive hostility, my Muslim coreligionists and I have, whether we admit it or not, gone into damage-control mode. To deflect the accusations of extremism against us, we explore every opportunity to find a chink in the armor of the other two Abrahamic faiths, as if to say to them, "Your houses are just as dirty." I, for one, found an unsettling satisfaction when I read of Pope Benedict XVI's reintroduction of the Tridentine Mass, wherein the priest prays for the conversion of the Jews to Christianity.[2] Three days later, Benedict XVI declared Catholicism as the only way to salvation.[3] From my numerous visits to Israel, I have learned that many religious Jews still subscribe to Meir Kahane's idea of expelling Arabs from Israel.[4] Intolerance, it seems, is the shared Achilles' heel of the Abrahamic faiths.

Many traditional Islamic scholars perceive modernity's secularism as a threat to "pure" Islam. They protect their view of religion by reliance on medievalist interpretations formulated during the first five centuries of the post-Qur'anic period. These interpretations typically present a denigrating view of the outsider. This othering is not restricted to those outside Islam; internecine Sunni-Shiite conflict, bloodthirsty in its intensity, has a long and continuing history. In this chapter, I show how two of Islam's highest authorities legitimate exclusivist othering, and I provide my own suggestions for a reexamination of the idea of religious tolerance. I primarily focus on my own faith tradition but, where possible, draw upon elements of shared narratives to suggest changes that are needed in the general outlook of the family of Abrahamic religions.

On July 3, 1997, after supposedly careful study of pluralism, the Permanent Assembly for Research and Responsa (Fatwas) in Riyadh, Saudi Arabia, under the direction of the grand mufti, Sheikh Abd al-Aziz Ibn Baaz, issued a long fatwa against religious diversity, summarized as follows:

1. Islam is the only true religion.
2. The Qur'an has abrogated all previous scriptures, among them, the "corrupted" Torah and the "forged" Gospel.
3. One must believe that all previous scriptures have been corrupted and abrogated. Were Moses alive, he would have had no recourse but to follow Muhammad.
4. Muhammad is the final prophet.
5. A Muslim must deem as a disbeliever anyone who does not accept Islam. Unless a Muslim believes that such a disbeliever, Jewish or Christian, is a denizen of hell, then that Muslim is also a disbeliever.
6. The idea behind pluralism is to destroy Islam.
7. Pluralism effaces the difference between Islam and disbelief.
8. If a Muslim supports pluralism, then he or she has committed manifest apostasy.
9. Pluralism is a demonstrably sinful idea, and it is therefore wrong for any Muslim to aid and abet it or to attend any conferences promoting it. It is also wrong for any Muslim to build a single structure to be used as a mosque, synagogue, and church.[5]

In 1998, a group of Shiite Muslims from Toronto, Canada, sought a ruling from Ayatollah Sayyid Ali Husaini Sistani regarding the writings of

Abdulaziz Sachedina, a professor of Islamic studies at the University of Virginia. Until that time, Sachedina had been one of the most sought-after speakers among Shia and Sunni groups. The questioned writings were collected in a binder under five rubrics, one of which was "Religious Pluralism." Among the statements taken from an academic journal article was Sachedina's claim that the idea of Islam as the only monotheistic tradition offering an indubitable guarantee of salvation is actually a post-Qur'anic construct.[6] Deemed particularly troubling was the professor's interpretation of a particular verse in the Qur'an; he argued that the verse in question referred to Islam not in exclusivist terms but rather as a path of natural religiosity and submission to the divine will.[7] (Interestingly, Islam's most famous exegete, Muhammad al-Tabari, also noted this interpretation, but that universalist approach was later overshadowed by particularism.)[8]

The ayatollah's position was that if Muslim youth were exposed to Sachedina's teachings that all Abrahamic religions are equally truthful, they might be encouraged to convert to Christianity or Judaism.[9] After prolonged discussions with Sachedina, who had traveled to Najaf to defend against the charges, Ayatollah Sistani forbade the professor from expressing any public opinions in matters dealing with Islam and from making speeches in mosques. Specifically, on August 21, 1998, the ayatollah ruled that "whereas his [Sachedina's] views on issues presented are based on incorrect understandings and are incompatible with religious and academic standards, and cause confusion in minds of the true believers, they are all enjoined to refrain from inviting him to lecture at religious gatherings and not to consult him for answers on questions regarding creed."[10]

The exclusivism of the foregoing two fatwas is in line with traditional Islamic exegesis. In this regard, Islam is not unique, for all three faiths give weight to traditional interpretation, sometimes deeming sacrosanct the views of those medieval men, even though their collective worldview was shaped by their temporal settings and bigotries. In defense of his reintroduction of the Tridentine Mass, for example, Pope Benedict XVI explained, "What earlier generations held as sacred remains sacred and great for us too, and it cannot be, all of a sudden, entirely forbidden or even considered harmful."[11] In like fashion, the exclusive claim of many Jews to the land of Israel lies in traditional interpretations of the Torah.[12]

All three Abrahamic faiths practice othering; indeed, the identities of the righteous, those whom God loves, are almost always defined at the expense of a hapless "other." To be sure, there are scriptural verses of tolerance toward the outsider: after all, the Bible counsels against maltreatment of the stranger (as in Exodus 22:21, 23:9), and the Qur'an even allows intermarriage with, and entry to heaven for, the other (Qur'an 2:62, 5:5). Such treatment, however, comes as condescension; ultimately, the "other" is never on an equal footing with those who see themselves as blessed by God. The other's life has to be controlled by those who perceive themselves as God's righteous and be destroyed if it ever gets out of hand. Even in the shared Abrahamic narrative, otherness is underlined by the persona and treatment of Hagar (see Genesis 16 and 21). The meaning of her name says it all: *ha-gar*, "the stranger," "the other." This Egyptian and her child are relegated to the desert, far away from those whom God has specially blessed.

As a Muslim, I am particularly troubled by the Islamic sanctification of authority of the past. For while the Qur'an does have its polemical verses, it allows for a generally tolerable modus vivendi with others. Shortly after Muhammad's death, however, the oral tradition arose and gradually acquired de facto supremacy over the Qur'an. This oral tradition—functionally defined as the words, deeds, and tacit approvals of Muhammad that are not in the Qur'an but reported by his companions—is known as the Hadith.[13] In early Islamic history, the Hadith fulfilled a certain need: it served to explain why Muslims were conquerors and why they ruled various regions.

Contrary to the Qur'anic verses on inclusivism, the oral tradition taught absolute exclusivism, explaining away the Qur'anic recognition of other religions in terms of abrogation and supersession: all other messages were replaced by the coming of Muhammad.[14] The traditional authorities do not view the Hadith in terms of temporality or spatiality: for them it transcends time and place. This outcome means that for many Muslims in today's world, their belief in the Hadith transforms them into walking anachronisms. The Hadith does not tell them how to live as a minority or how to function as Muslims while acknowledging the political and legislative power of secular states.

The history of interaction among Judaism, Christianity, and Islam knows animosity rather than cordiality as the norm. The frequency of contemporary interfaith trialogues seems to indicate that the obvious may have sunk in: conflict has only resulted in bloodshed and malice, without the triumph of any one religion over the other. Pluralism is a reality of modernity—at least in North America and Europe—and it is evident that

Islam must rethink its traditional view of the outsider. This "rethinking," however, ought not to carry with it any taint of rejection of the scripture, for as I have argued earlier, the Qur'an itself is not exclusivist. Indeed, any learned Muslim can quote from the sacred text verse after verse that, unless warped by the oral tradition, does not allow for any other understanding than pluralism, acceptance of the other on equal footing.[15] These perspectives fit well with the astute observation that Ismail al-Faruqi (1921–1986) made years ago: today the primacy of focus in interfaith discussion must be on the ethical rather than the theological.[16] This focus makes room for pluralism, as Jews, Christians, and Muslims increasingly agree that their shared Abrahamic narratives should lead to a new estimation of the outsider.

Importantly, emphasis on the ethical rather than the theological makes the concept of tolerance problematic. Tolerance connotes being required, even forced, to accommodate something that is objectionable. As Adam Seligman explains: "Tolerance with its historical associations of suffering the presence of what is detestable (in the eyes of God and mankind) is . . . too feeble a thing to promote. Pluralism and the celebration of difference: that is what is called for rather than the insipid call to tolerance."[17]

For many of us, theology is something that can be argued about without any definite conclusions, hence the different creeds within some religions. However, while we may argue about the ethical, we must admit that it has certain shared ideas that preclude descent into bias and bigotry. In the aforementioned Ibn Baaz fatwa of July 1997, the Arabic rendition of "pluralism" was *wahdat al-adyan*—literally translated as "the oneness of religions." This translation reflects the fear of the translator more than it does linguistic correctness. Pluralism is in fact the acknowledgment of the variety of religions, but out of fear that Islam would be compromised, the translator for Ibn Baaz seems to have abandoned a more correct *ta'adudiyya* for the egregiously erroneous *wahdat al-adyan*. In like manner too, the Sistani edict spoke about Sachedina's views being incompatible with academic standards. This statement seems more in the line of polemic where disparagement of an opponent takes precedence over fidelity to truth. After all, Sachedina has satisfied all the rigorous criteria for obtaining a Western Ph.D., indeed questioning elements of his faith as only a highly qualified academic can do. From within the walls of his religious enclave, Sistani has no right to impugn Sachedina's academic standards. In both fatwas, a stronger adherence to ethics—very much a part of the

Islamic idea of propriety—might have prevented the mistranslation and the problematic assessment of Sachedina's scholarship.

Can Judaism, Christianity, and Islam be genuinely pluralistic, accepting the intrinsic religious value of other traditions? The question seems simple enough, and one is urged to answer with a resounding affirmative. Optimism about that outcome, however, depends on the degree to which adherents of the Abrahamic traditions can change, in particular by understanding, affirming, and enacting the conviction that the best form of religious pluralism does not mean sacrificing our individual and even communal identities. Rather, such a pluralism entails the recognition that a truly wise God speaks in ways that allow, indeed require, human beings to seek the Divine according to their own cultural and faith constructs, fallible or incomplete though they may be.

Acknowledgment of the necessity of change and the potential of a changed outlook, however, must not come with any expectation of precipitous metamorphosis. We also have to admit that our political reality affects our religious worldview. From its inception, for example, the United States has disparaged "the other." With genocidal dehumanization, the nation's land was wrested from its indigenous people. The country's establishment and growth produced new inimical "others." One war followed another. In a state of multiple wars at the time of this writing, the United States has enjoyed relatively few periods of peace. A long history plagued by creations of a hated other makes it difficult to expect sudden harmony—religious or otherwise—in American perceptions of the outsider.

Judaism, Christianity, and Islam share the story of Abraham's greeting God's messengers who came to him as strangers. It would have been normal for Abraham to be wary, but instead he hurried to prepare the fatted calf for them (Genesis 18:1–8). From a Muslim point of view, I focus on the fact that Abraham greeted these strangers with "salaam"—peace— and that what transpired was not conventional courtesy but the utmost in hospitality (Qur'an 11:69). In his encounter with the strangers, Abraham discovered God's will. The encounter gave him glimpses about how the Divine mind works and taught him to intercede with God for the safety of the doomed, many, if not all of them, strangers to Abraham himself. Abraham, it must be noted, did not hold back his hospitality until he had established a common belief system between the strangers and himself; rather, he demonstrated his admirable human compassion from the beginning, when he had not yet ascertained who they were. This element of the story in particular needs to be highlighted.

Where religious pluralism is concerned, another instructive biblical narrative—also shared by the three Abrahamic traditions—involves Sodom and Gomorrah (see Genesis 19 and Qur'an 11). The Genesis story relates how Lot offered to "the men of Sodom, both young and old, all the people to the last man," his daughters "who have not known a man" so that "the men of the city" could "do to them as [they] please." Given Lot's choice to sacrifice the honor of his daughters, theologians have long faced questions regarding his fitness to be a true man of God. Reexamining the narrative from an alternative ethical perspective may allow us to see a greater reason for the story's presence in scriptures. Lot's hospitality to strangers, who were actually angels of God, went far beyond giving them shelter. Was he willing to sacrifice his own daughters and therefore the honor of his tribe, so that his guests would not be disrespected or harmed? Could it be that no sacrifice would more fully illustrate the ethics of hospitality toward the stranger and, by extension, the idea of pluralism?

I close these reflections by recalling a Chautauqua conference I attended in the summer of 2007. There I saw genuine pluralistic interaction blossom. People of the Abrahamic faiths listened to one another's narratives and asked questions without prejudice and presupposition. There was not agreement on everything, but I remember how I felt transported to a different world. My daughter and I interpreted the Qur'anic explanation of why humans were created as different tribes and peoples rather than as an undifferentiated community: so that we might find happiness in our diversity (Qur'an 49:13). We had no identity crisis; we knew we were different, yet we felt welcome. We were living the religion of good action rather than that of vapid theology. I will not argue the issue, but I seriously doubt that there will be a day when "the wolf shall live with the lamb, the leopard shall lie down with the kid, the calf and the lion and the fatling together, and a little child shall lead them" (Isaiah 11:6). Was the idea to express an actual prophecy or to create the vision of an ideal toward which to continuously strive? Certainty is immaterial here. What matters is that we, who claim to honor and respect Abraham, really follow his tradition and step up from tolerance to pluralism.

CONTRIBUTORS' QUESTIONS FOR KHALEEL MOHAMMED

1. You write that ethics, rather than theology, must be primary in interfaith discussions. Does this claim suggest that ethical differences among the faiths are less vexed than theological differences? Further, if, as you say, "certainty is immaterial," vis-à-vis *theological* differences, is it equally immaterial vis-à-vis *ethical* differences? Your essay seems grounded on the premise that ethics is a firmer foundation for religion than theology is, yet it is often a particular ethical perspective that attracts someone to a particular theology. Might ethics, therefore, be as contingent as faith? If not, what is the foundation for such a trans-theological ethics? Particularly in light of the Holocaust and twenty-first-century violence that has links to the three major monotheistic traditions, can we say that this foundation is less vexed than that which has given rise to theological differences?

2. The story of Lot and your interpretation of it raise cutting-edge questions about possible limits of hospitality—and thus authentic trialogue—within the Abrahamic traditions:

   a) The story, as you tell it, can be read as a man putting the honor of other men above that of his daughters. What kind of ethics would legitimize Lot's actions? If this story can be used to promote religious pluralism, might that be partly because a male-centered narrative is a feature that all three religions share? Can one read this text in such a way that does not leave the female reader outside the conversation?

   b) Does Lot's protection of his guests ethically "trump" his responsibilities as a father? In terms of interfaith dialogue/trialogue, how might one balance caring for one's own community with the desire to reach out to the other? When the two come into conflict, which poses the higher ethical demand?

RESPONSE BY KHALEEL MOHAMMED

All of the Abrahamic faiths include theological debate that erupts after the death of their founders and after the establishment of the religions' foundational scriptures. Indeed, theology is not defined, at least not entirely and absolutely, by religions' founding figures and sacred texts. As Ignaz Goldziher put it, "Prophets are not theologians."[18] While typically using scripture as a reference, theology is inherently problematic because it remains arguable and inconclusive. Consensus on major theological points is often lacking among members of the same faith. If they cannot agree on theology—and history shows the often violent results of their acrimonious disputations—then how can we expect theology to be any less vexed among members of different faiths?

Pluralism holds that we properly may have different versions of what we consider to be truth. None of those versions, moreover, is sufficient to produce absolute certainty regarding particular religious beliefs. Nevertheless, despite all the religious differences among the three Abrahamic traditions, shared moral outlooks exist. To be sure, differences can still be found in the ethical perspectives of Judaism, Christianity, and Islam, but when basic understanding of good and evil is concerned, similarities— sometimes confused with sameness—seem to predominate.

I find it difficult to accept the premise (as presented in one of the questions put to me) that a particular ethical perspective might attract someone to a particular theology. This relationship presupposes ethical differences among the Abrahamic traditions that are more radical than critical scrutiny can sustain. The Christian who believes that Jesus will return, the Jew who rejects this idea, and the Muslim who has conflicting ideas on the subject will all agree—despite their theological differences about Jesus' return—that life is sacred, rape is wrong, and injustice is evil. This ethical agreement, it seems to me, indicates beyond the shadow of a doubt that if certainty is immaterial regarding theology, it is not as immaterial regarding ethical differences. For me as a Muslim, the Qur'anic verse 2:177 seems to apply to all the Abrahamic religions:

> It is not righteousness that ye turn your faces to the East and the West;
> but righteous is he who believeth in Allah and the Last Day and the
> angels and the Scripture and the prophets; and giveth wealth, for love of
> Him, to kinsfolk and to orphans and the needy and the wayfarer and to
> those who ask, and to set slaves free; and observeth proper worship and
> payeth the poor-due. And those who keep their treaty when they make
> one, and the patient in tribulation and adversity and time of stress. Such
> are they who are sincere. Such are the Allah-fearing.

This verse emphasizes that outward rituals are of secondary importance and that it is our ethical perspective, in concordance with certain acts of belief (hence the term *ethical monotheism*), that underlines our righteousness.

Going beyond the Abrahamic religions, I need only to refer to Buddhism and Jainism to underline my contention that ethics is far less contingent than particular religious faith affirmations. Neither of those religions focuses on theology, but both contain truly admirable ethics. Arguably, the Dalai Lama is a most respected person in our world today, and this high regard results from his ethics more than from his "theology," a term that may even be inappropriate in his case. Among other things, these non-Abrahamic religions—and their ethical viewpoints—show that ethics transcends "Divine command" theologies.[19]

With regard to the Shoah, I think it resulted from warped Judeophobic theology devoid of ethical reflection.[20] A similar Islamophobic theology manifests itself presently. Had ethics been properly weighted, no Shoah would have taken place, nor would we see the currently pervasive Islamophobia. Theological discussions typically underscore differences and do little to make the world better. Given that each faith has so many theologies, and pluralism is concerned more with *interfaith* rather than *intrafaith* encounters, I feel that a quest for harmony can be successful only when, as a body made up of different religions, we apply our common ethical worldviews to solve the problems of our globalized community.

The second cluster of questions above concentrates on my interpretation of the biblical story about Sodom and particularly on my views regarding Lot and his daughters. Responses to these questions permit me to clarify and expand my understanding of this narrative and its implications for religious pluralism. Unlike Jewish and Christian interpretations of the story about Sodom and Lot, which rarely, if ever, take the Qur'anic version and Islamic sensibilities into account, my analysis depends on a Qur'anic perspective. For all their similarities, these two scriptural accounts and their implications are scarcely identical and their aims may be quite different.

The biblical narrative in Genesis is recounting an event, not mandating an ethic. Furthermore, the story of Lot in Genesis cannot be considered only in light of the event of the strangers' visit. The later incest between Lot and his daughters and the resultant tribes of the Moabites and the Ammonites (see Genesis 19:30–38) is also crucial. As Michael D. Coogan points out, this part of Lot's saga is "a scurrilous rationalization of Israelite superiority."[21] The Qur'anic version does not say that Lot offered his daughters to be ravaged. According to the Qur'an, when Lot presents his daughters, he emphasizes their purity and asks if there is not a single righteous person among the mob (Qur'an 11:78). The Qur'anic language suggests no invitation to rape. The Qur'an, however, does indicate that Sodom's crime was robbery and sexual defilement of strangers (Qur'an 29:29). In desperation, Lot is depicted as trying to get the townspeople to desist from such depravity, but their response is disdainful: "You know full well that we do not desire nor need your daughters" (Qur'an 11:79). Lot, therefore, is aware that the men have their own wives and will not have his daughters, but are only bent on molesting the strangers. His plea simply manifests the desperate hope, like that of his uncle Abraham, that he can find some way to avoid Sodom's destruction.

From Lot's lament in Surah 11:77, it seems that he is aware that the emissaries are not mere men, but are representatives from the Lord (Qur'an 11:77–78); one cannot therefore read into the narrative a case of putting the honor of men before that of his daughters. The idea behind the Qur'anic version is to tell a story of punishment for wrongdoing. No breach of ethics is permitted. Even if one were to disagree with my interpretation of there being no invitation to rape, Lot's role as a father is secondary to his being a messenger and wishing to save the city. As the Islamic maxim states, "The private hardship is borne in order to ward off the communal harm."[22]

Only a "presentism" forced upon the biblical and Qur'anic narratives can make them more inclusive of the female reader. Both the Bible and the Qur'an emerged from and were addressed to androcentric societies and their attendant suppositions. Perhaps we can make the reading more inclusive by focusing less on the gender of the visitors and the mob and by emphasizing that abuse of guests, among other abominations, warranted Sodom's destruction. The issue of making the reading more palatable for modern tastes is what makes the "double movement" theory of Fazlur Rahman so cogent: that we attempt not to rewrite the story but to understand its motive(s), its setting, and seek to extrapolate an ethic that can apply to our time.[23]

On the issue of balancing my own faith community's interests against reaching out to the other, I rely on the Qur'an's mandate: "Stand up for justice, even if it be against yourself, your parents and kin" (Qur'an 4:135, 5:8). One has to look at the issue at hand and act upon what is perceived to be righteous. This stance rejects insistence on sameness of faith, which only legitimates divisive particularism and reinforces "othering," and gives priority to religious pluralism.

NOTES

1   In the summer of 1989, Mohammed Arkoun noted the mass media campaigns against extremism in Islam, with almost no coverage of liberal Islam. See Mohammed Arkoun, "New Perspectives for a Jewish-Christian-Muslim Dialogue," *Journal of Ecumenical Studies* 26, no. 3 (Summer 1989): 523–29; reprinted in *Muslims in Dialogue: The Evolution of a Dialogue*, ed. Leonard Swidler (Lewiston, N.Y.: Edwin Mellen Press, 1992), 224–29. Edward Said also noted that "malicious generalizations about Islam have become the last acceptable form of denigration of foreign culture in the West; what is said about the Muslim mind, or character, or religion, or culture as a whole cannot now be said in mainstream discussion about Africans, Jews, other Orientals, or Asians." Edward Said, *Covering Islam: How the Media and the Experts Determine How We See the Rest of the World* (New York: Vintage Books, 1997), xi–xii.

2   Ian Fisher, "Pope Revives Old Latin Mass, Sparks Jewish Concern," *San Diego Union Tribune*, July 8, 2007.

3   Nicole Winfield, "Pope Affirms Catholicism as Only Way to Salvation," *San Diego Union Tribune*, July 11, 2007.

4   Raphael Mergui and Philippe Simonnot, *Israel's Ayatollahs: Meir Kahane and the Far Right in Israel* (London: Saqi Books, 1987), 49.

5   "Pluralism: A Baseless Call and Pervasive Apostasy," *Al-Da'wa* (Riyadh), July 3, 1997, 22–23.

6   "The Presentation Submitted to the Marja'" (Safari Mosque, Toronto, n.d.), 1.

7   Ibid., 7.

8   See Wilfred Cantwell Smith, *The Meaning and End of Religion* (New York: Macmillan, 1965), 112–13.

9   See Abdulaziz Sachedina, "What Happened in Najaf?" Available online at http://www.uga.edu/islam/sachedina_silencing.html. In this essay, Sachedina provides his account of what happened during the investigation of his scholarship in August 1998.

10   "The Presentation," 48. See also *Al-Haqq Newsletter* (Islamic Humanitarian Services, Ontario), July–December 1999, 8.

11   Fisher, "Pope Revives Old Latin Mass."

12   Mergui and Simonnot, *Israel's Ayatollahs*, 49.

13   Mahmud al-Tahhan, *Taysir Mustalah al-Hadith* [Notes on the Science of Hadith] (Riyadh: Matawan al-Ma'arif, 1987), 15. See also John Burton, *An Introduction to the Hadith* (Edinburgh: Edinburg University Press, 1994), 19.

14   See item 3 in the Ibn Baaz fatwa, cited above in this chapter.

15   A few examples are Qur'an 2:62, 136, 281; 3:3; 5:51.

16   Ismail al-Faruqi, "Islam and Christianity: Dialogue or Diatribe," *Journal of Ecumenical Studies* 5, no. 1 (Winter 1968): 45–77; reprinted in Swidler, ed., *Muslims in Dialogue*, 1–35.

17   Adam Seligman, "Tolerance, Liberalism, and the Problem of Boundaries," *Society* 41, no. 2 (January–February 2004): 12–16.

18 Ignaz Goldziher, *Introduction to Islamic Theology and Law*, trans. Andras and Ruth Hamori (Princeton, N.J.: Princeton University Press, 1981), 67.

19 From the Socratic question of whether things are good because God says they are good or whether they are intrinsically good.

20 I use the Hebrew term instead of *Holocaust* to focus on the event for what it was: a catastrophe.

21 Michael D. Coogan, "Lot," in *The Oxford Companion to the Bible*, ed. Bruce M. Metzger and Michael D. Coogan (New York: Oxford University Press, 1993), 467.

22 Muhammad al-Burnu, *Al-Wajiz fi Idah Qawa'id al-Fiqh al-Kulliyah* [A Concise Explanation of the Major Fiqh Maxims] (Riyadh: Maktabat al-Ma'arif, 1989), 206. See also Khaleel Mohammed, "The Islamic Law Maxims," *Islamic Studies* 44, no. 2 (Summer 2005): 191–208.

23 Fazlur Rahman, *Islam and Modernity: Transformation of an Intellectual Tradition* (Chicago: University of Chicago Press, 1982), 5–9.

18

Interreligious Dialogue beyond Absolutism, Relativism, and Particularism

A Catholic Approach to Religious Diversity

DIDIER POLLEFEYT

Catholic approaches to interreligious dialogue begin with three models for understanding religious diversity: exclusivism, inclusivism, and pluralism.[1] With regard to non-Christian religions, however, this typology has become a stumbling block for authentic encounter and dialogue with the religious other. After a critical analysis of this typological approach and the crisis it provokes, I attempt to develop new perspectives on interreligious encounter that go beyond theological absolutism (usually attributed to exclusivism and inclusivism), relativism (usually attributed to pluralism), and the declaration of the impossibility of dialogue (usually attributed to particularism).

The first model of religious diversity is traditionally called exclusivism. Exclusivists are convinced that believers of other religions or nonbelievers can only be saved when they convert to the only true religion, namely, the religion exclusivists confess. For Christian exclusivists, this position means that people can only be saved when they convert to Christianity and accept, explicitly, Jesus as Christ and Redeemer. This Christian exclusivism is for the most part not only Christological in nature but also ecclesiological: *extra ecclesiam nulla salus* (no salvation outside the Church). This view entails that Christians have the obligation to proclaim the Christian message to everyone because truth is revealed only through Christ and the Church.

Exclusivism is no longer the official position of the Catholic Church, but it can still be found in several—especially evangelical—Christian churches, as well as in some non-Christian religious traditions.[2] The central idea is that God has revealed himself as a unique mediator or medium and that only through the explicit recognition of this mediator or medium can one find liberation or salvation. In the course of history, however, it was primarily the Christian tradition that developed an exclusivistic theology, accompanied by powerful institutional structures—a theology sometimes resulting in a religious colonialism that employed violence as a means to its end.

In contrast to exclusivism, inclusivism does not deny in advance the value of non-Christian religions. The central idea of Christian and specifically Catholic inclusivism is that salvation outside Christianity is possible, but only thanks to the salvific work of God through Jesus Christ. Inclusivism accepts the idea that God wanted salvation for all people in all times and places and that God's salvific way can take many forms. *Explicit* knowledge of Christ is not necessary for one to be saved. For this reason, one cannot in advance reject all other religions. This approach was initially developed before and during the time of the Second Vatican Council (1962–1965) by the Catholic theologian Karl Rahner: "But if it is true that a person who becomes the object of the Church's missionary efforts is or may be already someone on the way towards his salvation, . . . and if it is at the same time true that this salvation . . . is Christ's salvation, since there is no other salvation—then it must be possible to be . . . an anonymous Christian."[3]

Since the Second Vatican Council, this inclusivistic position has become the official position of the Catholic Church. In the 1964 Vatican II document *Lumen Gentium*, the "Dogmatic Constitution on the Church," we read that "those also can attain to [everlasting] salvation who through no fault of their own do not know the Gospel of Christ or His Church, yet sincerely seek God and moved by grace strive by their deeds to do His will as it is known to them [by] the dictates of [their] conscience."[4]

Inclusivism makes room for religious freedom and interreligious dialogue. For Pope John Paul II, interreligious dialogue, based on the inclusivistic paradigm, is an instrument of peace. In his speech in Assisi, Italy, on the World Day for Peace (October 26, 1986), John Paul II asked for "respect for one's personal conscience, rejecting all forms of coercion or discrimination with regard to faith, freedom to practice one's own religion and give witness to it, as well as appreciation and esteem for all genuine traditions."[5] For John Paul II, this engagement in interreligious dialogue is not in conflict with the proclamations of Christ.

Inclusivism has been criticized as a position that is not truly open to the reality of the other or because it would restrict its openness solely to what is compatible in the other with one's own religious identity. As philosopher of religion John Hick notes: "Inclusivism . . . [still] rests upon the claim to Christianity's unique finality as the locus of the only divine revelation and the only adequate saving event. Non-Christians can be saved because, unknown to them, Christ is secretly 'in a way united' with them."[6] Theologian Paul F. Knitter adds that "when one already has the fullness of truth, there can't be still too much to learn [in interreligious encounters]."[7] The central critique against inclusivism is that it does not take into account adequately the religious self-understanding of the other as other. With this point in mind, theologian Roger Burggraeve criticizes both exclusivism and inclusivism along the same lines, confronting these paradigms in a manner similar to the philosophical critique offered by the contemporary French thinker Emmanuel Levinas: "Dialogue starts by resisting the inclination to exclude the other (exclusivism) or by reducing the other to ourselves (inclusivism)."[8] Coming from a Muslim perspective, Bülent Şenay argues that inclusivism is often seen as a form of Christian imperialism. "On this understanding," Şenay writes, "it is not Buddhism that saves, but Christ in Buddhism, and Hindus are not saved by their beliefs, but in spite of them."[9]

The inclusivistic theology of religions has many variants, which include important recent developments. I refer in particular to Jacques Dupuis's Catholic "inclusivistic pluralism," Mark Heim's Protestant Trinitarian theology, and Paul Griffiths's Catholic "open inclusivism."[10] Dupuis's logocentric approach, one of the newest developments in a rethinking of the inclusivistic position, stresses that "the transcendent, illuminating power of the divine Logos, operative throughout human history, accounts for the salvation of human beings even before the manifestation of the Logos in the flesh [Jesus Christ]. . . . The divine Logos continues, even today, to sow his seeds among peoples."[11] At the same time, we see here how "open inclusivism" reaches its limits. The Vatican's Congregation for the Doctrine of the Faith issued a warning that was published in Dupuis's book:

It must . . . be firmly believed that Jesus of Nazareth, Son of Mary and
only Saviour of the world, is the Son and Word of the Father. For the
unity of the divine plan of salvation centred in Jesus Christ, it must
also be held that the salvific action of the Word is accomplished in and
through Jesus Christ, the Incarnate Son of the Father, as mediator of salvation for all humanity. It is therefore contrary to the Catholic faith not
only to posit a separation between the Word and Jesus, or between the
Word's salvific activity and that of Jesus, but also to maintain that there is
a salvific activity of the Word as such in his divinity, independent of the
humanity of the Incarnate Word.[12]

The developments in and critiques of inclusivistic theology need to
be seen in relation to pluralism, a third paradigm. Pluralists sometimes
maintain that only their approach allows for authentic dialogue. Arguably,
the central idea of pluralistic theology is the equality of all religions. All
religions are but partial expressions of the Ultimate Reality. All religions
are parallel paths to salvation insofar as they are agents working to move
human beings away from reliance on ego and orienting them, instead,
toward the goal of seeking Ultimate Reality.

This pluralist paradigm also has been the object of severe criticism.
Gavin D'Costa has argued, for example, that agnosticism is the inevitable outcome of pluralism because pluralism dismisses all religious particularity, "first from the particularity of the incarnation, then from the
particularity of a theistic God, and then from the particularity of any religious claim, be it Christian or non-Christian."[13] Pluralism risks becoming
exclusivistic for all those who do not accept the pluralistic presuppositions
for realizing authentic dialogue. The most convinced believers within a
particular religious tradition are likely to have problems with the relativistic understanding of their religion by pluralist thinkers, but, paradoxically, they may also be considered by pluralists to be unfit for dialogue.
This dilemma requires one to ask whether the pluralistic position allows
for dialogue with a religious other who is radically other. Pluralism may
turn out to be less different from inclusivism or exclusivism than appears
to be the case at first glance. Pluralist thinking typically is based on the
idea of a common ground, but John Cobb rightly warns against this idea
as the foundation for interreligious dialogue. "Real dialogue," says Cobb,
"involves listening to genuine strange ideas, whereas the assumption of

common ground limits the strangeness of what can be heard. The listener who is convinced of common ground will not be able to hear the full novelty of what is said."[14]

Especially in Christian circles, most discussion about the nature of interreligious dialogue positions itself between inclusivism and pluralism, which still leaves dialogue imprisoned within the typology of exclusivism, inclusivism, and pluralism. Importantly, Christian scholars created this typology to reflect on Christian questions, especially questions related to the possibility of salvation for the non-Christian believer. But this soteriological question is a Christian question, a point that led George Lindbeck to identify the typology's "soteriological fixation" as an expression of Christian superiority.[15] The orientation of Judaism or Islam can hardly be described as an orientation toward salvation as it is understood within a Christian framework. So the critique concerning respect for the self-understanding of the other should be addressed not to inclusivism alone, but rather toward the entire enterprise of dialogue/trialogue, which should not be dominated by categories and concerns peculiar to one religion alone.

Criticism of the three-part typology led to another approach to interreligious dialogue, one centered on the particularity of religious systems. This position cannot be located within the traditional typology. "Rather," as Paul Griffiths indicates, "it attempts to change the terms of the debate itself."[16] The goal of the particularist in interreligious dialogue is no longer to reduce differences to some common denominator or ground, but to discover, accept, and respect the differences among partners in dialogue. Lindbeck may be the most eminent proponent of this position. Religions are not just different schemas for expressing human experience of the divine; rather, each is a different framework for the expression of a radically different religious experience. For Lindbeck, religion is an external word (*verbum externum*) that shapes the self.[17] He compares religions to linguistic systems, which also are always particular. Religious believers are people who have learned to speak a particular religious language; no general or universal religious language exists. Furthermore, Lindbeck argues, religious languages, unlike natural languages, are untranslatable; they are intra-semiotic, intra-textual, and all-encompassing. He stresses that "nothing can be translated out of this [biblical] idiom into some supposedly independent communicative system without perversion, diminution or incoherence of meaning."[18] The consequence of this position is the impossibility of interreligious dialogue. Lindbeck's conclusion is clear:

"Not only do they [the religions] no longer share a common theme such as salvation, but the shared universe of discourse forged to discuss that theme disintegrates. . . . Those for whom conversation is the key to solving interreligious problems are likely to be disappointed."[19] Lindbeck clearly draws the consequences of his own theology for interreligious dialogue. A radical particularism means the end of interreligious dialogue since there is nothing common to talk about. We are even lacking a common language with which to understand one another. In this position, we see how the dominance of sameness is exchanged for the dominance of otherness.

The fact that this particularism renders interreligious dialogue impossible is not per se an argument against it. Perhaps dialogue is impossible. But the following questions should be asked: Do the presuppositions that Lindbeck uses to understand religion do justice to the essence of the dynamics of religions itself? Are religions closed, untranslatable, and all-absorbing linguistic systems, creating different worlds that cannot engage in dialogue with one another?

Several elements in the self-understanding of religions produce answers to these questions. First, from the monotheistic perspective, all human beings are created in the image of God and are connected with one another. Also in an eschatological perspective, the aim of the biblical God is oriented toward the unity of the whole of creation. This outlook means that the first and last words are given not to separation or otherness but to unity and interconnectedness. Linguistic systems include efforts to refer to God, to explain or to express the relation that people experience with something or someone outside themselves. So religious systems are not auto-referential, but rather refer to a God or a divine reality experienced as outside or beyond any linguistic system. Precisely because of this external reference, different religions can talk to one another about how they experience and express this "outside" or "beyond." It is even possible to hold a discussion on the "truth" in relation to this reference to the "outside" or "beyond."

Further, religious linguistic systems are not completely separated from one another historically. There are many linguistic, cultural, and theological overlaps and mutual influences. The grammar of faith and the practice of the different religions did not develop in near isolation.[20] Finally, religious traditions are not static entities. Precisely because they refer to a living reality outside themselves, and because the context in which reality is experienced is constantly changing, religions are flexible systems. Traditions are therefore dynamic realities that can change in response to new challenges and in interaction with other traditions.[21] Lindbeck's approach risks making religions "traditions without God." Religions risk becoming auto-referential instead of hetero-referential systems, systems that can become either violent or indifferent toward all that is different and that cannot be absorbed into one's own system.

In *Sur la traduction (On Translation)*, the French Protestant philosopher Paul Ricoeur analyzes the problem of the untranslatable character of languages. He is well aware of both the opportunities and the risks of translation.[22] Ricoeur also is hopeful concerning the possibility of translation from one linguistic system to another. However, no translation is possible without the risk—indeed, the reality—of losing meaning, changing meaning, perverting meaning vis-à-vis the original text. Ricoeur recognizes that the perfect translation is impossible, but that outcome does not necessitate the affirmation of unbridgeable differences (42). Far from ending only in the loss of meaning, the activity of translation can discover new meanings, including meanings in scripture itself. Furthermore, in the effort of translating in engagement with the other, new meanings can appear that were not clear or revealed until dialogue or trialogue ensued, not even to those who speak the original language. Thus Ricoeur speaks about an "enlargement of the horizon of one's proper language" (15); he accents "linguistic hospitality" and receiving the other in one's own religious understanding of reality (20).

This line of thought suggests that one should be aware that every interreligious translation is a dangerous enterprise, for in the course of translation, one runs the risk of losing or perverting religious meanings, thus becoming untruthful vis-à-vis one's tradition.[23] Since experience and language can never be disconnected completely, even speaking about one's own religion and about the religion of the other will in some way begin from and remain colored by one's own original language. Hence inclusivism, in some way, is always inescapable for religious believers who enter into interreligious dialogue. If, for example, the Christocentric reference is "translated away" in the dialogue, Christians would have betrayed their own religion, since the activity of the logos in Christ for the salvation of all persons belongs to the essence of Christianity. But the fact that the perfect translation does not exist can never be an excuse for simply remaining in one's own closed linguistic or religious system and failing to enter into the process of translation. A religion that refuses in principle to translate itself time and again destroys its fundamental dynamic, which is born out of the dialectic between sameness and otherness.

Religious diversity that extends beyond commonality even can become more a blessing than a curse, as a rereading of the biblical story of the Tower of Babel (Genesis 11:1–9) suggests. The inhabitants of Babel tried to create meaning by realizing a common project based on one common language: the building of a tower "that reaches to the heavens" (Genesis 11:4). When God saw this idolatry of a world in no need of translation anymore, he confused their languages so that they were no longer able to understand one another. God created otherness. The inhabitants of Babel became strangers to one another; the dream of a common destiny and project was definitively lost.

Traditionally, this story is read as emphasizing God's punishment for human hubris. But an alternative reading would emphasize that in the building of the tower, God saw how humanity was looking for the infinite in the wrong place, namely, by reducing the infinite to a common ground at the cost of otherness. God redirected humanity to real transcendence, a transcendence that is only possible through the experience of the stranger. The other represents an invitation to break open my own closed linguistic world time and again; I am invited to enter into a "translational" or inter-religious relation. In this translational movement I can (re)discover God, at the point and at the moment that my loyalty is tested to the limit.

The Christian story of Pentecost (Acts 2:1–13) often has been understood as an undoing of the story of Babel. However, Pentecost should rather have been read as a confirmation of God's decision to bring into the world different languages but not necessarily to confound understanding and appreciation of difference. Now everyone can speak his or her language, but thanks to careful translational activities, people can start not only to respect and understand one another but also to learn from one another.[24] This prospect should change the agenda of the theology of religions in a fundamental way.

CONTRIBUTORS' QUESTIONS FOR DIDIER POLLEFEYT

1. With regard to Lindbeck's understanding of religions as linguistic systems, you ask, "Are religions closed, untranslatable, and all-absorbing linguistic systems, creating different worlds that cannot engage in dialogue with one another?" You respond by contending that religions-

as-linguistic-systems aim to refer to the external experience of the "beyond," the "outside," the "divine" or God. However, in arguing for religions as linguistic systems, are you referring to the entire "package" of each religion, including its scripture, history, culture, and practices, or are you referring to the particular devotion, reasoning, and practice of each human individual toward that which is beyond? Further, do religions always refer to the same "beyond"? How can you support your understanding of religions-as-linguistic-systems in light of the apparent negation of the core teachings of one religion by another? In a post-Holocaust world whose historical context includes twenty-first-century violence implicating all three Abrahamic traditions, what key challenges to authentic trialogue rooted in experience of the "beyond" do you anticipate?

2. If a non-Christian should seek out a Catholic Christian and declare his or her longing to convert to Christianity, is it theologically within the realm of possibility for the Catholic to turn him or her away, saying, "No, you have wisdom and salvation in your own tradition"? If not, then doesn't Christian theology end up appropriating the Other or the stranger, making any dialogical/trialogical relation impossible?

RESPONSE BY DIDIER POLLEFEYT

The central challenge presented to my essay is whether "religions always refer to the same 'beyond.'" My essay criticizes both a too easily positive and a too easily negative response to this question. In the popular understanding of interreligious dialogue, a spontaneously given and positive answer to this question is based mostly on the pluralistic paradigm. As the pluralist John Hick argues, the different religions "describe not the ultimate as it is in itself but as it is conceived in the variety of ways made possible by our varied human mentalities and cultures."[25] In other words, different religions represent different human perspectives on the "beyond," on "the ultimate," or on "the Real."[26] In this understanding, each religion has "a particular devotion, reasoning, and practice . . . toward that which is beyond." This pluralistic perspective often presents itself as the only alternative to the intolerance of both exclusivism and inclusivism. This approach implies that religious systems are *only* relative, cultural-historical conceptualizations of religious experiences of the "beyond," of the ultimate divine reality that forms the common ground and source of all religions. The presupposition of the pluralistic paradigm is thus that one should be prepared to accept the relativity of one's own faith position as a precondition for participation in authentic dialogue. The risk of this position is that in its reaction against exclusivists and inclusivists—who both attempt to convert others because they cannot deal with religious difference—pluralism reproduces within itself the intolerance against which it pretends to fight.

Often, we see how the dialogical process shifts from an encounter among representatives from different religious traditions to an encounter among the representatives of one common theological paradigm across religions: pluralism. Pluralism excludes on principle all other opinions and approaches. But, on the other hand, a too easy "yes" to the question "Do religions always refer to the same 'beyond'?" also risks imposing a specific belief on all believers, a belief in a "common ground." Such a common ground presupposes, at the very least, a relativization—if not a rejection and replacement—of the particularity of one's own religious perspective. J. Augustine DiNoia explains how this pluralist approach violates the "logic" of authentic interreligious dialogue: "Participation in such [authentic] dialogue demands at least recognition of 'the other *as* other' . . . and perhaps the acknowledgment of incompatibility among some doctrine-expressing sentences of some religious communities."[27]

I introduce the linguistic approach as a corrective to the sometimes uncritical way that interreligious dialogue starts with belief in "the same beyond." For Lindbeck, "it is just as hard to think of religions as it is to think of cultures or languages as having a single generic or universal experiential essence of which particular religions—or cultures or languages—are varied manifestations or modifications. One can in this outlook no more be religious in general than one can speak language in general."[28] Lindbeck makes us aware of the particularity of religious systems in a radical way. For Lindbeck, religions do not reveal in different ways the same experience; rather, they involve diverse experiences.[29] In this approach, no "same beyond" exists. The relationship between different religions becomes a relationship between different realities or "packages" that use completely different and autonomous language systems, including coherent scriptures, histories, and practices. Particular religious languages "absorb" reality. Religious language cannot be translated outside its own realm. For this reason, Lindbeck thinks, the meanings within one religion cannot be translated into those of another. Lindbeck himself speaks of a "balkanization" of the dialogue.[30]

The analysis of religions as linguistic systems sharpens awareness that we cannot too easily speak of any "same beyond" to which all religions refer. Ultimately, however, I reject this understanding of religions because it destroys the dialogical dimension of religions and religious believers, and it violates one of the most central characteristics of any religious system, namely, that religions say something about reality outside themselves. Religious systems refer to something or someone "beyond" their own linguistic structures. For a monotheistic believer, for example, believing in God is not the same as believing in Mickey Mouse, because Mickey Mouse simply does not exist outside the narrative construct of its creator. For a monotheistic believer, God is not just a construct, created, born, or imprisoned within a linguistic system. On the contrary, the strongest religious experiences occur when God comes from the outside, from the stranger, who questions and breaks open religious systems in the name of a greater truth.

My position is that all sound religions refer to *a beyond*, but (contra Lindbeck) not necessarily and automatically in the *same way* to What or Who is beyond (with regard to monotheistic religions), or (pro Lindbeck) not necessarily and automatically to the *same beyond* (with regard to non-monotheistic religions). This outlook helps explain why religions are not analogous to clothes that one can easily change and also why religious systems are incommensurable on many points. In my view, interreligious dialogue is possible, and it can be fruitful, but only so long as the participants agree that no one has direct and unmediated access to a reality "beyond" and that this reality will finally remain unknown and mysterious for every person and religious system.

Interreligious dialogue is a communicative and hermeneutical activity. This observation does not exclude speaking about "truth" in such dialogue, since we can still have discussion regarding the adequacy and the consistency of different human mediations of (religious) reality. Our relation to (religious) reality is always mediated by a linguistic system that opens, colors, and cocreates—but also limits and even confuses and darkens—our understanding of the reality outside ourselves. Significantly, this position allows for an inclusivism that permits a believer to escape from his or her insider's perspective. As a Christian, for example, I cannot understand reality without affirming the ultimate significance of Christ and his Spirit for the salvation of all humankind, even if non-Christians do not explicitly know or acknowledge this significance. This inclusivistic position also exists in Judaism and Islam. For almost two thousand years, the rabbinic tradition has asserted that righteousness was established in God's covenant with Noah: anyone who keeps the seven commandments of this covenant will be saved, no matter to what religion he or she belongs. And the Qur'an, revealed through Muhammad, states: "Those with Faith, those who are Jews, and the Christians and Sabaeans all who have Faith in Allah and the Last Day and act rightly, will have their reward with their Lord. They will feel no fear and will know no sorrow."[31] We see here that the particularity of our own religious systems—Christ, the commandments, Allah—remains our point of reference for interreligious dialogue. At the same time, one must be alert to the danger of reading, understanding, and appreciating others only in one's own religious terms.

The introduction of the idea of "translation" in interreligious dialogue is a way to escape the paradox between (1) the idea of the radical incommensurability of religious systems (with nothing "beyond" the linguistic system) and consequently the impossibility of interreligious dialogue and (2) the idea of a common ground (with the "same beyond" for all religions). The notion of "translation" is a way to deal with the tension between otherness and sameness in our understanding of religious identities. Within this perspective, to engage in authentic interreligious dialogue means to attempt to translate one's religious understanding of reality to someone who is not participating in the same religious system and to open oneself to the efforts of the other to engage in the same task of translation. As every translator knows, translation is a precarious enterprise; finally, and in principle, it fails. Perfect translations do not exist. Translation is immensely risky. Its inevitable shortcomings mean that we can never completely transcend our own particularity, that the other will never understand me completely, and that every translation runs the risk of being unfaithful to the original text. Nevertheless, translation can still be a source of enrichment and can even result in the discovery of new meanings within one's own religious system.

With regard to the questions posed about conversion, I do not think that conversion always means that one does not respect the other. Conversion and interreligious dialogue need not be exclusive of one another. As a Christian, I am well aware of the many (individual and collective) forms of superficial, pragmatic, imposed, and even violent conversion in the history of my tradition. But these negative and unacceptable forms of mission and conversion do not exclude the possibility and even the beauty of many conversions of a person into a religion, or the conversion of an individual from one religion to another. Accepting a convert into one's religious community can be an act of hospitality, a source of new challenges, meanings, and joy.

Again, references to language and translation can be helpful. Authentic conversion occurs when someone learns a new or another religious language and when at a certain point one becomes "absorbed" by its reality. He or she then begins to think, speak, act, and live in that new religious universe and starts to experience reality itself from the new and other perspective. Of course, just as one needs to learn to speak a language adequately, one needs to learn a religious language adequately. This explains why conversion always needs to be a personal and gradual process, one that requires careful guidance from the believing community. In the Catholic Church, the so-called Rite of Christian Initiation of Adults (RCIA) is the official order for initiation of the unbaptized. It is a process that gradually reveals the story of God's salvation for the unbaptized through initiation into the mystery of Jesus' life, death, and resurrection. As a translational activity, interreligious dialogue neither should nor can exclude the possibility of authentic conversion (in all possible directions). And, indeed, sometimes so-called converts speak the new religious language for the wrong reasons and speak it so poorly, so distortedly, that it is better to advise such converts to stay (temporarily or permanently) within their original philosophical or religious language. Conversion is not the explicit, primary, or only goal of interreligious dialogue. Many other goals have priority: full respect of differences, mutual enrichment, and cross-fertilization of ideas. But the possibility and authenticity of religious conversion has its place in interreligious dialogue, too.

NOTES

1 This typology was first introduced in Alan Race, *Christians and Religious Pluralism: Patterns in the Christian Theology of Religions* (London: SCM Press, 1983).

2 See, for example, Lausanne Committee for World Evangelization, http://www.lausanne.org.

3 Karl Rahner, *Theological Investigations* (London: Darton, 1964), 1:75–76.

4 Second Vatican Council, *Lumen Gentium*, "Dogmatic Constitution on the Church," 1964, sec. 16. Available online at http://www.vatican.va/archive/hist_councils/ii_vatican_council/documents/vat-ii_const_19641121_lumen-gentium_en.html.

5   Pope John Paul II, "Address at Assisi," in *Interreligious Dialogue: The Official Teaching of the Catholic Church (1963–1995)*, ed. Francesco Gioia (Boston: Pauline Books, 1997), 532.

6   John Hick, *Disputed Questions in Theology and the Philosophy of Religion* (London: Macmillan, 1993), 84.

7   Paul F. Knitter, *Jesus and the Other Names: Christian Mission and Global Responsibility* (Maryknoll, N.Y.: Orbis Books, 1996), 142.

8   Roger Burggraeve, "Alterity Makes the Difference: Ethical and Metaphysical Conditions for an Authentic Interreligious Dialogue and Learning," in *Interreligious Learning*, ed. Didier Pollefeyt (Leuven, Belgium: Peeters, 2007), 237.

9   Bülent Şenay, "Teaching World Religions: Reflexive 'Interreligious Learning': Phenomenological Theology and Methodological Agnosticism," in Pollefeyt, ed., *Interreligious Learning*, 220.

10 Jacques Dupuis, *Toward a Christian Theology of Religious Pluralism* (Maryknoll, N.Y.: Orbis Books, 1997); Mark Heim, *Salvations: Truth and Difference in Religion* (Maryknoll, N.Y.: Orbis Books, 1995); Paul Griffiths, *Problems of Religious Diversity* (Malden, Mass.: Blackwell, 2001).

11 Dupuis, *Toward a Christian Theology of Religious Pluralism*, 320.

12 Vatican, Congregation for the Doctrine of the Faith, "Notification on the Book *Toward a Christian Theology of Religious Pluralism*," 2001, sec. 1.2. Available online at http://www.vatican.va/roman_curia/congregations/cfaith/documents/rc_con_cfaith_doc_20010124_dupuis_en.html.

13 Gavin D'Costa, *The Meeting of Religions and the Trinity* (Edinburgh: T & T Clark, 2000), 28.

14 John Cobb, "Dialogue without Common Ground," in *Weltoffenheit des christlichen Glaubens* [Openness to the World of Christian Faith], ed. Imelda Abbt and Alfred Jäger (Tübingen: Katzmann, 1987), 148.

15 George Lindbeck, "The Gospel's Uniqueness: Election and Untranslatability," *Modern Theology* 13, no. 4 (1997): 425.

16 Paul Griffiths, "The Properly Christian Response to Religious Plurality," *Anglican Theological Review* 79, no. 1 (1997): 3.

17 See ibid., 3.

18 Lindbeck, "The Gospel's Uniqueness," 429.

19 Ibid.

20 Jerome Stone, "Philip Hefner and the Modernist/Postmodernist Divide," *Zygon: Journal of Religion and Science* 39, no. 4 (2004): 767.

21 John Cobb, "Incommensurability: Can Comparative Religious Ethics Help?" *Buddhist-Christian Studies* 16 (1996): 45.

22 Paul Ricoeur, *Sur la traduction* (Paris: Bayard, 2004).

23 This point is strongly argued in Marianne Moyaert, "Een zekere fragiliteit? Interreligieuze dialoog en de spanning tussen openheid en identiteit" [A Certain Fragility? Interreligious Dialogue and the Tension between Identity and Openness] (Ph.D. diss., Faculty of Theology, Katholieke Universiteit Leuven, 2007; promotor: Didier Pollefeyt).

24 Didier Pollefeyt, "Voorbij afschuw en verschoning" [Beyond Horror and Excuse] (Ph.D. diss., Faculty of Theology, Katholieke Universiteit Leuven, 1995; promotor: Roger Burggraeve), 532, 584.

25 John Hick, *Disputed Questions in Theology and the Philosophy of Religion* (New Haven, Conn.: Yale University Press, 1993), 165.

26 Ibid., 178.

27 J. Augustine DiNoia, "Teaching Differences," *Journal of Religion* 73, no. 1 (1993): 64–65.

28 George Lindbeck, *The Nature of Doctrine: Religion and Theology in a Postliberal Age* (Philadelphia: Westminster John Knox Press, 1984), 23.

29 "French Revolutionary *fraternité* are not diverse modifications of a single fundamental human awareness, emotion, attitude, or sentiment, but are radically (i.e., from the root) distinct ways of experiencing and being oriented toward self, neighbor, and cosmos." Ibid., 40.

30 Lindbeck, "The Gospel's Uniqueness," 427.

31 Qur'an, *Suratal-Baqara*, 2:62.

Epilogue

What Should Be Remembered?

LEONARD GROB AND JOHN K. ROTH

> . . . If anything can, it is memory that will save humanity.
> —Elie Wiesel, Nobel Lecture, 1986

As *Encountering the Stranger* draws to a close, what is worth remembering about this book? Its readers, of course, will provide the most important responses to that question, but Elie Wiesel's proposition—"If anything can, it is memory that will save humanity"—resonates well with the volume's prologue, a point of departure stressing that "dialogue is the way" when interactions among the Abrahamic traditions are in play.

Judaism, Christianity, and Islam—including interaction and dialogue within and among them—are steeped in memory and in particular memories. Indeed, absent the human capacity to remember and the specificity of the memories that are ours, those religious traditions neither would nor could exist. The importance of memory, however, is even more fundamental than that. Absent memory and memories, for instance, there would be no strangers, and that result would obtain because no one would have a recognizable personal identity. Memory is finite, fallible, and frail; particular memories are not always reliable, and they may be subject to distortion and deception, partly because forgetfulness and forgetting are often their companions. Nevertheless, without memory and memories, one can scarcely imagine the existence of language(s), religion(s), and ethics. No dialogue would be possible. In fact, there would be no humanity.

With the presence of memory and memories, however, not only do humanity, language(s), and religion(s) emerge and evolve, but they do so in amazing particularity. That particularity produces and reflects the richness and beauty of diverse traditions and cultures, but that same particularity makes us strange to one another. Senses of strangeness both separate and relate human beings. Those senses, rooted in memory and memories, can turn people into strangers who become threats. When human relations trend in that direction, the ensuing whirlwind frequently reaps discrimination, hatred, and violence. The history of religions—often with the particularities of Judaism, Christianity, and Islam at the forefront—bears witness to such destructive encounters, which already, unfortunately, have scarred the twenty-first century and created ominous portents for the times ahead.

Given the stress and strain, the threats and fears that besiege contemporary life, humanity's future is as problematic and precarious as it has ever been. If that claim is credible, and plenty of evidence exists to affirm that it is, then does Wiesel's proposition about memory make sense? Could memory save humanity? Could the very reality that does so much to make us strangers to one another contain what is needed and necessary to make human beings affirm, at least as a governing hope, that—to recall words by Tommy Sands from this book's third part—"there are no strangers here, just friends that you never knew"? It is worth remembering that *Encountering the Stranger* answers *yes* to those questions in at least two ways.

First, reflecting Martin Buber's insight that "one can enter into relation only with being which has been set at a distance," the pages of this book show how particular people—Jews, Christians, and Muslims—all of whom were once distant from one another and whose backgrounds, traditions, and beliefs remain quite different, became friends by making their diversity not an occasion for suspicion and hostility but an opportunity for discovery and hospitality.[1] Those experiences did not eliminate differences or even disagreements among the contributors to this volume, but they did make us see and understand better that memory and memories of who we are in our particularity can deepen appreciation for the value of respect for others and can produce the enhanced self-respect that results from welcoming and befriending the stranger.

The friendships formed as eighteen people—strangers all at one time or another—came to know one another by talking, sharing, and writing together are not enough to change the world very much, let alone to save humanity. But such friendships are important nonetheless because those relationships, deepened through dialogue, and the work done in these pages indicate a second, immensely significant way in which this book says *yes* to the question "Could memory save humanity?"

Reaching far beyond the impact that eighteen people alone could have, *Encountering the Stranger*'s most important insight is that Judaism, Christianity, and Islam all contain teachings and traditions that, if remembered and practiced, can transform human existence by giving priority to hospitality. The book amplifies and extends that point partly by recalling the injustice, suffering, and waste that accumulate and poison human relations when any religious tradition becomes exclusive and seeks to impose dominance on others. Alternatively, the book shows something else that is eminently important to remember, namely, that when people practice their religious traditions most authentically, most consistently in terms of the priorities of those traditions at their best, the result is likely to be one that increases compassion, justice, and inclusiveness. When failure to practice religion in those ways takes place, a destructive reality that, unfortunately, is not likely to disappear soon, the need for perspectives of the kind found in these pages becomes all the greater.

Safeguarding, valuing, welcoming the stranger—those themes and outlooks guided the unfolding of this book's contents. All three of the Abrahamic traditions can help their adherents make progress in those directions, and, at their best, those traditions can model for all humanity welcoming dispositions and hospitable practices that lead strangers to become friends. The likelihood of such results hinges on deciding and taking to heart what should be remembered.

NOTE

1   The quotation is from Buber's 1950 essay "Distance and Relation." See *Martin Buber on Psychology and Psychotherapy: Essays, Letters, and Dialogue*, ed. Judith Buber Agassi (Syracuse, N.Y.: Syracuse University Press, 1999), 4.

Selected Bibliography

This bibliography supplements the works cited by the contributors to this volume. Restricted to recent publications, typically those that have appeared in the twenty-first century and after the pivotal events of September 11, 2001, the books and websites noted here are primarily of two kinds. Some concentrate on contributions to trialogue among the Abrahamic traditions: Judaism, Christianity, and Islam. Discussions that concentrate on two, but not all three, of these traditions—Jewish-Christian or Jewish-Muslim dialogue, for example—are more numerous, but they are not the focus of this bibliography. The works identified below emphasize trialogical content and interaction. Other books and websites in this select bibliography deal with topics and approaches that are especially relevant to the outlooks in *Encountering the Stranger*, even though these works are not examples of trialogical content and interaction.

Banchoff, Thomas, ed. *Religious Pluralism, Globalization, and World Politics.* New York: Oxford University Press, 2008.

Barrett, Kevin, John B. Cobb, Jr., and Sandra B. Lubarsky, eds. *9/11 and American Empire: Christians, Jews, and Muslims Speak Out.* Northampton, Mass.: Olive Branch Press, 2007.

Berger, Alan L., ed. *Trialogue and Terror: Judaism, Christianity, and Islam after 9/11.* Eugene, Ore.: Wipf and Stock, 2012.

Boase, Roger, ed. *Islam and Global Dialogue: Religious Pluralism and the Pursuit of Peace.* Burlington, Vt.: Ashgate, 2005.

Brill, Alan. *Judaism and World Religions: Encountering Christianity, Islam, and Eastern Traditions.* New York: Palgrave Macmillan, 2012.

Byrne, Máire. *The Names of God in Judaism, Christianity, and Islam: A Basis for Interfaith Dialogue*. New York: Continuum, 2011.

Chittister, Joan, Saadi Shaker Chisti, and Arthur Waskow. *The Tent of Abraham: Stories of Hope and Peace for Jews, Christians, and Muslims*. Boston: Beacon Press, 2006.

Clark, Kelly James, ed. *Abraham's Children: Liberty and Tolerance in an Age of Religious Conflict*. New Haven, Conn.: Yale University Press, 2012.

A Common Word between Us and You. Amman, Jordan: The Royal Aal al-Bayt Institute for Islamic Thought, 2009. Home page retrieved at http://www.acommon word.com

Coppola, David L., ed. *What Do We Want the Other to Teach about Us?* Fairfield, Conn.: Sacred Heart University Press, 2006.

Cornille, Catherine. *The Im-possibility of Interreligious Dialogue*. New York: Crossroad, 2008.

Esposito, John L. *The Future of Islam*. New York: Oxford University Press, 2010.

Esposito, John L., and Ibrahim Kalin, eds. *Islamophobia: The Challenge of Pluralism in the Twenty-First Century*. New York: Oxford University Press, 2011.

Feiler, Bruce S. *Abraham: A Journey to the Heart of Three Faiths*. New York: William Morrow, 2002.

Firestone, Reuven. *Who Are the Real Chosen People? The Meaning of Chosenness in Judaism, Christianity, and Islam*. Woodstock, Vt.: SkyLight Paths Publishing, 2008.

Gopin, Mark. *Between Eden and Armageddon: The Future of World Religions, Violence, and Peacemaking*. New York: Oxford University Press, 2000.

———. *Holy War, Holy Peace: How Religion Can Bring Peace to the Middle East*. New York: Oxford University Press, 2002.

Greble, Emily. *Sarajevo, 1941–1945: Muslims, Christians, and Jews in Hitler's Europe*. Ithaca, N.Y.: Cornell University Press, 2011.

Grob, Leonard, and John K. Roth, eds. *Anguished Hope: Holocaust Scholars Confront the Palestinian-Israeli Conflict*. Grand Rapids, Mich.: Wm. B. Eerdmans, 2008.

Heck, Paul L. *Common Ground: Islam, Christianity, and Religious Pluralism*. Washington, D.C.: Georgetown University Press, 2009.

Heft, James L., ed. *Beyond Violence: Religious Sources of Social Transformation in Judaism, Christianity, and Islam*. New York: Fordham University Press, 2004.

———, ed. *Catholicism and Interreligious Dialogue*. New York: Oxford University Press, 2011.

———, ed. *Passing on the Faith: Transforming Traditions for the Next Generation of Jews, Christians, and Muslims*. New York: Fordham University Press, 2006.

Heft, James L., Reuven Firestone, and Omid Safi, eds. *Learned Ignorance: Intellectual Humility among Jews, Christians, and Muslims*. New York: Oxford University Press, 2011.

Hinze, Bradford E., and Irfan A. Omar, eds. *Heirs of Abraham: The Future of Muslim, Jewish, and Christian Relations*. Maryknoll, N.Y.: Orbis Books, 2005.

Idliby, Ranya, Suzanne Oliver, and Priscilla Warner. *The Faith Club: A Muslim, a Christian, a Jew—Three Women Search for Understanding*. New York: Free Press, 2007.

Inter-Religious Dialogue. Website of the *Journal of Inter-Religious Dialogue*. Home page retrieved at http://irdialogue.org.

Kimball, Charles. *When Religion Becomes Evil*. Rev. ed. New York: HarperCollins, 2008.

Knitter, Paul F., ed. *The Myth of Religious Superiority: A Multifaith Exploration*. Maryknoll, N.Y.: Orbis Books, 2005.

Magonet, Jonathan. *Talking to the Other: Jewish Interfaith Dialogue with Muslims and Christians*. London: I. B. Taurus, 2003.

Marty, Martin E. *When Faiths Collide*. Oxford: Blackwell, 2005.

Meister, Chad V., ed. *The Oxford Handbook of Religious Diversity*. New York: Oxford University Press, 2010.

Mudge, Lewis S. *The Gift of Responsibility: The Promise of Dialogue among Christians, Jews, and Muslims*. New York: Continuum, 2008.

Niebuhr, Gustav. *Beyond Tolerance: Searching for Interfaith Understanding in America*. New York: Viking, 2008.

Ochs, Peter, and William Stacy Johnson, eds. *Crisis, Call, and Leadership in the Abrahamic Traditions*. New York: Palgrave Macmillan, 2009.

Patheos: A Website of the Balanced Views of Religions and Spirituality with Faith. Home page retrieved at http://www.patheos.com.

Patterson, David. *A Genealogy of Evil: Anti-Semitism from Nazism to Islamic Jihad*. New York: Cambridge University Press, 2011.

Peters, Francis E. *The Children of Abraham: Judaism, Christianity, Islam*. New ed. Princeton, N.J.: Princeton University Press, 2004.

———. *The Monotheists: Jews, Christians, and Muslims in Conflict and Competition*. Princeton, N.J.: Princeton University Press, 2003.

———. *The Voice, the Word, the Books: The Sacred Scripture of the Jews, Christians, and Muslims*. Princeton, N.J.: Princeton University Press, 2007.

Pratt, Douglas. *The Challenge of Islam: Encounters in Interfaith Dialogue*. Burlington, Vt.: Ashgate, 2005.

Reedijk, Rachel. *Routes and Roots: Identity Construction and the Jewish-Christian-Muslim Dialogue*. New York: Rodopi, 2010.

Roggema, Barbara, Marcel Poorthuis, and Pim Valkenberg. *The Three Rings: Textual Studies in the Historical Trialogue of Judaism, Christianity, and Islam*. Leuven, Belgium: Peeters, 2005.

Rubenstein, Richard L. *Jihad and Genocide*. Lanham, Md.: Rowman and Littlefield, 2010.

Solomon, Norman, Richard Harries, and Tim Winter, eds. *Abraham's Children: Jews, Christians, and Muslims in Conversation*. London: T & T Clark, 2005.

Steinkerchner, Scott. *Beyond Agreement: Interreligious Dialogue amid Persistent Differences*. Lanham, Md.: Rowman and Littlefield, 2010.

Studies in Interreligious Dialogue. Home page retrieved at http://poj.peeters-leuven .be/content.php?url=journal&journal_code=SID.

Swidler, Leonard, Khalid Duran, and Reuven Firestone. *Trialogue: Jews, Christians, and Muslims in Dialogue*. New London, Conn.: Twenty-Third Publications, 2007.

Vaux, Kenneth L. *Jew, Christian, Muslim: Faithful Unification or Fateful Trifurcation? Word, Way, Worship, and War in the Abrahamic Faiths.* Eugene, Ore.: Wipf and Stock, 2003.

————. *Journey into an Interfaith World: Jews, Christians, and Muslims in a World Come of Age.* Eugene, Ore.: Wipf and Stock, 2010.

Volf, Miroslav, ed. *Do We Worship the Same God? Jews, Christians, and Muslims in Dialogue.* Grand Rapids, Mich.: Wm. B. Eerdmans, 2012.

Vries, Hent de. *Religion and Violence: Philosophical Perspectives from Kant to Derrida.* Baltimore, Md.: Johns Hopkins University Press, 2002.

Editors and Contributors

LEONARD GROB is professor emeritus of philosophy at Fairleigh Dickinson University. He has published numerous articles dealing with the thought of Martin Buber and Emmanuel Levinas and is the coeditor of two collections of essays rooted in Buber's thought: *Education for Peace: Testimonies from World Religions* and *Women's and Men's Liberation: Testimonies of Spirit*. Within the field of Holocaust studies, Grob has authored articles and book chapters on topics such as post-Holocaust education, ethics after the Holocaust, post-Holocaust theodicy, and philosophical reflections on rescuers. Since 1996, Grob has served as co-organizer, along with Henry F. Knight, of the biennial Stephen S. Weinstein Holocaust Symposium (formerly the Pastora Goldner Holocaust Symposium) in Wroxton, England. He has also been involved in projects devoted to encouraging Israeli-Palestinian dialogue. Grob is the coeditor of *Teen Voices from the Holy Land: Who Am I to You?*, a volume of Israeli and Palestinian children's narratives. In 2008, Grob and John K. Roth published *Anguished Hope: Holocaust Scholars Confront the Palestinian-Israeli Conflict*, a collection of essays focused on the Holocaust and the ongoing issues in the Middle East.

JOHN K. ROTH is the Edward J. Sexton Professor Emeritus of Philosophy and the founding director of the Center for the Study of the Holocaust, Genocide, and Human Rights (now the Center for Human Rights Leadership) at Claremont McKenna College, where he taught from 1966 through 2006. In 2007–2008, he served as the Robert and Carolyn Frederick Distinguished Visiting Professor of Ethics at DePauw University in Greencastle, Indiana. In addition to service on the United States Holocaust Memorial Council and on the editorial board of *Holocaust and Genocide Studies*, he has published hundreds of articles and reviews and authored, coauthored, or edited more than forty books, including *Genocide and Human Rights: A Philosophical Guide*; *Gray Zones: Ambiguity and Compromise in the Holocaust and Its Aftermath*; *Ethics during and after the Holocaust: In the Shadow of Birkenau*; and *The Oxford Handbook of Holocaust Studies*. Roth has been a visiting professor of Holocaust studies at the University of Haifa, Israel, and his Holocaust-related research appointments have included a 2001 Koerner Visiting Fellowship at the Oxford Centre for Hebrew and Jewish Studies in England as well as a 2004–2005 appointment as the Ina Levine Invitational Scholar at the Center for Advanced Holocaust Studies, United States Holocaust Memorial Museum, Washington, D.C. In 1988, Roth was named U.S. National Professor of the Year by the Council for Advancement and Support of Education and the Carnegie Foundation for the Advancement of Teaching.

CONTRIBUTORS

RACHEL N. BAUM is adjunct assistant professor of Jewish studies and Hebrew studies at the University of Wisconsin–Milwaukee, where she also coordinates the Jewish studies major. Baum's research focuses on the emotions of post-Holocaust Jewish identity. She has published a number of essays, including chapters in *Between Hope and Despair: Pedagogy and the Remembrance of Historical Trauma*, edited by Roger I. Simon, Sharon Rosenberg, and Claudia Eppert, and *After-Words: Post-Holocaust Struggles with Forgiveness, Reconciliation, Justice*, edited by David Patterson and John K. Roth. Baum has also presented her work at the Scholars' Conference on the Holocaust and the Churches; the University of Oregon's "Ethics and the Holocaust" conference; and the Holocaust Educational Foundation's "Lessons and Legacies" conference, among others. Baum currently serves on the executive committee of Milwaukee's Holocaust Education and Resource Center and is an educator in its Holocaust Study Institute. She is currently working on a project about the recreation of Jewish life in virtual worlds such as Second Life.

MARGARET BREARLEY read modern languages at Oxford University. She was awarded a DAAD (German Academic Exchange Service) scholarship to Münster University, Germany, and received her Ph.D. from Cambridge University. From 1973, Brearley was a lecturer in German medieval and Renaissance literature at Birmingham University, taking early retirement in 1986 to found and direct the West Midlands Israel Information Centre. She has held academic posts at the Centre for Judaism and Jewish-Christian Relations, Selly Oak Colleges (1987–1992), and the Institute of Jewish Affairs, London (1992–1996). Brearley has lectured in Israel, Germany, Finland, and the United States and throughout Great Britain. She has published numerous articles and book chapters, especially on anti-Judaism, genocide, the Holocaust, and the Roma people. Brearley founded a day-care center for the mentally ill in 1979 and has been a consultant to several films and documentaries, a judge for the Times Preacher of the Year award, an honorary advisor on the Holocaust to the Archbishops' Council (2001–2004), and an honorary research fellow at University College, London (2006–2009).

BRITTA FREDE-WENGER teaches in the fields of religion and English at an upper-level Catholic high school in southwestern Germany, where she also coordinates the school's intercultural programs. Frede-Wenger received her Ph.D. in Catholic theology at the University of Tübingen, Germany, where her dissertation concentrated on the post-Holocaust Jewish thought of Emil L. Fackenheim. This work was awarded the Promotionspreis "Religion und Ethik" (2. Preis) by the University of Erfurt, Germany; it was published in 2005 under the title *Glauben und Denken im Angesicht von Auschwitz: Eine Auseinandersetzung mit dem Werk von Emil L. Fackenheim* (Belief and Thought in the Face of Auschwitz: A Discussion of the Work of Emil L. Fackenheim). Frede-Wenger worked as an academic assistant to the Catholic theological faculty in Tübingen as well as for the Akademie der Diözese Rottenburg-Stuttgart. She has conducted numerous workshops in adult education and teacher training. Frede-Wenger was an advisor to York University's Mark and Gail Appel Program in Holocaust and Antiracist Education and is a member of the Stephen S. Weinstein Holocaust Symposium at Wroxton College. Her publications include contributions to *Anguished Hope: Holocaust Scholars Confront the Palestinian-Israeli Conflict*, edited by Leonard Grob and John K. Roth.

HENRY GREENSPAN is a consulting psychologist, lecturer in social theory and practice, and playwright at the University of Michigan in Ann Arbor. He has been teaching and writing about Holocaust survivors for more than thirty years, engaging survivors not through onetime "testimonies" but through sustained conversation often over many years. His most recent books include the second and enlarged edition of *On Listening to Holocaust Survivors: Beyond Testimony* and, with Agi Rubin, *Reflections: Auschwitz, Memory, and a Life Recreated.* His play *Remnants*, which was broadcast in the United States on National Public Radio, has been staged at more than two hundred venues worldwide. Recently, he has been working closely with a large project in Montreal that, partly inspired by his approach, has been gathering the accounts of Holocaust survivors as well as survivors of the Rwandan and Cambodian genocides and political violence in Haiti.

PETER J. HAAS holds the Abba Hillel Silver Chair of Jewish Studies at Case Western Reserve University, where he also directs the Samuel Rosenthal Center for Judaic Studies. Haas took ordination as a Reform rabbi from Hebrew Union College in Cincinnati in 1974. He then served for three years as an active-duty chaplain in the United States Army, developing an interest in moral philosophy and moral education. Upon completion of his military duty, he enrolled in the graduate program in religion at Brown University, receiving his Ph.D. in Jewish studies in 1980. Haas taught at Vanderbilt University in Nashville, Tennessee, from 1980 until 1999, when he went to Case Western Reserve University. Among his most important writings are *Morality after Auschwitz: The Radical Challenge of the Nazi Ethic* and *Human Rights and the World's Major Religions: The Jewish Tradition*, along with contributions to *Ethics after the Holocaust*. Haas's ongoing research interests include the relationship between science and religion in the contemporary world. He has delivered presentations at numerous conferences in Israel, as well as in England, Italy, Germany, and Belgium, and has also served as president of Scholars for Peace in the Middle East (SPME).

RIFFAT HASSAN is professor emerita of religious studies at the University of Louisville. She was born in Pakistan and educated in England, specializing in the philosophy of the progressive Muslim thinker Muhammad Iqbal. Widely recognized as a pioneer of feminist theology in the context of the Islamic tradition, Hassan is also an activist who has traveled extensively, addressing diverse audiences about the Qur'an's strong affirmation of human rights and the imperative to build justice- and compassion-centered societies. From 2002 to 2009, Hassan developed and directed two major peace-building programs involving South Asian Muslim scholars, religious leaders, and community activists together with their American counterparts. The U.S. State Department regards these programs as models for future exchanges involving Muslims and Americans. Hassan's ongoing projects include the completion and consolidation of her research work and providing leadership training to Muslim women and youth. She is the author or editor of several volumes, including, most recently, *Pakistan Progressive: The Politics of Ethnicity in Pakistan*.

ZAYN KASSAM is professor of religious studies at Pomona College in Claremont, California. A specialist in Islamic studies, she teaches courses on gender in Islam and Muslim societies and on Islamic philosophy and mysticism, as well as courses on religion and the environment. Kassam published the volume on Islam in the six-book series *Introduction to the World's Major Religions* as well as an edited work on Islam, women, and activism. She is also the author of various articles dealing with gender issues, ethics, and the teaching of Islam. The recipient of numerous teaching awards, including the American Academy of Religion's 2005 Excellence in Teaching Award, Kassam is a member of the Claremont Interfaith Mideast Peace Group and serves on the boards of the *Journal of Religion, Conflict and Peace* and the *Journal of Feminist Studies in Religion*. Her current research project examines the situation of Muslim women in the context of globalization.

HENRY F. KNIGHT is the director of the Cohen Center for Holocaust and Genocide Studies at Keene State College, where he teaches courses included in the first undergraduate major in Holocaust and genocide studies in the United States and directs the Cohen Center's co-curricular programming. Knight is cochair of the biennial Stephen S. Weinstein Holocaust Symposium (formerly the Pastora Goldner Holocaust Symposium) that he and Leonard Grob, of Fairleigh Dickenson University, cofounded in 1996. He serves on the Church Relations Committee of the United States Holocaust Memorial Museum in Washington, D.C., and several other national and international advisory committees related to Holocaust studies. Knight is the author of *Celebrating Holy Week in a Post-Holocaust World* and, with Zev Garber, *Confessing Christ in a Post-Holocaust World*.

HUBERT G. LOCKE is dean and professor emeritus, Evans School of Public Affairs, University of Washington, where he also served as associate dean of the College of Arts and Sciences and vice provost for academic affairs. He holds degrees from Wayne State University, the University of Chicago, and the University of Michigan as well as honorary degrees from six institutions. Locke is the author of a number of books related to the German Church during the Nazi era, including *Exile in the Fatherland: The Prison Letters of Martin Niemöller*. Among his extensive writings on the Holocaust are *Learning from History: A Black Christian's Perspectives on the Holocaust* and *Searching for God in Godforsaken Times and Places*. Locke has been visiting professor of religion at Whitman College and the Ida E. King Distinguished Professor of Holocaust Studies at the Richard Stockton College of New Jersey. In 2003 and again in 2010, he served as acting president of the Pacific School of Religion.

ROCHELLE L. MILLEN is professor of religion at Wittenberg University. She is the author of *Women, Birth, and Death in Jewish Law and Practice*; the editor of *New Perspectives on the Holocaust: A Guide for Teachers and Scholars*; and the coeditor of *Testimony, Tensions, and* Tikkun: *Teaching the Holocaust in Colleges and Universities*. Millen is cofounder of the Religion, Holocaust, and Genocide Group of the American Academy of Religion, which she cochaired for seven years. Millen serves on the academic advisory board of the Hadassah-Brandeis Institute and is a member of the Board of the Ohio Council on Holocaust Education. She serves on the editorial board of the Stephen S. Weinstein Series in Post-Holocaust Studies of the University of Washington Press. Millen is a member of the Church Relations Committee of the United States Holocaust Memorial Museum. She chairs the Professional Development Committee for the Columbus Jewish Federation and, in 1995, received the Samuel Belkin Memorial Award for Professional Achievement from Stern College for Women of Yeshiva University. Currently, Millen is working on a volume about interwar Poland, in which she utilizes private correspondence from the period 1930–1936.

KHALEEL MOHAMMED is associate professor of religious studies at San Diego State University. He is also a core faculty member of the university's master's degree program in homeland security and participates in the Center for Islamic and Arabic Studies. Mohammed read Islamic law at the Muhammad bin Saud Islamic University in Saudi Arabia and has studied in Yemen, Mauritania, and Syria. He holds an M.A. in the history and philosophy of religion from Concordia University and a Ph.D. in Islamic law from McGill University. From 2001 to 2003, Mohammed was a Kraft-Hiatt Postdoctoral Fellow at Brandeis University. He has written several journal articles, coauthored *Coming to Terms with the Qur'an* (with Andrew Rippin), and translated Ayatollah Husayn Fadlullah's *World of Our Youth*. Mohammed has delivered presentations internationally at numerous academic conferences. His current interests are in Islamic law maxims and the comparative narratology of the Hebrew Bible and the Qur'an.

DAVID PATTERSON holds the Hillel Feinberg Chair in Holocaust Studies at the University of Texas at Dallas. A winner of the National Jewish Book Award and the Koret Jewish Book Award, Patterson has published more than thirty books and more than 130 articles and book chapters on philosophy, literature, Judaism, and the Holocaust. His writings have been anthologized in *Yom Kippur Readings, Holocaust Theology, The Holocaust: Readings and Interpretations,* and *Great Jewish Quotations.* Patterson's most recent books include *A Genealogy of Evil: Antisemitism from Nazism to Islamic Jihad; Emil L. Fackenheim: A Jewish Philosopher's Response to the Holocaust; Open Wounds: The Crisis of Jewish Thought in the Aftermath of Auschwitz; Wrestling with the Angel: Toward a Jewish Understanding of the Nazi Assault on the Name;* and *Hebrew Language and Jewish Thought.*

DIDIER POLLEFEYT is professor of pastoral theology and theology of Jewish-Christian relations at the Katholieke Universiteit Leuven, Belgium, where he also serves as the vice dean of the Faculty of Theology. Pollefeyt teaches courses on Jewish-Christian dialogue, post-Holocaust theology, and religious education and chairs the Academic Center for Teachers' Training in Religion. In addition to his numerous articles on post-Holocaust ethics and theology, his recent books include *Incredible Forgiveness: Christian Ethics between Fanaticism and Reconciliation; Hermeneutics and Religious Education; Interreligious Learning;* and *Never Revoked: Nostra Aetate as Ongoing Challenge for Jewish-Christian Dialogue.*

BÜLENT ŞENAY holds a Ph.D. in religious studies from Lancaster University, the United Kingdom, where his doctoral dissertation was "Messianic Jews—Hybridity, Identity, and Tradition." He began his teaching career as a lecturer of Islamic studies and Muslim ethics at the University College of St. Martin's in the United Kingdom (1996–1999). Şenay continued as associate professor of history of religion on the Faculty of Islamic Theology, Uludağ University, Bursa, Turkey (2000–2008). He has authored numerous publications and has lectured on subjects such as the "religious other," teaching religion in multicultural/plural society, and identity and religion in Europe. Şenay serves currently as counselor for religious affairs in the Netherlands and is a participant at both the academic and diplomatic levels in the Intercultural Exchange Project of the Council of Europe in Strasbourg. He was recently named William James Visiting Professor at Bayreuth University, Germany, and visiting professor in the Department of Near Eastern Studies at Princeton University. Şenay's research interests and writing agenda are focused on religion in multicultural societies and on identity and religion in Europe.

SANA TAYYEN is currently a Ph.D. student in the philosophy of religion and theology program at Claremont Graduate University in Claremont, California. She received her M.A. in liberal arts from the University of Memphis. While at Claremont, Tayyen has served as research assistant at the Institute for Signifying Scriptures and at Pomona College. Her work ranges from a comparative dissertation on the theologies of St. Thomas Aquinas and Imam al-Ghazali to an ethnographic study of Arab American Muslim and Christian communities. Tayyen's research interests are in the areas of interreligious communication and comparative theology, focusing on challenges confronting religious identity and interreligious communal coexistence.

BASSAM TIBI, a political scientist, was born in Damascus, immigrated to Germany, and became a German citizen. His education in Arab-Muslim and European settings prepared him for the study of intercultural communication. Between 1973 and 2009, he served as the Georgia Augusta Professor for International Relations at Göttingen University. Tibi has held many visiting academic appointments, spanning four continents and including positions at Harvard, Princeton, and Yale as well as at universities in Yaoundé, Cameroon; Jakarta, Indonesia; and Singapore. His publications include more than twenty-five books, the most recent of which are *Islam's Predicament with Modernity* and *Islam and Islamism*. In 1995, the president of the Federal Republic of Germany awarded Tibi the German Cross of Merit, First Class, for his contribution to the betterment of intercivilizational communication between Islam and the West.

Index